Quiet, for a Tuesday

Solo in the Algerian Sahara

Tom Sheppard

The story:

Chapter 1	Maps and guides	9
Chapter 2	Heading west	23
Chapter 3	The Reggan bypass, Part 1	31
Chapter 4	The Reggan bypass, Part 2	49
Chapter 5	The phantom fort	61
Chapter 6	'3 Nov'	71
Chapter 7	Idj	85
Chapter 8	Idj to Wadi 'N'	99
Chapter 9	'6 Nov' to QFAT	105
Chapter 10	QFAT to Issedienne	117
Chapter 11	Issedienne to Guantanamo	129
Chapter 12	Death in the desert	149
Chapter 13	Rainbows	157
Chapter 14	Ezz-Tes	165
Chapter 15	North	177
Chapter 16	*vers* Timimoun	197
Chapter 17	Pieces of silver?	207
Chapter 18	Casbah	219
Chapter 19	Clancy Woods	231
Chapter 20	Algeria, the uncut gem	237

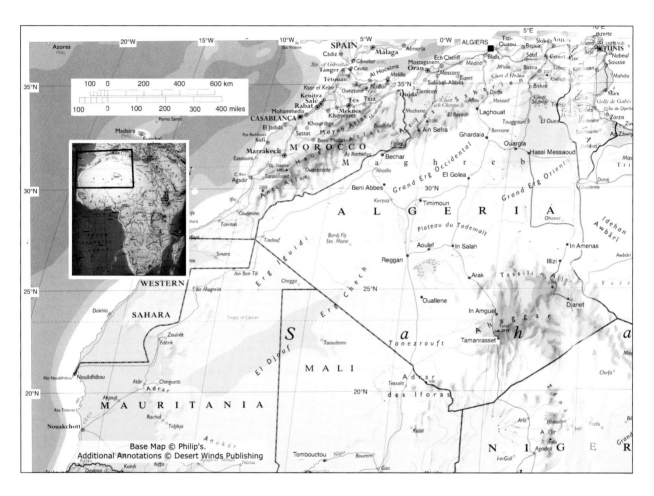

Algeria is about the size of western Europe. South of approximately 33° N, it is desert. Large areas of that desert are very beautiful.

Prologue

From the nav log:

28 Oct contd.

28866	1750	11m out of Reggan. 26°xx.xx'N, 0°xx.xx'E.
		Leaving road to camp on 150°T.
288xx	1758	Camp. 26°xx.xx'N, 0°xx.xx'E. Fuel: .8 tank

Wed 29 Oct 03		**E Reggan to In Salah**
		28867-29014 = 147 miles

Fuel:		Tank .8 plus 6 full cans (120 litres)
Water:		Can 3b (Taghit) 2 litres. Rest full (65 litres)
Wake up:	0655	24.8°C. Sunrise c. 0705, 107°M
Tyres:		2.55 bar @ 27°C

288xx	0820	Off. Back to road - c. 1 mile.
288xx	0835	Lat.xxx Long.xxx Just passed graded rd S.
288xx	0842	26°xx.xx'N, 0°xx.xx'E. Crossing low valley with low hills hdg S.
		Coming from E this would be just past the Reggan xx sign.

*   *   *   *

Three years pass.

1. Maps and guides

'Forever', said Mohammed wearily, allowing himself a just perceptible shrug of resignation, a rare latitude in his role as translator that hinted at a certain personal interpretation of the situation. In the context of his local knowledge, though, a gesture that spoke volumes and clicked my morale down another notch.

The office was dim, the windows closed and shuttered against the glaring heat of the day. Four energy-saving folded-tube devices attempted to light its corners. One had failed. A grander bulb in the centre of the ceiling, a droopy pear-shaped object resembling the principal physical attribute of a stud bull, flickered in a variety of colours in response, presumably, to component malfunction or fluctuating mains voltage.

'What was the date of your entry into Algeria in 1961?' the captain asked, as if therein lay the key to my assumed current profession of espionage. To add professional finesse to the list of about 12 or 15 previous visits I had made to Algeria over the years he was attempting to attach dates and ports of arrival and departure.

In Salah. The street.

We were at In Salah, sometimes called Ain Salah, 'ain' being one of the Arabic words for well. If you use 'In Salah' as I do you have to be careful to say 'at' rather than 'in' to avoid confusion and unwarranted correction of the manuscript. Either way, I always had a soft spot for In Salah – even now when it was again the place of my deten ... . Detention is the wrong word, with its overtones of clanging doors and bare light bulbs. A word encapsulating the concept of involuntary extension of stay would be better. But poor old In Salah, once an important crossroads of caravan routes, now relegated to the status of a fuelling stop and an only marginally involved

In Salah market and (right) the duty sand dune in position over the main road from Algiers.

spectator to the BP/Sonatrach and Halliburton gas exploration and extraction activities to the north and around. When locations were handed out In Salah drew the short straw. Though on this occasion on its best behaviour, In Salah's weather was more usually a minor but stoically accepted hell of high temperature, strong north-easterly sand-wind – *vente-sable* as they called it locally – and chronically poor visibility. The sand-wind, in the course of its apparent resolve continuously to redistribute the silica content of the entire Sahara, contrived to maintain, within the city limits, a token permanent dune across the main north-south ribbon of tarmac connecting the Mediterranean coast to Algeria's distant south, a thousand miles into the great desert.

I'd been here a number of times. Always to the accompaniment of flying sand. Was it just my bad luck, I'd often wondered? But no. A few years earlier, after a trip I'd done in an unrelentingly windy and dust-laden April, I'd checked the meteorological data. There, at the very peak of the seasonal wind-speed diagrams and temperature gradient charts, In Salah took pride of place. Nor was the topography helpful. In the near 700-mile span of the dividers south from Algiers on the coast, the terrain rose to the High Atlas, dipped slightly at the Hauts Plateaux, tripped over the Atlas Saharien, skimmed the sea of great sand dunes comprising the Grands Ergs, zoomed over the bleak, black stony Tademait Plateau before stepping down, and down again, to In Salah's resting place, the Plaine de Tidikelt.

Plain 'plain' would be the better word to describe this low-lying, visually uninspiring west-east stretch where nature's Amazing Landscapes department had taken a day off after what it had achieved further south. Traversed now by a firm, smooth tarmac road linking In Salah to Aoulef and Reggan 150 miles to the west, this was the region where I'd been almost simultaneously very unfortunate and very lucky 15 years earlier. In a hellish, brown-sky blow at a withering 44°C the front wheel of my underpowered 350cc motorcycle had dug into the soft churned sand and sent me over the handlebars closely pursued by a weighty rucksack that on impact had a go at separating my cervical vertebrae. Where – *'Pas de trafic ici'*, they'd said earlier – almost exactly five minutes later a Toyota with an English-speaking Algerian among its passengers came to my rescue.

And where, a few hours after that, in further defiance of *'Pas de traffic ici'*, an empty pickup also loomed out of the night to take the damaged me and the damaged bike to Aoulef to recover. It even had a bale of alfalfa in the back to lean the bike against. Not for the first time I murmured to myself something about there being Someone Up There ... .

Right now, in the dimly lit office at In Salah, my problems concerned Someone Down Here. But this was Episode 2. I had had a similar problem – Episode 1 – the year before, farther to the east – questioning in dim offices, lots of chin-scratching, delays and an embarrassing absorption of gendarmerie manpower and budget.

Freelancing, solo, like the proverbial John Denver bird on the wing across vast clear-horizon off-tracks regions of the Algerian Sahara – it had been 540 miles fuel-point to fuel-point – I came to roost at the BP/Sonatrach gas field near In Amenas, at the specific invitation of Shane Yavari, American/Iranian engineer and all-round exceptional person, who I had first met at the BP Teguentur gas plant north of In Salah two years previously. Now, as then, he (and BP, bless them both) offered me hospitality, a shower and a bed for the night. Like a kid in a toyshop, I soaked up a tour of the incredible engineering activity associated with such enterprises the next morning. But BP's new security regulations did not permit them to just let me go on from there, especially up the Gassi Touil corridor

In Amenas gas field ; plumbing on a grand scale.

leading north to Hassi Messaoud where the pipelines from 50 oil fields converged.

BP handed me over to the Algerian Gendarmerie at In Amenas to check out. I'd been in the building only 10 minutes but could contain myself no longer.

'J'ai penseé que vous êtes Michael Owen!' I said, trying to un-rivet my gaze from the spitting image of the great footballer standing behind the reception counter in a smart olive-green pullover and white belt. Gales of laughter exploding from his colleagues attested this was not the first time someone had remarked on the likeness. Big smiles all round. Another ill-lit office, the subliminal flicker and green

tinge of fluorescent strip lighting, a throbbing air conditioner, high mounted, spilling cold air down onto the overstuffed armchair I sat on the edge of at the head man's behest. A lengthy report grinding out like those shots you used to see in the movies of ticker tape coming off a machine; on where I'd been, who I was. All in Arabic. In an act of extraordinary faith I signed it when bidden so to do, understanding nothing of what had been written. After due consideration the gendarmerie at In Amenas felt they should escort me through these sensitive areas. It meant a preliminary night stop at In Amenas's charmingly ramshackle one-star hotel on the last night of the Ramadan fast. As usual the plumbing was a disaster, the blankets were unbelievably soft and cuddly, the bed comfortable. Kind, concerned other guests showing me where everything was at the spartan pre-dawn breakfast next morning.

Arriving bang on time, the escort comprised a vehicle front and rear, big green and white Nissan Patrols, three men in each changing at the border of each gendarmerie's area of authority to be replaced by another two vehicles and another six men. A long shadow to my left, flying, blurring over the uneven ground, kept station with my G-Wagen as we sped north to a rising sun, right and a little behind me. In the next two days the change of escort happened nine times. Eighteen vehicles. All those men; all for one visitor. Me. Sometimes we waited out in the desert for the new vehicles and crews to arrive. The young gendarmes en route were eager to know what I was doing, why I was there. They had views and questions. 'I think English colonialism was better than French.' 'What is Algeria's image in

*'Your country is
very beautiful.'*

the west?' Ordinary lads; conscripts doing their military service.

At many of the stops the drivers partook of post-Ramadan Eid hospitality before the changeover; tiny cakes and coffee from their colleagues, like mince pies and sherry at Christmas. Eid was a four-day holiday and I was embarrassed to be taking their time. Another night stop at the hotel in Hassi Messaoud, Algeria's oilsville and collecting point for the dozens of pipeline feeds from the oilfields to the south and east. As I checked in: Bang! Bang! Cr-rack-crack-crack! Outside. 'Aaagh! *Terroristes!*' I said, feigning alarm and wondering for a nanosecond if my joke was perhaps a bit too edgy. The gendarmes laughed as the 8-10-year-old '*terroristes*' outside threw more celebratory Eid fireworks around the street.

My escort lasted 1185 kilometres all the way from In Amenas, through Berriane to Laghouat, on the first two days of the Eid holidays. I shut my eyes tight and curled my toes at the cost. I cringed at the Euro-quivalent for a Middle Eastern visitor in the UK: 'Right, sunshine, you'll be spending the holidays in this nice cosy cell won't you, and we'll sort you out later then. When we've got time, eh?' Not here, though. Polite and considerate.

Now, at In Salah, confined to Captain Rahmouni's darkened cavern with the weirdly pulsating centre light we went through it all again. Yes I had been to Algeria many times. This was my sixteenth journey, I enthused. I just loved the Sahara, the space, the tranquillity, the landscape. In England, too many people, too much noise, too many cars. Your country is very beautiful. I have proposed to UNESCO and the Algerian Government

the establishment of a Protected Area. This was my sixth trip in the Mercedes 4x4 G-Wagen since 2001, entering the last few times at Algiers port on a boat from Marseilles and heading due south, through the hills, stopping at Laghouat. Camping along the way. Normally there was a convoy system at El Golea southbound but this time apparently not, and I was allowed through so there seemed reason to believe there were new easier rules.

Yes of course I have maps and GPS to keep track of where I am. The captain wouldn't have known about Mark Thatcher even if my execrable French could have managed the right tenses to tell him about the dangers of not knowing where you were in the desert.

In the timescale blur that often assails you in the sudden, sideways-jump of unexpected and long-drawn-out situations like this I began to wonder how I actually came to find myself here being grilled by Captain Rahmouni. It was the day before that it all started to go wrong, at the southern end of the Tademait Plateau crossing, these days not much more than a rather tedious couple of hundred miles' tarmac south from El Golea. Once it had been a bone-jarring, pot-holed track plagued by flour-fine dust and heavy trucks dragging clouds of it in their wake to blind you and challenge the efficacy of your engine air filter. Ain al Hadjadj is the military checkpoint at the top of the breathtaking descent of the *falaise* as you hit the final 100km southbound to In Salah.

The view from the edge of the plateau is magnificent, the road zig-zagging away into the haze, skirting west of the two great conical peaks that are outcrops from the escarpment. For the hundredth time your admiration for the road engineers is kindled. The big trucks creep down the road cut into the side of the cliffs in the lowest gear they can find, a snail's pace with a roaring engine, foot well clear of the brake. Last time I was here a long 42-tonner (nominal!) laden with sacks of grain eased down the long slope. Popped on top of the load like a Dinky toy and held with flimsy ropes, a Renault 4. As it crept through hairpin after hairpin the truck drew to a halt near the bottom. I could just hear the hiss and pssshhhhh of the brakes from my vantage point. It being that time of the day, the driver, solo with his vast weight of cargo and machinery, opened the cab door, climbed down, spread his mat, faced east and, as his faith demanded, said his prayers. It made me feel very humble.

The gendarmes at the Ain al Hadjadj checkpoint didn't get too many foreigners through and didn't quite know what to do when I first arrived. Shrugging the sling of his automatic rifle further up onto his shoulder and grinning away the slight embarrassment of coming, from habit, to the left window instead of the right, the smile and outstretched hand were followed by a down-to-business *'Papier!'*. The passport jogged them, after a pause and a nervous thumbing through, into calling *le lieutenant*.

'Where -' (oh, good grief, not that ...) '-is your guide?'

Like a fine bone-china cup hitting a tiled floor from six feet the optimism of the previous four days' bureaucracy-free travel shattered. I had grappled many times – with varying success – with what was about to unfold. You have to go back four years to attempt the first layer of

Looking south toward In Salah from Ain al Hadjadj.

comprehension. In the spring and early summer of 2003 seven separate groups of 'adventure tourists' in 4x4s and vans had successively been kidnapped by bandits in the Sahara, in a region thought to be to the west of Illizi.

The total of personnel who disappeared was no less than 32. Throughout the summer of 2003 the bandits and the Algerian army played cat and mouse round the desert. Naturally, with its usual blindness to Algeria, the British press did not even report the initial incidents and certainly never followed up on the developing drama. Internet stories and German press quotes, however, bounced back and forth about what was going on – with the customary caveats and lack of confirmation to go with conflicting versions of the action. Eventually about three months into the saga the Algerian special forces recaptured half the party that had by then split into two groups.

The remainder enjoyed, and that's possibly not quite the right word, an escape-and-evasion tour of the desert through the heat of the summer, one dying from the heat in the process, so the stories went. Eventually the group was run to earth in neighbouring Mali, way to the south-west, and after an exchange of emissaries with different messages – one of which, in one direction, was rumoured to include the payment of 5.5 million euros – the hostages were released. Around 18 months later stories came out that the leader, rakishly known as Razzak the Para, had been captured in Chad. Libya, Chad and Algeria argued the toss as to who should have him. The resolution of the argument took longer than the typically short attention span of the press.

Between the captives' release and the news about Razzak being apprehended, I had planned, in that same autumn of '03, another Sahara trip. On a personal level I groaned at all the goings-on, feeling certain that much sucking of teeth and all manner of draconian regulations would prevail to prevent my returning. Astonishingly, nothing changed. I roamed the desert virtually at will soaking up its beauty, revelling in the awe-inspiring landscapes, camping under the stars, seeking and plotting the ancient French tracks tantalisingly marked on the old maps I'd bought so long ago. Like an echo bouncing back across a vast canyon, completely out of phase, it took another two years before any discernible regulatory revisions took place.

There was around these years considerable routine extremist, bad-guy, bandit activity and accordingly there were already general rules about joining a convoy coming south from

The El Golea convoy, southbound and impatient.

El Golea over the Tademait. On the parallel southbound route to the west through Bechar, Adrar and Reggan there were no rules, apparently.

With a wackiness that came to characterise the whole scenario, the El Golea convoy of 50-60 assembled vehicles and their delayed, frustrated drivers were released like the proverbial greyhounds on a Wednesday or a Sunday morning at 0800 hours, aimed at In Salah 250 miles to the south. Within 10 miles the convoy – a disparate agglomeration of heavy trucks, 2-tonners, medium trucks and the odd light 4x4 – was no more. It simply was not a convoy. The fast vehicles sped off, the slow ones plodded, those in the middle were alone. There were no escorts or whippers-in and what was even more bizarre, if you were coming back, south to north, no convoys were even assembled; you went as you pleased. Similarly at In Salah. Southbound, by 2005, a 'guide' was obligatory. Northbound it apparently did not matter. I sought desperately a rationale that could possibly make sense of this extraordinary set-up. Perhaps, I wondered, it was that the tankers southbound were full and therefore a juicy hijack or bomb target and coming back they would be empty. And perhaps something was lost in translation but the word 'guide' was not quite appropriate. For a start the route south from In Salah was a perfectly straightforward tarmac road, albeit badly damaged in places. Secondly, the 'guides' were usually no more than drivers and had little knowledge of the surrounding countryside and certainly were not capable of understanding a map.

On the other hand, camping once a mile or so off the road in the rocks 50km north of In Salah to photograph the rugged landscapes and catch a moonrise behind a huge flat-top mesa to the east, I heard the wavering drone of what sounded like a hundred Lancaster bombers coming in from the north. At first there was nothing to see and then, where the

Northbound tanker, empty, descends off the Tademait south of El Golea.

road dropped down between the flanks of a rock cutting, I saw a fuel tanker emerge – one of the great 25,000-litre articulated trucks that seem to comprise half the traffic on the road to Tamanrasset. Then another followed close behind. And another. And another. I counted 32 tankers travelling at a spacing of no more than 50 metres until this astonishing convoy occupied all of the road that I could see from where I stood. I reached for the binoculars and there were armed soldiers front and rear. Someone, somewhere was taking the threat very seriously.

And wisely. However small the risk, the hijacking of just one of these mobile holocausts would have been a catastrophic coup for the bandits and the extreme caution was sensible.

But my painstakingly planned expeditions after that November '03 trip were in danger of expensive disruption from the strange, randomly applied and unfathomable regulations that were invoked at odd places down the route for visitors. I made a point never to disobey instructions or break the law. Avoiding the instructions in the first place, however – avoiding putting people in the position of having to implement often illogical rules that had obviously not been thought through – seemed the sensible way out. It kept the gendarmerie off the hook and me on course for the wide open spaces.

I had adopted this tactic once before, coming north from Tombouctou more than 25 years earlier; a kind of don't-ask-don't-tell, you can't be responsible if you don't know about it. There is no road or track north from Tombouctou that went where, or anything like as far, as I wanted to go so I would have to go cross-country – for a considerable distance. I wanted to cross the vast desert that separated the fabled ancient city in Mali from Reggan in Algeria, a little to the east of north – a matter of some 900 miles off-tracks. To request permission would, for a start, almost certainly have met with a refusal. If the authorities had agreed there would have been an implied measure of responsibility for my safety. The Commandant du Circle had already been most kind and accommodating, letting me have a little top-up fuel from their meagre stocks for my journey from the Niger river to the middle of the Tanezrouft. He had enough on his plate taking care of civil affairs in the small dusty settlement and it would not have been fair to burden

him additionally with the wanderlust whims of a lone English traveller smitten with the vastness of the Sahara. I left them with the impression I was heading east on the track to Gao and crept out of the town, north before dawn, to start my journey. It seemed to me the right way to do things; the responsibility was then just mine.

Post-2003, in Algeria, there was also the question of who manned the roadblocks – the army, the police or the gendarmerie. In that order they were easy or difficult to deal with. They all sang from different hymn sheets; I had ample grounds for the impression that they were in competition with each other. The army were best. Finding you out in the wilderness they would approach tactically, rightly regarding a single oddball vehicle out in the sticks as suspicious until they'd had a good look. They were solicitous for your safety but accepted, if you had the right equipment and attitude, that you were a sensible visitor and had made the right judgements.

On one occasion, a certain collusion by an artful and helpful English-speaking Algerian communications engineer on my behalf, whom fate in its munificence had allocated to the same 'guide' as me southbound from In Salah, had resulted in my being 'freed' at Arak to follow my carefully planned route out into the desert. Four exhilarating hours later, 20 miles from the nearest tarmac with an inspiring silhouette of jagged peaks fronting a equally inspirational Saharan sunset, I was celebrating my liberty with a hedonistic cup of lemon tea when a sudden noisy mix of dust, metallic rattle and squealing brakes announced the arrival of an Algerian army patrol. Whether it was planned that way I don't know but they came out of the setting sun and were on me before I knew what was going on, suddenly surrounding the G-Wagen. A thorough look to see how many people they were dealing with and who they might be quickly resulted in the classic Algerian change-the-grip-on-your-rifle-to-shake-hands situation which invariably prevailed. Within minutes good natured joshing was the order of the day. Drinking lemon tea during

Tombouctou-Reggan direct. Do-it-yourself border crossing at 22°36'N, 01°07'W.

Desert
interception. The
Izouret-Arak
patrol.

Ramadan before the sun has gone down! Agh! And me feigning abject penitence. Each of the soldiers seemed to have a little plastic camera and group photos were next on the list, to which I was invited to join. 'D'accord,' I said, mug in hand and sticking out my elbow. 'Comme Tony Blair!' Much laughter seemed to indicate the soldiers not only knew who Tony Blair was but they'd noticed his propensity for coming out of Number 10 with a coffee mug in his hand. I wondered how many British squaddies would know who the prime minister, or even president, of Algeria was.

Their curiosity satisfied – after quite a lot of prodding around in my possessions and ooh-what's-this queries – the merry band sped off home in the direction of Arak 40 miles or so north-east across the desert. I did wonder if their arrival had been entirely coincidental as I had made a point of telling the army folks at Arak after my release from the 'guide' exactly where I was planning to go – including the names of the peaks which they, as local specialists, would know. I didn't want anyone thinking later that I was pulling the wool over their eyes. Either way, they seemed a good cheerful bunch with an entirely professional approach without what came across as – to use the well-worn phrase – the 'excessive zeal' manifested by the gendarmes.

•   •   •

'My guide?', I said, to le lieutenant's glare. Dragged from the shelter of the little hut atop the windy ridge at Ain al Hadjadj where the road dipped down so spectacularly, I had an uneasy premonition that le lieutenant was going to mean a degree of trouble. Forcing the smile I hoped would calm him, I pointed to my GPS and maps and said, 'These are my guides! The road is straight and tarmac, In Salah is only 100km!'.

'You have maps? Pass me the maps! Military maps!'

'Of course I have maps! Your country is big and I must know where I am! Not military maps. I bought them in shops. In London, Paris and in Algiers. Twenty, thirty years ago.' Despite my impending predicament I found myself bursting with laughter inside as I found myself speaking like the Red Indians in the movies talking to Charlton Heston. How about, 'My people come from land of grey skies, many cars ... ' That ought to do it. The truth was it suited my terrible French. Short sentences, slowly and clearly. If you screwed up the tenses it was only one sentence at a time.

'Let me see. Give them to me!'

'Of course! Here ... ' My premonition began turning to unease as le lieutenant strode away. I waited. And waited some more. It took four hours for the escort to arrive from In

Salah. Three big gendarmerie Nissans and six men. Four hours later again, my questioning at the gendarmerie HQ at In Salah was still under way. Now it was Captain Rahmouni in the dimly lit office with the flickering bulb.

'What are these marks? These figures?'

'Ah. They're position fixes and the dates I was there. And the odometer readings of the wagon; you know, the kilometres?'

'And this?' The moment was like something from a TV spy drama, the great dénouement where, with the hint of a superior smile and the smallest twitch of an eyebrow, the spycatcher has nailed his man. Rahmouni produced a yellow Post-it Note from the folds of the map with pencilled writing, a sketch and scribbles on it: 'Track' ... 'valve' ... 'pipeline' ... 'junction' ... 'Krechba'. At first I had no idea what it was or where it had come from. Then it slowly came back.

'Ah! Teguentur! ... I was there in ...'

'You were in Teguentur? The gas facility to the north?' Why? What were you doing there; at Teg?'

It didn't take a specially incisive intellect to see which way the conversation – 'interrogation' seemed too strong a term till then – was going. Not only was I a spy with military maps but I had been to the secure area around the Teguentur gas field with sketch maps on where to place explosives and thus bring Algeria's economy to a spectacular blazing halt overnight and probably initiate a Third World War for good measure.

'Well yes. Three years ago. Shane Yavari. BP. They asked me there. Or rather I asked if I could see what ... '

'Why? What was your interest in this?'

Even as it formed in my mind, I knew how feeble the answer would sound. On a par with – no, far worse than – the invariably asked question as to why I went to the Sahara in the first place. The overwhelming majority of Algerians, brought up for generations past on the danger, the hostility, the heat, the thirst that the great desert represented, had little desire to visit the wide open spaces and much preferred the security and the life of towns, the company of street cafés, the fellowship of family. To a degree it was understandable that heritage going back centuries should produce such a view. Few had opened their eyes to the beauty and tranquillity of the desert. Only the Touareg, it seemed, happy to call at towns like Tamanrasset to do a little trading, buy a few supplies, preferred this magnificent environment as their normal living space. So I was always having to explain. And now; what was my interest in Teguentur?

'I'm just ... ', I cringed, '... fascinated by big engineering. I've always wanted to see ... and BP were kind enough to ... ', I tailed off as further suspicion hardened Rahmouni's stern glare.

'I need to study these maps some more tonight.' And I was dismissed. In Salah's Tidikelt Hotel was the usual Algerian up-country mix of rickety furred-up plumbing, water turned off, frightening electrics hanging out of the wall, rattling, uncontrollable air conditioners (if they worked at all) and delightful people. I managed to get some supper and Ahmed – it seems demeaning just to refer to him as the head waiter – greeted me like an old friend.

Rahmouni called again. His 'superior', 650km to the south (sitting in a high-backed chair and stroking a white cat, I assumed) had summoned us to Tamanrasset. 'Tomorrow morning; we leave In Salah at seven.'

I woke at two. In truth the tossing and turning that went before could hardly be classed as sleep. I was losing patience. This whole damn thing was getting to be ludicrous. I had planned to go to Tamanrasset eventually but not with some non-stop breakneck convoy of escorts at their customary 65mph over roads that in parts were a broken, rutted, sea of potholes. Four hundred miles there and 400 miles back. If they wished to drive in that manner they were welcome; they had not bought the vehicles they used. Nor were they grossing three tonnes. It was time politely to stick my toes in. I was a visitor, a tourist, not a spy with military maps. This was country and landscape that I had planned for many months, and incurred considerable cost, to visit and savour slowly; not to tear through in a cloud of dust non-stop and risk damage to my vehicle in the process.

Not trusting my French to put it over adequately or courteously, I slaved with a dictionary till gone three and handed Rahmouni the note in the morning. I would be happy to stay as long as required, give whatever information they thought they needed and speak to whoever they wished me to speak to at In Salah until they were ready to return the two maps they had taken. I said, however, that I must have an English-speaking interpreter. The only one I knew was Mohammed Dahmani, BP's local rep, but if they knew any other English speakers that would be fine. To his credit, Rahmouni took it well and said he would be in touch with his advisers – intelligence people, I gathered – and, returning to the gendarmerie HQ with his convoy, would call me later.

The session lasted all day. Did I have any other maps? Naturally! Could they see round the vehicle? Of course! I showed them everything. The rescue aids, the Thuraya satellite phone, the rescue beacon, the rocket flares, the cans of fuel and water, the rations, the recovery gear. I brought out my carefully catalogued map and satellite image collection which they lit upon eagerly and wanted to examine back in the gloomy office. This, I said, was no more than any sensible person would have in a vehicle that was going to the Sahara region on an extended trip. I was not about to get lost and trigger an emergency. I drove with extreme care – as I had done for over 40 years on desert trips without mishap – but if an accident occurred, I could alert the authorities and had plenty of food and water reserves on which to survive until they got there.

Mohammed Dahmani, by amazing good luck, was in town. I had not seen him since we first met five years earlier and though I always called when I passed through In Salah I had always done so, it seemed, when he was away on business. Like the fine fellow he was, he turned up to help me communicate more fluently and try to put Rahmouni's mind at ease. He looked tired and in poor spirits, still recovering from a bizarre attack by hooligans in his office 18 months previously. He had been stabbed and BP had rushed him to hospital at Hassi Messaoud where he stayed for a month. For a start he was able to confirm Shane Yavari's existence at Teguentur and that I had visited there at BP's invitation. He explained that my precious maps bore pencilled navigation annotations dating back 27 years and that there was nothing sinister about that. The satellite shots were more intuitive to read than some of the mapping and he was able to tell Rahmouni that this was all free download off the internet. Though this was a little before Google Earth, the LandSat shots I had (the same base material) were from a Maryland University website and I had taken endless hours at home to geo-ref each shot, applying a latitude and longitude grid from the French IGN (*Institut Géographique Nationale*) maps that I had bought all those years ago. (Those endless hours and the impression they made would pay off before too long.)

I showed Rahmouni landscape photographs I had taken on previous trips and a copy of my book *Four-by-four Driving* with all the detail about using a 4x4 in the desert. It was all taken to the office next door where a heavily-built man in combat fatigues sceptically scanned the material and muttered I know not what in Arabic to Rahmouni. He and the others, disconcertingly, nodded. But we seemed to be getting somewhere. Again I was allowed to return to the hotel. And I permitted my spirits to rise.

Surely, holding nothing back, making it clear I was a self-funded writer and photographer, I had convinced them of who I was and why I was there. 'Another desert-loving Englishman!' as Faisal in *Lawrence of Arabia* said. At worst I would have to have a 'guide' to get to Tamanrasset – I had planned, back in the UK, that this might be the situation – but then, taking advantage of the bizarre rules applying to south-north travel that somehow didn't apply if you're going the other way, I could, northbound, meander slowly among the landscapes I loved at my leisure.

Early evening Rahmouni phoned and wanted to see me for 'another 30 minutes'. My spirits rose some more. This would be the wrap. When I arrived my precious collection of large-scale (1:200k) IGNs were scattered all over Rahmouni's desk. There were about 75 of these sheets in all, monumental cartography lovingly and diligently produced by the French in the '50s, '60s and '70s. The task of producing this map coverage for a country the size of western Europe amounted to a great deal more than just accumulating the mountains of aerial photography that resulted from endless flying hours over the largest desert in the world. It would not have been like setting a satellite to take shots at specific intervals, orbit after orbit, and transmit them back to a nice air-conditioned lab somewhere in the US.

Taken from noisy, vibrating, piston-engined aircraft by human crews who, looking out of the window at the seemingly infinite rock-scattered beige haze below, must have wondered at times if the task would ever end, these pictures had to be anchored with ground survey. Parties had to be down on the ground later taking astro shots of exceptional precision using a theodolite, stars and time checks with no room for error. For their extended and repeated trips into the desert they'll have travelled with local Touareg who could name the peaks, the valleys, the *sebkhas*, the wadis, the plains – all to be recorded on the final map sheets – something no satellite could do. If these crews and cartographers could ever have conceived of the idea of satellite imagery and GPS for position fixing they would have taken well-deserved pride, later, in seeing the superlative accuracy of their work when I was able to compare the two technologies.

Rahmouni had summoned the patient and helpful Mohammed Dahmani again to translate and, instead of a quick conclusion, had – as if to keep me on edge – more questions to ask. At length, however, he said the magic words.

'You are free to go. To Tamanrasset. Without a guide. And you can camp along the way; not too far from the road, of course!'

'That's fantastic!' I said. 'I guess you had to satisfy yourselves about who I was and what I was doing.'

As I started gathering up the maps and returning them to their carefully sequenced order in the map cases, Rahmouni said a few words to Mohammed in Arabic.

Mohammed said: 'They are keeping the maps.'

'They're *what*?'

'They have to keep the maps. All of them. And the satellite pictures.'

I felt as though I had been turned to stone. 'What do you mean? How long for?'

'Forever', said Mohammed wearily, allowing himself a just perceptible shrug of resignation, a rare latitude in his role as translator ...

2. Heading west

Captain Rahmouni was basically a nice man. He didn't want to part on bad terms and came out to smile and shake hands before I made my way glumly back to the hotel. Old as the hills as excuses go – and here it was probably genuine – he'd just been following orders from Mr Big down in Tamanrasset. Knowing how much it meant to me he had said I could go on to Tamanrasset, on my own, camping en route, without a guide. He agreed to tell the police post outside In Salah, *le barrage* on the road south, to let me through next morning. And, at my request, to try to get through to the army checkpoint 100km further south at the nothing place that had once been near the well at Hassi el Khenig. (Not that it had moved; just that the well at Hassi el Khenig didn't seem to exist any more.)

Not parting on bad terms, unfortunately, seemed to involve painting an unrealistically rosy picture for me; the familiar Middle Eastern trait of, for the kindest motives, telling you what they thought you wanted to hear.

Naïve self-delusion or deliberate deception, I knew not which, but the police post outside In Salah at *le barrage* had not, of course, been informed and, without a guide, they sent me back after my bright, early and, if not optimistic, at least fingers-crossed start in the morning. An awful sinking feeling of inevitability came over me as I envisaged a gloomy and bad-tempered return to Algiers. The hell with them, I thought. Rushing around dilapidated tarmac roads with an impatient stranger in the passenger seat was not the aim of the trip. Not only was I back to square one, I was back to square-one-minus-one for my maps, my satellite images and all the results of my detailed and laborious planning were gone. Even if one existed who would not expect to cover the 400 miles to Tamanrasset all in one breakneck, exhausting, chassis-battering non-stop take, where could a 'guide' be found on the spur of the moment like this? Going back to remonstrate with Captain Rahmouni was not an option; it would get me nowhere.

The only map I had, dragged from my bag, was a ridiculous tourist publication devoid of detail and at a laughably small scale – 1:2.3 million. I was thus in the Sahara with no usable means of orientation. The middle of the Sahara – for that accurately describes In Salah, a dusty little town surrounded by a lot of desert stretching a very long way in every direction. For the moment I was on a tarmac road that could lead me on to Tamanrasset – *barrage* and army checkpoint permitting – and then straight back, on tarmac road, to Algiers. That was not why I had come to Algeria. Tarmac roads were only a means to an end. A conduit and jumping-off point for access to the wilderness, the real Sahara.

A plan had begun to form the previous night while I digested the implications of my now mapless state. That was when I thought I'd be getting to Tamanrasset; a plan for the northbound return, bizarrely free of the obligatory guide.

Now, driving disconsolately back from *le barrage* to the police station, my brain in a whirl, a secondary plan materialised for not even getting to Tam, which appeared to be the present likelihood.

I had brought with me all the navigation logs from my previous five trips to remote Saharan Algeria in the G-Wagen. I had the en route position fixes and waypoints from each trip in the logs and many of them on the GPS data storage. Hundreds of them; latitude and longitude positions in degrees, minutes and decimals of a minute to three figures. I also had, as well as the excellent Lowrance 3500c marine GPS unit I'd hard-wired into the Mercedes, a standby hand-held GPS. I had written many times that GPS is only as good as the maps you use it on. What good is a fix if you can't relate it to the terrain on a map?

But what if you already had the navigational fixes, a succession of waypoints, that you had visited and established before? You could maybe retrace an old route on a kind of join-the-dots principle. Join the dots; join the position fixes and drive from one to the other. It depended on the distance between the dots, the complexity of the terrain, where they were relative to each other and your desired route and how accurately they'd been recorded. In 2003 and 2005 I had established some routes that I'd have been more than happy to revisit. And I was beginning to realise, with all that work, all those hours putting in the latitude and longitude lines on the satellite shots before I set off, that I had a recall of the maps and satellite print-outs, together with the past and planned routes themselves that, to my surprise, was almost photographic.

Or, and here was to be the rub, I certainly thought so at the time. It seemed as though something might be salvaged from the wreckage. Going off-tracks in the Sahara: no maps. How wise was that, whatever else you had on board? You really did have to stand back at times like this, take a hard look and put things in context.

And with the hard look, I started to reflect. With all this drama – despite the hassle, storm in a teacup would be the better term – there was bound to be a no-smoke-without-fire aftermath. Would I ever get a visa for Algeria again? Could this be my last trip? Should I not make the most of it on those grounds alone?

•   •   •

I took this somewhat pessimistic view about visa procurement because it had happened in Libya several years earlier: just a sensible test of the rescue beacon, sanctioned by the UK authorities with whom it was registered. And then it had all turned to powder. Of my first, wide-eyed, moist-eyed, introduction to the breathtaking beauty of the desert, I had written, many years before after a crew trip in a Royal Air Force Beverley:

> 'Ahead, as the great aircraft droned on, the first scything cut of the sun on the horizon skimmed rays of pale light across the desert, colour emerging from the thin grey haze. Below us Uweinat's gaunt rocks cast mile-long shadows over the sand; a small line of dunes down to our right showed slip faces to the sun, scalloped shadow backing each bright crescent. The Sahara in all its vast majesty – serene, awesome, beautiful ... . It was like witnessing the birth of the world.'

So I had contrived to go there on the ground. Again and again. Uweinat – Jebel Uweinat – is on the join of Egypt, Libya and Sudan, on the tip of that right angle at Egypt's south-western frontier that the border describes. Uweinat is a vast granite and sandstone massif of towering outcrops, plateaux and eroded peaks with a fringe of giant boulders at its feet and winding valleys of sand and rock tapering to impossible conclusion at the flanks of the

Jebel Uweinat,. massive bastion of the border between Libya, Egypt and Sudan and host to thousands of rock paintings and engravings.

mountain. It rises 4000 feet above the flat surrounding plain, and measures around 20km west to east and a dozen north to south. It is high enough to trigger and store its own rainfall. On my first trip there in 1960 with the RAF desert rescue team, we saw the thin galvanised pipe and cistern that had been installed by the Italians during the Second World War to lead the water down from a natural reservoir higher up the mountain.

But Uweinat was alive with rock art – engravings and paintings, many hundreds of them, going back 8-9000 years. First reported by Egyptian explorer Hassenein Bey on his pioneering expeditions in the 1920s, they were listed in more detail with surveyed positions by Ralph Bagnold in the 1930s on his epic desert journeys in two-wheel drive Ford Model 'A's, trips that were among the forerunners of wheeled desert exploration. The catalogue of this beautiful and prolific rock art has been hugely expanded and painstakingly recorded, photographically and with GPS co-ordinates, by Andras Zboray on his numerous expeditions with co-opted tourist visitors in very recent years.

I thought, now, at In Salah, of my own trip to Libya in 1998. After years of trying I had finally got a visa from the Libyan Consulate to return to Uweinat. My passport was annotated with special permission to visit the massif to examine the paintings. So rare was this authorisation that I determined to make the most of the opportunity and visit as much of the Libyan desert as I could en route. Though my goal of Uweinat, and its rock art was in the far south-east of the country, I started 1100 miles to the west with the track from Ghadames down the border with Algeria, working my way then east to the extinct volcano of Wau en Namus and through the Rebiana Sand Sea to Kufra. The Kufra that I had first visited in 1960. For the solo journey I took an EPIRB (Emergency Position Indicating Radio Beacon) of the kind used by ocean yachtsmen. My route was to take me to very remote

Camels heading north, Libya. Probably looking for something a little more appetising.

regions in all four corners of Libya and it seemed a good idea to check the functioning of the beacon at predetermined spots along the route so that any subsequent non-appearance could be bracketed relative to my last check-in. Usually emergency beacons are kept strictly for emergency situations but if advance permission is sought, tests can be made. I had obtained the clearance.

The knock on the door came at 0245. As with my visit to the BP gas plant at Teguentur that had so horrified Captain Rahmouni, my fascination with huge civil engineering projects found me with the contractors at Tazerbo, learning about the staggering Great Man-made River Project that tapped ancient aquifers in the southern Libyan desert and piped the water in three-metre-diameter concrete pipes all the way to the coast at Benghazi and Tripoli. This seems to be the kind of thing expatriate Brit engineers do very well. All over the globe tight little communities of British professionals, dedicated, tolerant, resilient, rumble into remote compounds in dusty Toyotas at the end of a long working day, take off their hard hats and yellow jackets, kick the clogged doormats of their Portakabins, blow the dust off their computer keyboards and send queries, chasers or reports back to HQ on how the project is going and ask where the hell those parts are.

My bearded, energetic, genial and charismatic host here in bleakly isolated Tazerbo was Pat Conroy-Hargrave. He offered a night of Brown and Root hospitality, a shower and a meal cooked by the equally irreplaceable, cheerful and unsinkable Filipino cooks without whom such organisations – just like BP at Teguentur and In Amenas – would be brought to their knees, deafened by their rumbling stomachs. We had thought bringing out a strange electronic device such as my EPIRB for the test might arouse unfounded suspicions and Pat colluded in my meeting the 2000 hrs pre-arranged check transmission by secreting the device under a cardboard box on the roof of the cabin for its appointed period of test.

At 0246 I was being asked by the Libyan security staff if I had set off an electronic device. A transmission had been picked up in Benghazi at 2011 and the fix showed it had come from the Tazerbo camp.

I think I was being arrested. Certainly I would be helping the police with their enquiries at Kufra 150 miles to the south. My wild-eyed escort later in the day, piratical of visage, drove his Toyota with panache, trailing a thin plume of sand, stopping only to pray at dusk and attend to a fuel filter problem. He must have done it in the right order as we were soon on our way again heading into the night south toward Kufra at a wholly inappropriate speed and now over a wholly unacceptable example of road disrepair and degradation.

Ah, they said, we understand your position (they had the co-ordinates too!) but EPIRB test transmissions are only allowed in the first five minutes of every hour. Are you sure? I said. They were sure. I was not. After all I had had specific permission from the RAF Rescue

Co-ordination Centre at Kinloss. But the Libyans were right. I'd been given the wrong information. After apologies, a four-day wait for further authorisation and the somewhat unwelcome addition of a military escort I was on my way to Uweinat in convoy with an ill-equipped army Toyota heading south-east over the wide sandy plains and bands of evil small dunes that separated Kufra from the great mountain.

They were wonderful – the captain, the soldier driver and Moussa the 'guide'. Moussa was actually a member of the *mukhabarat*, the secret police, but he was able to direct me to the most readily accessible rock paintings at Karcur Ibrahim – one of Uweinat's named valleys – and with that magic endorsement on my visa they agreed to let me off the leash while they took a rest at the untidy, tin-strewn, plastic-bag-littered collection of Portakabins that comprised the border post. I seemed to have won some credibility since whenever, on the way down, one of our party got stuck in the sand it was always the escort Toyota, and they didn't have shovels or sand channels or even tyre pressure gauges and inflators. I supplied them all plus a strong and willing shoulder to the back of their wagon to get it moving again – even, later, a tow-rope to pull their reluctant engine with its clapped-out battery into life. I tried my best to render the assistance without looking like a smart-ass to their guardians of the vast desert wastes.

It was like being given just half an hour to zip around the Hermitage in St Petersburg. Making my way round to the northern fringes of Uweinat on my own I had a now-or-never decision to make and, though I pondered during the night I camped, I didn't doubt the outcome. Sitting precisely on the Egyptian border with the minor Holy Grail of the Karcur Tahl valley just a few miles round the corner to the east where Hassenein Bey and Ralph Bagnold had recorded some of the first dramatic and beautiful rock carvings to be discovered, I was not able to resist trying to find them. I fancied, too, that Moussa's leaving me alone like this and hinting at what lay to the east – in Egypt – was a kind of blind eye to what he was sure I would want to do.

A small tatty tangle of barbed wire at a low saddle marked, inaccurately, the border where I tip-toed across. It was as though the GPS had been programmed to send out a jangling alarm but when I saw the latitude and longitude read-out it instantly alerted me to its being part of the co-ordinates on a map I had photographed at the British Museum Reading Room years before, showing Bagnold's original route round Uweinat in 1927. A lone tree, an opening to a south-easterly defile and then a wide valley moving through south to south-west into Karcur Tahl itself.

The security chief at Kufra had said it had rained three weeks earlier at Uweinat. I beamed and knew what to expect. The valley was a mass of low, cool green plants and delicate yellow flowers, the scattering of trees, like the rocks themselves, washed down and free from their usual coating of dust. Beyond, where the valley narrowed and led up into the mountain, the eastern plateau of Uweinat loomed majestically against a clear dark-blue sky like a great

The miracle wrought by rain at Uweinat. Karcur Talh valley three weeks after the downpour.

Rock engravings, Karcur Talh valley at Jebel Uweinat as photographed by Bagnold c.1927 and recently. 8000 years ago herds of graceful giraffe were the norm. What a wonderful thought.

benevolent guardian.

I drove slowly and cautiously down the wadi scarcely believing that 38 years after first reading about them I was finally in this extraordinary place scanning the north-facing flanks of the rocks where the carvings were known to be. Suddenly they were there, not 20 yards away. I had somehow expected them to be hugely inaccessible, hidden, overgrown and difficult to find. Unlike rock paintings which were always in overhangs or sheltered spots protected from the erosive effects of wind, sand and weather, engravings were often on easily seen rock faces and virtually immune from the effects of the weather. Here, they were at head height, right alongside the wadi bed where people could walk. And a little further on, the same carvings pictured in Bagnold's book 60 years before. The cattle, the ostriches, the beautifully rendered herd of giraffes – intertwining necks like waving stalks of corn so evocative as almost to be an animation of the scene.

•   •   •

'Ah, the minefield!' I was talking later to Stefan Kröpelin of the Heinrich Barth Institute, in Cologne.

'Pardon?'

The map I asked him to send me confirmed it. Stefan's colleagues had worked in the area north-east of Uweinat, on the Egyptian side. During a spat between Egypt and their Libyan neighbours mines had been laid in that area, right up to the edge of the mountain. *Geo* magazine's October 2000 edition which Stefan also sent me showed the result of getting it wrong: a Mercedes G-Wagen in flames and burnt almost to a skeleton when the photograph was taken. I had apparently been to Karcur Tahl through a minefield.

And back.

It had been a good trip, though, albeit the Land Rover had scared me again. A rash of random, engine-wrecking cam-belt failures, due to pulley misalignment and known to the manufacturers had not been brought to the notice of owners. Only through the grapevine had I heard and been able to have the remedial modification carried out before the trip. The company's ethics did not impress me, especially against the background of their up-market posturing with the Range Rover and Discovery. In the desert the Defender's high fuel consumption under load and the lack of cross-axle differential locks had been a constant problem and a significant limit to performance in challenging conditions. On my return the Land Rover was sold, ending a 36 year association with the marque, and I bought the

Mercedes G-Wagen that would later renew my acquaintance with the Algerian Sahara. But the 6000 miles around all four corners of Libya, a unique opportunity to see the extraordinary Wau en Namus crater, the Great Man-made River Project, and make a return to Uweinat would lead, in due course, to persuading UNESCO to support my proposal for a protected area at Uweinat to safeguard the rock art. They mounted a tri-national conference and workshop in Tripoli to get the three concerned nations on board.

A few months after my visit I wanted to return, invited by some oil geologists to join their prospecting expedition in the far south of the country – a once-in-a-lifetime opportunity. Even with their corporate clout they were unable to obtain a visa for me. Despite the EPIRB incident having been a perfectly sensible test conducted at the wrong time only because of some incorrect information from elsewhere, there was apparently 'a file' on me.

That was Libya; then. And it didn't take a vivid imagination to see the In Salah maps episode leading to a similar situation in Algeria should I ever want to visit again. A note on a file, a subtle embargo. I didn't know it at the time but somewhere a letter had apparently already been written.

•   •   •

So my reflections at In Salah had me thinking there'd be a problem next time. Or more to the point, possibly – probably – there wouldn't be a next time. As in Libya, this was likely to be my last trip. Accusations of having 'military maps', questioning on who I was, why I had been to Teguentur, where I had been in Algeria, the apparently cardinal sin of going to the old fort at Ain Guettara and wanting just to be alone to savour the peace and magnificence of the Sahara and photograph its beauty in my own time.

In Salah shops wake up for the afternoon's trading.

When I reached the police commissariat, turned back from *le barrage*, the counterweighted steel bar across the road on the southern edge of town, the cheerful, easy going policeman there was sympathetic. This was not the gendarmerie. Gendarmes wore olive green, the police wore dark blue (and the army camouflaged fatigues). As I fumbled through the usual signing-in procedure and gave all the details I'd given a hundred times before to the good-humoured policeman, my brain was humming and on a different plane. I knew this could be my last opportunity. I had come with specific plans and routes in mind – that included, by an amusing stroke of irony, visiting another 'old fort' – Ouallene. Was there a chance I could still make these plans work? The question was a mere formality, part of a justifying process, as I sought to embark on an objective sequence of reasoning. Of course there was a chance. I'd be going, if my plan was workable, not only and exactly to places – GPS fix points – where I had been before but on an inverted, modified version of my original planned routes. Plan 'A' would be mutating.

I'd be making some leaps between the widely-spaced waypoints (very widely-spaced, actually) from different previous trips. The first could hardly have been more 'widely spaced' – a giant 200-mile first leg south from the region of Reggan over the Tanezrouft – then jumping from halfway down past-route A to a point on past-route B, possibly connecting cross-country with past-route C. The satellite shot preparation that had taken so long back in UK over the past four or five months was well enough engraved on my mind's eye that I could visualise it all. Vitally important and with enormous good fortune, I had written down the co-ordinates of the waypoint at the end of the southbound 200-mile leg in one of my notebooks; and the majority of it was over the benign Tanezrouft plain – once you got on to it. That still left a 120-mile gap to the next waypoint and a number of significant others but I had a pretty clear mental picture of what terrain to expect.

'Maybe I should go to the west towards Aoulef and Reggan?' I said, probing casually for a reaction from the policeman. I had no wish to break any rules, despite the extreme difficulty of finding out what the rules were and why they applied in one direction and not the other. But if the splendid Captain Rahmouni could resort to well-intentioned deception then I was not averse to a little fancy footwork myself to avoid possible bureaucratic conflict. For the happy policeman had said, yes, there was no problem in the direction of Aoulef and Reggan: no checks, no guides required. That would be fine, he said. It is beautiful!

The craziness of the regulations seemed to have no end and, still desperately searching for some rationale, I concluded (tentatively) that the rules about guides perhaps not only applied to southbound traffic to Tamanrasset alone but also varied from one *wilaya* to another. The Tamanrasset *wilaya* (or region of governance) extended north to In Salah but only a little way to the west. Going in that direction, if what the policeman said was true, I'd be in the clear. Where before I had been hoping, once I'd got south to Tam, to strike back north-west on a huge 500-mile sweep to Reggan, now I would first go west towards Reggan and then broadly in the opposite direction – 500 miles south-east through the desert, down towards Tamanrasset. From Plan 'A' I had pin-balled rapidly through a crumbling Plan 'B', 'C' and 'D', and was somewhere around Plan 'E' by now. I did not propose, however, to tempt providence by bumbling into Reggan, hitting another unpredictable administrative Armco and being sent away.

I had come to explore this route and one other, on my own and at my own pace so that I could concentrate, await the light and the weather to savour the regal, majestic, dignified, achingly beautiful landscape and record it through a lens. There seemed now, after a traumatic four or five days, to be a chance of doing it. Albeit at some risk.

There was, of course, the small question of the maps and of having to establish the Reggan bypass. Reggan bypass? I hoped nobody would mind. I liked the sound of that: the Reggan bypass.

3. The Reggan bypass. Part 1

I've noticed it before. The sheer will to communicate works minor miracles and brooks no hindrance from little details like a language barrier. I have managed, barely able reliably to pronounce the name of their hideously complex language, Tamachek, to establish health, provenance, destination, and boundless goodwill with Touareg I have met in the Sahara without being able to speak a word in their tongue.

There were others; little details and obstacles to comprehension, that is, in the context of my current situation where I'd be the first to admit my potential fluency should have been considerably better than in the case of a meeting with desert Touareg. First there was my lousy hearing where the chopped-off higher frequency responses almost hit the bottom of the audiogram. Then my skeletal French, the echo in the new Police Commissariat building at In Salah and – I hope I don't do him an injustice here – the possibly less than perfect diction, swallowed consonants and limited vocabulary of the cheerful policeman who was supplying me invaluable intelligence about the route west towards Reggan via Aoulef. Probably because they do not speak it at the seemingly obligatory 200 miles an hour as they do in France, I usually found I could understand Algerians speaking French more easily than I could understand Frenchmen.

But the cheerful policeman had been right. Mostly. Though his assertion that the way west was beautiful denoted a degree of local pride not supported by the appearance of this bleak, featureless route under what was now a harsh, glaring, short-shadowed midday blaze of light, certainly I found no checkpoints, barriers, *barrages* or other disruptions to a steady, quiet, thoughtful, fuel-sipping 45mph potter towards Aoulef and Reggan. Despite its three-tonne all-up weight and 2.9-litre five-cylinder turbocharged diesel engine, my Mercedes G-Wagen – this was the type 461 with a *kastenwagen* (van) body, what I liked to call 'the civil engineers' version' to distinguish it from the sybaritic, leather and wood, silly engines, Range-Rover-wannabe Type 463 sported by others – could turn in an impressive

Initial plan – 'Plan A' →   Final plan – 'Plan E' ➜   Other expeditions →

The original plan – 'Plan A' shown pale blue here – comprised two sectors with a refuel at Arak. This, several iterations later, was inverted and melded – if fuel and other considerations such as the realities of mapless navigation allowed – into a single segment: 'Plan E' in red, destination Tamanrasset.

miles-per-gallon when the horrors of its aerodynamic profile were minimised by driving slowly. Cd-half-rho-V-squared-S, the formula for calculating aerodynamic drag, was engraved somewhere on the inside of my skull from earlier Air Force and model aircraft days and the V-squared bit meant that if you doubled the speed, the drag rose by a factor of four – 2-squared. And a big 'S' didn't help much either, the frontal cross-sectional area.

Miles-per-gallon – mpg – was of vital (in every literal sense of the word) importance on a trip like this. The fuel I carried and the formula by which I calculated my range was probably more important than my water supply. After all, what good is water if you are stranded without fuel 100 miles short of your destination out in the Sahara? Mpg was calculated at every refuelling and the fuel (and water) state was monitored daily and entered in the nav log. Consistency was the goal. Unlike the Land Rover Defender 90 with the 300Tdi engine, which in Libya had alarmed me with its sharp rise in fuel consumption in difficult conditions, the Merc on correctly deflated BFGoodrich 265/75 16R All-Terrain tyres maintained a calm and dependable fuel consumption of around 23-25 miles per Imperial gallon on all the off-tracks sectors of the six major Saharan journeys it had purred reliably through over the previous seven years.

Born of my RAF short-range jet fighter training, the one thing you made sure you got right was your fuel state – unless you wanted to end your career as the pilot of a high-speed, rakishly styled, heavyweight glider. The formula was well tried over the years: planned sector distance multiplied by 'terrain factor', plus 25 per cent, plus 100 miles; all divided by the likely (worst) mpg gave the number of gallons to take. 'Terrain factor' was a guesstimated increase in distance-covered according to the kind of terrain encountered. In dunes, for example (avoid them like the plague if you can), TF might be 1.5 to 2.0; but on firm flat desert it would be down at 1.1.

Despite the Merc's consistency, I usually used 20 or 22 mpg as the divider for an extra margin. You could work backwards from a 'full fuel' state – here a 95-litre fuel tank and six internally stowed 20-litre jerry cans – to give a max range figure. And lest this – around 750 miles in the case of the G-Wagen at 22 mpg – should seem too generous in the light of the planned sector distance, think of your state of mind as you near the end of so long a leg, still off-tracks, still not in sight of your destination, with six empty cans on board and a fuel gauge showing low. You don't fool with fuel.

I had reason to believe there was diesel at Aoulef and would certainly top up there, 90 miles west of In Salah, if I could, albeit my basic calculations indicated I could make it to In Amguel – or certainly to a decision point for an alternate fuel source – without.

Basically there are two north-south Sahara routes – shown on the map opposite dropping down respectively from In Salah and Reggan. The eastern route – the main one – runs just about due south from Algiers through Ghardaia, El Golea, In Salah, Arak, In Amguel, Tamanrasset, south to cross into Niger at In Guezzam, through Agadez and on to Nigeria. Farther west by about 250 miles, the Tanezrouft route, aimed at Mali, starts conceptually at Bechar (map p6), around 550 miles south-west of Algiers. It then heads south through Adrar and Reggan before encountering the vast flat Tanezrouft, crosses into Mali after 400 miles and there's another 100 miles before Tessalit and the chance to refuel.

I'd crossed between the two routes previously, west to east in 1979. My petrol-swigging V8 Range Rover in the previous year, 1978, had logged 907 miles between Tombouctou and Reggan, cross-country, off-tracks just about all the way. The trailer I needed to assuage its indecent thirst had contributed to too many of the scary moments arising from such a long and minimally mapped crossing and, southbound through the Tanezrouft towards Tamanrasset in 1979 the vehicle, now on fatter 7.50x16 Michelin XS tyres, towed nothing

but a cloud of dust behind it. Though the maps were still very broad brush and at a toe-curlingly small scale of 1:1m, the indications had been that crossing from the Tanezrouft to the eastern route should not present too much trouble. So long as it was done 200 miles or so south from Reggan, between about 22° and 23°N and with the assistance of the track running south-west from the Hoggar mountains toward Mali which I aimed to join about halfway along its length. In truth it was thus more cutting the corner, albeit quite a large one, than forging a new route.

Twenty-seven years later the basic plan – only 'Plan A' as it turned out (the pale blue line and arrow on the map overleaf) – was to cross in the opposite direction, from the Tamanrasset road to the Tanezrouft but a lot farther north where a much more demanding way through had to be found. This meant picking a route between the massifs, escarpments,

Old tech: see-thru sun compass, based on the classic Coles, DR plot-out from the nav log on graph paper (or map), night astro with a T2 theodolite.

34

outcrops, dune areas and wadis. But now I had (at least when I started) satellite shots that I had geo-reffed (overlaid latitude and longitude) together with much better maps – specifically, the old but excellent French IGN 1:200,000 series made in the '50s and '60s, for no better maps had been produced since.

I now also had GPS for constant position readouts (and homing to my own look-ahead waypoints) rather than the time-consuming, once-a-day evening fix that a heavy, bulky and vulnerable theodolite yielded with star shots. Now it was 2006 and in the previous five years I had done five Algeria expeditions in the Merc, two of which – 2001 and 2003 – took in narrow swathes of terrain that lay between the two Sahara north-south routes.

If the presentation of a Holy Grail on a purple cushion was sought by a desert wanderer, especially after several decades savouring the beauty and vastness of such regions with definitively old-tech navigation aids, it would take the form of GPS and Google Earth printouts, geo-referenced with a fine latitude and longitude grid. You have to have done it the old way, for a long time, to appreciate the miracle this represents. Google Earth and other LandSat printouts, carefully catalogued alongside my IGN maps were flagged, underlined, diamond-studded items on the 23 pages of my equipment list when I packed and weighed the G-Wagen at the planning stage of the trip. When you've navigated with a bubble sextant, a sun compass, dead-reckoning nav plot-outs on bits of graph paper – or later, if you can borrow one, experienced the brain-wilting burden of theodolite astro and a nine-star position fix after a long hot day – the luxury, the precision, the reliability, the repeatability of GPS and an appropriate map or satellite printout to use it on is, in every sense of the phrase, a life-saver of such technological elegance and beauty it is hard to find a sufficiency of superlatives with which to lavish praise.

New tech: GPS (Lowrance 3500) and annotated LandSat images. (This shot from an earlier trip; on this expedition no Google Earth images were available to photograph!) It all still needs very careful plotting.

Now, as I squinted against the harsh midday glare heading to Aoulef, leaving In Salah behind to the east, passing the spot where I'd had the bike accident 15 years earlier before the road had been firmed-up, smoothed and sealed, I had, alas, no maps, no LandSat images and no Google Earth. So I was still weighing things up.

There was much to think about, mainly the wisdom or otherwise of what I was proposing to do: setting off without maps through country most of which I had never seen before on a trip which would be not less than 500 miles in extent. The 2001 and 2003 expeditions in the same 250,000-square-mile patch yielded experience only in narrow strip form; strips maybe five to ten miles wide if the visibility had been good. How different from the 1978 and 1979 scenario was the see-how-it-goes route that I was

proposing to embark upon? Were not those trips themselves risky to the point of foolishness – solo, no radio, no-one aware of where I was heading, no rescue aids except flares and a heliograph and only 1:1m mapping? They didn't seem so at the time. A challenge, yes, to be planned in detail and tackled with great care. Someone – a young MT corporal at RAF El Adem in Libya in 1969, as I recall – said he could see no reason why you couldn't drive round the world off-tracks if you drove carefully and within the limits of yourself and your vehicle. A wise young man was he, mature beyond his years. And certainly it was a creed I have followed on all my trips.

But what were the pluses? What special assets did I have now? I had the route logs of the 2001 and 2003 trips and a record of every GPS fix I'd taken on those journeys – albeit only a few were relevant to this route. I thus had a sprinkling of fixes I could use as waypoints to home-in on; join-the-dots, as I termed it. Even the nearest dots, though, were

The electronic awesome foursome. McMurdo 406 EPIRB, Thuraya, standby hand-held GPS (Lowrance H20c) and 'notebook' recorder.

a long way off. Something like 350 miles from Reggan – south and east – was the closest one to feature in my logs. You could get it terminally wrong in the desert within the space of five or ten miles so that was a hell of a long way to be sniffing the air before getting to terrain I knew with any certainty. Against this was the fact that the Tanezrouft was famous for being huge and flat. And, jewel in the somewhat tenuous crown, there was the grubby note on one of my notebooks giving the co-ordinates in latitude and longitude of the southernmost Tanezrouft waypoint I'd need to get to before turning east towards Ouallen.

I always smiled when I thought of Ouallen; a straw for cartographers to clutch at. A name to put in an otherwise empty space on the map of the southern Sahara. I had often wondered what it was, so way off the beaten track on a route going nowhere and doing what? Doubtless, I concluded, an old, abandoned French fort that would yield my dream finds – the remnants of an old biplane, a tattered tricolor still flapping from a mast, sand-blasted wine bottles littering the surrounding area, the rusting chassis of a Dodge Power Wagon. My curiosity about Ouallen, certain to be deserted now, was a significant, if minor, factor in my urge to follow the route I had chosen.

And the other thing – one of the major pluses – was the near obsession with which I had, at the planning stage, studied the maps and satellite shots of the terrain leading to and beyond Ouallen. My memory was so clear I could see it all. I couldn't see the latitude and longitude lines but the overall picture was one of reaching my noted coordinates, heading to Ouallen through a gap in a prominent ridge, and, in broad terms then continuing east with a major and almost unbroken range of rock hills and escarpments to the north until I got to a previous waypoint representing my camping spot on 3rd of November 2003 – '3 Nov' as I called it. Then again, no map or satellite shot – whether or not I had them – could give the actual detail of the going. Was it stony? Rocky? How big were the rocks? What about sand? Vegetation? Endless areas of 'touffe-touffe', the suspension-wracking grass tumps a foot – or three feet – high? This you knew only when you got there.

(And what if, without maps, I found myself in a maze of difficult terrain and, with no grand overview that cartography or satellite pictures provided, was unable to determine which direction I should go to get out? I did not think of this as I headed towards Aoulef but would have cause to ponder it in a state of some trauma later on.)

My brain boiled. The debate went on. And on; even as I drove west. This time, as on the last three trips, I had an EPIRB – like the one that got me into trouble in Libya – and a Thuraya satellite phone. An EPIRB (Emergency Position Indicating Radio Beacon), when activated, sends a UHF signal that is picked up by a satellite and relayed to rescue centres worldwide. If the EPIRB has been registered with a code, as mine had with the UK coastguard, the code would indicate who it was and give a rough position to within 10km. But an EPIRB is an all-or-nothing device for only the direst emergencies where the emergency is critical and time-vital. There are in-between situations when outside assistance is needed but, with adequate supplies on hand, there is no need for the rescue team itself (if there is one) to be put at risk with undue haste, tearing across the desert having accidents. There are also times when you just need to talk to someone to get specialist advice.

So I got a Thuraya. Gone are the days of dishes and fold-out antennae; satellite phones now are the size that ordinary mobiles were a few years ago. And Abu Dhabi-based Thuraya, running two geo-stationary satellites serving Europe, the northern half of Africa and the Middle East, charges less than competitors with world coverage.

It was an interesting balance of criteria. I was, I felt, better off on balance than in 1979; but there's no substitute for maps. As if I ever doubted it.

I had at this point, essentially, two aims. One, to make the journey I had planned for so long to a new and wild part of the Sahara and, now the other, to avoid encountering and upsetting those who, for well-meaning reasons, would wish to prevent my doing so. The latter had me more on edge than the former. I guess I had, too, to acknowledge that among these concerned reasons was the statistical possibility of problems with 'bandits' – for want of a better (or more pejorative) word – who sometimes gave in to the attractions of kidnapping, ransom demands and vehicle hijacking. Recent history being what it was, there was little doubt the Algerian Government would be loath to 'lose' another tourist or suffer an 'incident' when they were discernibly pouring the balm of assumed normality over the general security situation. The men on the ground at the sharp end, specifically the gendarmerie, had their orders and minimising risk to visitors was, for sure, high on their list of priorities. Stepping around these people without upsetting them, if I could unobtrusively do so rather than into their restrictive arms, kept them in the clear and me on course to see some of the most beautiful landscape on the planet.

What about the bad guys, though? My 'security perimeter' was under my camp bed, under my pillow and laughably primitive – a stout stick and a miniflare rocket. Sleeping in the open under the stars as I did, my worst-imaginable event would be waking to the sound of harsh metallic clicks and the blinding glare of a torch shone into my face. What would they want? If they actually were the bad guys, probably the vehicle. There was a long record of this kind of episode. Overall I relied on the generally oddball, sore-thumb aura of my operation to reduce my target appeal – first, a rare Mercedes G-Wagen, right-hand

drive, (the 'sore thumb'; a thieveable Toyota would blend in with the local population far better); and second, a solo, aging and skinny *étranger* at the wheel, obviously not an expat oilfield engineer worth a fat ransom from his rich western-owned oil company.

The stout stick was fractionally better than not having a stout stick but the red rescue flare, secreted in a glove at the top end of my sleeping bag where I fervently hoped it would not spontaneously ignite, could be aimed at the ground by the bad guys' feet or into air according to the demands of the situation. If they eventually prised the hidden vehicle keys from me they would discover, thanks to an unfindably hidden battery master switch which I set every night before turning in, that the wagon would not start 'because of some unknown fault' and hopefully the impasse would conclude peacefully with a manly handshake from both parties and a cup of coffee all round. I reckoned, almost seriously.

I never had to enact this James Bond charade but a peculiar incident in a remote area on the 2001 trip had me wondering later how close I had come. (High speed solo vehicle approaching from the west, way off the track, none of the usual greetings or politenesses, a brusque exchange and then roared off again. A brief sizing-up, I thought later; was I an oily-boy from Khanfoussa? Was I worth the effort? Odd wagon, that; no add-on tourist clobber or roof rack. Guy looks a bit old ... shit'd hit the fan ... better leave it.)

•   •   •

Aoulef at that time of day, high noon, was deserted, neat, clean and mud-coloured in the Tidikelt style of building, the main streets very wide and of beaten earth and dust. It would have been easier to find the fuel station if there had been someone to ask. Hard shadows blackened every doorway in the dry heat but a hint of movement at one yielded directions. The tank brimmed after only 14 litres but that was another 75 miles range up my sleeve. It also meant the Merc, since its last refuel at In Salah, had turned in a little over a chest-beating 34 mpg. A nice old boy took the money: 189 Algerian dinars; £1.39, about 10p a litre! The mileage on the odometer read 44757. It would be quite a bit more at my next fuel station refuelling.

It pays to be a nit-picker, to notice things; 'Life is about detail!' I keep saying and it probably drives people a little bit mad. (Chris, smashing chap, who did a superb job on my patio at home, wasn't very careful with his tools. I gave him a replacement drill bit for his electric drill after he'd broken his own. I cringed as he put the drill down, every time, point first on the ground. I wasn't going to granny him; maybe he knew, professionally, how strong they were; taken a course, perhaps. But then, predictably, as he put it down point first once more, the drill broke again. 'Chris! I could see that coming! Life is about detail! And it'd probably be safer if you did your bootlaces up before you step on one and fall over... !' We were well on joshing terms by then so he smiled, put the fag back in his mouth and did up his laces.)

At Aoulef and 44757 I thought back to that log entry on Wednesday 29 October 2003 when the mileage read 22875; those all-important words 'Just passed graded rd S.' That bit of detail paid off too. Thereby lay hours of study on the Google Earth images and the LandSat pictures downloaded from the Maryland University site. Not much more than a faint-contrast pixel wide on the image, I thought – no, I was sure – I could see a barely perceptible mark to coincide with the position of my log entry. It disappeared, as these tracks often do, but if it was there at all someone – quite a few people, if it was graded – had been that way before: south from the tarmac road toward the edge of the plateau that faced the Tanezrouft 15 miles or so to the east of Reggan.

If I was to avoid the potential problems that Reggan might bring in its wake I would have to drive around it; where there was no track. Reggan was on a plateau that rose on the northern edge of the Tanezrouft and I would have to find a way to tippy toe down off it without risk to the Merc, to myself or to what was to become a kind of

'Graded rd S'; not much to see – despite the enhanced, high-contrast image! 'Rubicon' would be the better title.

Scarlet Pimpernel existence in the area. The 'Graded rd S' was the beginning of the soon-to-be-established Reggan bypass.

Having no map or satellite image to base it on I had to set my generated waypoint on the detail from the 2003 log. I'd actually made that log entry some way down the road after seeing the track so there was now a cautious and rather anxious drive from the lat/long of the log entry towards Reggan, scanning the bleak terrain to the south. Suddenly it was there, not too obvious in the early afternoon near-overhead sun but clear enough when I really looked at it. God bless Google. God bless my 2003 log.

Just 'going round Reggan' wasn't quite as simple as the phrase alone made it sound. Part of what was imprinted on my memory about this well-studied part of the route, was the terrain a smidge to the east of the optimum route round Reggan. Alarmingly, dramatically, displayed on the LandSat images, but appropriately if you know that kind of terrain, was the Sebkha Azzel Matti, a huge area of salt marsh – and that was what was to the east of my best route. I really had to avoid that. Salt marsh is unimaginably frightening if you have seen the results of people getting it wrong. Salt marsh is like lemon meringue

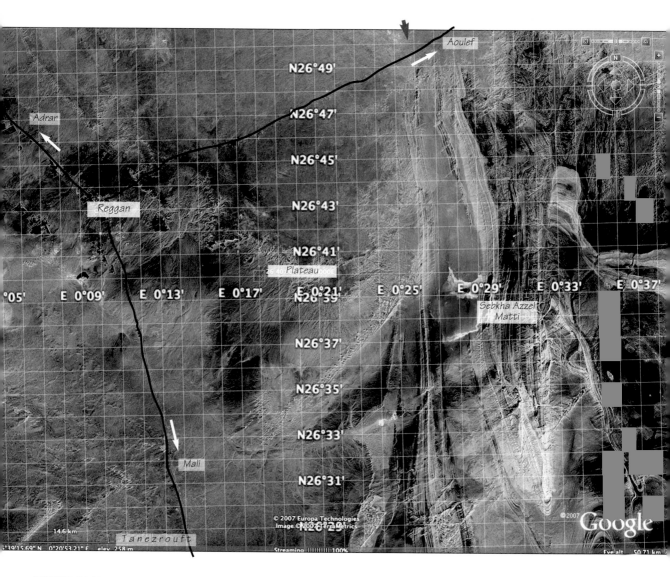

Image labels (on satellite map):
Aoulef
N26°49'
N26°47'
Adrar
N26°45'
N26°43'
Reggan
N26°41'
Plateau
°05' E 0°09' E 0°13' E 0°17' E 0°21' E 0°25' E 0°29' E 0°33' E 0°37'
N26°39'
Sebkha Azzel Matti
N26°37'
N26°35'
N26°33'
Mali
N26°31'
14.6 km
Tanezrouft
© 2007 Europa Technologies
Image © 2007 TerraMetrics
© 2007 Google
Eye alt 50.71 km

20/20 hindsight would have recalled this, as interpreted superbly by Google Earth. At the time I recalled most of it but without the lat/long grid – or scale. Each 'square' here equates to 1.16 statute miles.

pie; a thin crust on the top and a bottomless soft goo underneath. Break through that in a vehicle and you are, if you are lucky, sitting on your chassis, the wheels revolving slowly without giving traction in the goo beneath. If you are unlucky, the vehicle will sink further into the *sebkha* and be all but un-recoverable. Whilst *sebkha* could sometimes, when it was quite dry, support a vehicle, all too often it couldn't and it was very hard to tell the difference until the worst happened.

At all costs, I must avoid getting into the Sebkha Azzel Matti but following the ridges should take care of that. At the planning stage when I had about me all the images I needed, I planned to drop down off the plateau and hug its south-eastern profile, funnelling, if I could, between some ridges or dunes that paralleled each other in a generally south-western direction – at least south-west was what I thought I remembered

– that would lead me on to the Tanezrouft proper. There I would head south, displaced to the east of the Mali route by enough distance to remain out of sight of it. I dared not risk encountering any random checkpoints that would rumble the absence of any Reggan rubber stamping that may have been the norm for southbound traffic on the main route.

I crossed my Rubicon as I left the Aoulef-Reggan tarmac road onto the thin, insignificant graded track. 'Graded' was perhaps an overstatement but a blade had been down there leaving the characteristic small ridges either side, and if anyone had taken the trouble to do that the route must have had some significance. I suspected it may have been access to some oil, mineral or survey activity in the past. Despite all the objective debate and my carefully weighed, measured conclusion, there was a hard-to-ignore butterfly in my stomach as I glanced over at the passenger seat, usually three layers deep in map folders and saw it was bare.

As I turned on to south I was also all too aware that, with the sun on my right and being positioned down-sun from the airfield at Reggan just a few miles to the west, the white Merc would stand out as a bright white dot on the dark-brown terrain. I had learned this lesson before, leaving the road to camp. Going down-sun meant high visibility from passing vehicles. On that earlier occasion an army patrol had come roaring and rattling over from the road to see who I was but, in their usual way – being army rather than gendarmerie – had accepted my presence, equipment and attitude pragmatically and left me in peace, pointing out where they would be if I should require any assistance.

Tracks, graded or otherwise, have a surprisingly long life in the Sahara, years after they have last been used. I was grateful for a relatively smooth progression towards what I was sure would be a moderated way down the edge of the plateau, a descent of a couple of hundred feet. Then suddenly there was a hut in my one o'clock position. Army post? Look-out? Barrier to this very sort of diversion? As I got closer I saw to my relief that it was empty, no binocular-wielding, rifle-toting figure above the rail. What I next saw was a blow. The hut related to a hard-core building material collection site that had obviously played a part in the construction of the road from Reggan to Aoulef when it was realigned and tarmack-ed years before. The front-loaders had scooped rock and stones into trucks that had taken the material the four or five miles back to where the carriageway was being made. My 'graded track' effectively stopped. Here. It didn't lead down off the plateau at all.

By now it was around four o'clock. There would be other 'disappointments' before the day was out. The hard-core site, was, however, quite close to a kind of valley leading up the south-aligned ridge and that which sloped up without too much drama could be utilised for a careful descent too. Recceing on foot, I found that – bless its cotton socks, or at least its amazing feet and general desert savvy – a camel had scrambled up this way quite recently and, they being the local experts, who was I to argue with the choice of route? Though the tyres were warm I deflated a little to an indicated 2 bar for the sand/rock mix that lay below and, with low range and diff locks selected, straddled a small gully to edge my way down. I wouldn't have been able to get back up this slope but a glance, way over to the left, showed there was a likely looking return route if need be.

Down below and now on relatively smooth going, albeit with some rather iffy sand of uncertain firmness, there were enough southbound ridges to accord with my memory of this area on the satellite shots. I'd aim to be easing round to the right before too long to follow the fan-shaped southern profile of the plateau onto a south-west heading. For now my heading was south and the ridges to my right (west) were not crossable so I had no option but to follow their parallel pattern and hope they did not extend too far. In the back of my mind I hoped too that I was not on the wrong side of a structure I recalled separating the path south-west from what amounted to a channel pointing at the dreaded Sebkha Azzel Matti.

There was plenty to keep me busy, though, and keep back-of-my-mind thoughts right where they belonged. The sand, despite a benign appearance, was unpredictably soft in places and a ready boot of throttle was needed to respond instantly to the ominous sinkage that occasionally took place. The ridge to the west became uncompromisingly jagged and rose so that not only was it an uncrossable barrier but, with the sun sinking, its long shadow spread across the wide valley in which I now found myself somehow conveying a sense of foreboding. I was reading the country as I found it. With no maps and with nothing on which to plot the minute detail the GPS was giving me on actual position in latitude and longitude I had little alternative but to keep going and await my chance to strike south-west through the ridge to my right towards the Tanezrouft track.

Tension edged towards anxiety as the sand changed to that meringue-textured dark-brown crust redolent of a dried – hopefully fully dried – *sebkha*. From nowhere some old wheel tracks that had compressed the crust into something a little firmer appeared. Uselessly I stabbed the GPS to record a waypoint. At least I would have a record to plot later when I had something to plot it on. I didn't know then how soon I'd be using it again. The 'track' edged to the right and mercifully, as it disappeared – as tracks do in the desert – I was faced with a slight change in the texture of the ground, *sebkha* giving way to sand and even, ahead, a small ridge of dunes, curved, dainty, clean and beautiful; on their own in the low late afternoon sun and affording some firm going on the upwind side. Despite keeping right of the dunes, I was becoming mildly alarmed at the apparent lack of an opening to the south-west.

I was now 17 miles from the paved road to the north, trying hard not to give in to my usual difficulty grasping scale and my tendency to worry when things did not happen after short distances. The ground was rising slightly and, at last, a hint of an opportunity to make headway west presented itself. It was time to take action and, hitherto confined by the huge rock ridge to a heading of 160°, nothing like as far west as I felt correct, I swung the Merc right as far as I could where the terrain afforded the chance, the ridge reducing in height to meet a sandy area. After a little over a mile weaving among the undulations and still anxious, I was able to head right slightly towards a promising break in the terrain. Suddenly my unease abruptly spiked. In an attempt to beat the failing light I had hoped to get myself on to a clear route south-west before stacking for the day but as I sought a flatter area to camp, the Mercedes suddenly lurched left. The sand was giving way, too soft to bear the vehicle's weight. I pulled left again to let gravity help but it went deeper, sinking as the wheels spun momentarily in the loose particles. A brief try with more power confirmed my worst suspicions and, knowing I would probably only make things worse by even trying, an even briefer attempt to reverse out dropped the wagon a further inch or two into the sand. I cut the throttle abruptly with fire in the pit of my stomach knowing that to do otherwise would drastically worsen an already serious situation.

Logic and past experience took over but did not allay my rising alarm given the circumstances. The routine now would be well tried and well known and would take time. Deflate the tyres to the minimum 1.1 bar. Try, minimally, to see if that alone would do the trick for a reverse-out. Then it would be sand tracks out, dig at each wheel, probably – since the sinkage had been considerable – jack each wheel up to get the sand tracks in place, actually sliding them under each tyre in turn, diff locks front and rear and try again. There'd likely be a repeat after the Merc reached the end of the sand tracks. And another repeat. As I stepped from the wagon I realised I was now also trying an uphill extraction; in bad conditions.

It was hot. It was getting dark. The light was now so bad I couldn't properly see the true slope of the terrain I was dealing with, what had caused the lurch to the left, but a straight reverse-out was the obvious course of action. I badly wanted to get the wagon clear of the bogging so I could make camp knowing the worst was over. I began work immediately.

•　　•　　•

Water. Now there's a subject to discuss when thinking about deserts. Something quite interesting was about to happen. I never stop being amazed at the functional elegance and self-healing, self-regulating capabilities of the human body. When I lost an argument with gravity a couple of years back and my Yamaha fell on and broke my leg, not only did the bone immediately – it showed on the X-ray just four days later – get to work generating some kind of bone-mending stuff, but when things were looking about right it stopped. It knew what to do and when to stop doing it. Only the properly humble, and therefore rare among the white-coats fraternity, realise how little we actually know about the human body. Whilst we (they) think we have a grasp on the sheer mechanics of what – in some cases – is happening, what about the next level down? I have never heard an explanation of where all the cells and little tiny things get their motivation for what they do. Perhaps my sense of wonder outstripped my medical knowledge some long time ago. Perhaps I have not read enough about DNA. (Then again where does that actually come from and who did the design spec? If it really evolved from the primordial slime who or what gave it the nudge? And why?)

Having served overseas as RAF aircrew, boned up on desert survival training and also done much study prior to expeditions I have been on, I have heard and read much about water-consumption requirements. Consumption varies, of course, with workload and rockets when the ambient temperature goes above 40°C. The human thermoregulatory system works by using evaporative cooling, sweat – the latent heat of evaporation when

How low can you go? Just 1.1 bar. Rechecking the tyre pressures in the morning in preparation for the delicate reverse-out Unsung heroes, tyres must be looked after as if your life depended on them. It does.

water changes from a liquid into a gas or vapour; as in cold-feeling aerosol sprays. To maintain an 80kg human body at 38.6°C when it's 42° outside requires quite a lot of refrigerating evaporation and therefore quite a lot of water. Thus the books and pamphlets indicate an average person on an average workload in hot climates with night/day temperatures of 5/35°C will be needing 5-10 litres per day and around 50 per cent more than that in night/day temperatures of 25/45°C. Trying to bracket 'average' makes it all hugely difficult to be precise about it and, for certain, body mass is in there too. And for expedition planning purposes 'water consumption' has to include everything – cooking and washing.

Quietly puzzled but pleasantly surprised for the extra reserve it yielded, I found on the previous three or four trips that 3.8 litres had been my highest daily consumption figure with an astonishing 2.2 and 2.25 and numerous well-under-threes recorded. All the trips were in the September-December time of year with top temperatures around 38-42°C and workload comprised driving, spending quite a proportion of the day walking off into the middle distance or up a dune with heavy camera equipment to get the right photographic angle, perspective or light. I felt the solution (as it were) to this low consumption lay, in my strapping, skinny, Gulag-style physique – a muscle-rippling 67kg back in the UK that atrophied to a rib-and-vein flaunting 64-65kg on a trip. I was, without doubt, the lucky one with the benefits of skeletal physique there for all to see.

But two events made their way to the footnotes department. Seduced by the astonishing lozenge-shaped outline of the 20km long Tininirt massif on the satellite pictures rising like a vast rock whale from the surrounding desert – and the LandSat multi-spectrum imagery lending it a vivid red hue on a flank of the north-west valley cleft – I had given in to the 'gotta see it' alert it set flashing. Stopping, as usual at the end of a long hot day and straight away grabbing the camera rucksack and solid tripod before the light went, I set off to get pictures. Within minutes I became light headed and faint and nearly lost my balance. This was a different kind of alert. One which I recognised pretty quickly, crouching down to recover before walking carefully back to the wagon to find my water bottle.

It happened on another occasion too. Interesting; as though a line on the water reserves graph had suddenly been crossed, the needle on a gauge flicking into the red. Even low-volume, lightweight, skinny-wrinklies had their limits.

•   •   •

The wheels of the Merc seemed to have given up their principal role of keeping the wagon off the ground and were resolutely down into the soft sand, the axle casings only a centimetre or two above the surface. At this weight, each wheel was asking three quarters of a tonne flotation from the light windblown sand and its fragile crust – the latter now broken so the bearing strength was even less. There was much to do. First the tyres. To deflate to an indicated 1.1 bar (the lowest Michelin had cleared them to at this gross weight) while they were hot would be taking them past the lower limit, predicated 'cold', but I guessed 1.4 at this temperature would probably be right.

'How much should I let them down?' I had shouted on my very first desert trip with the RAF Desert Rescue team in 1960 when bidden to deflate a bogged Land Rover in the Libyan Sand Sea. 'Till they look soft!' came the don't-bother-me-with-details reply from the harassed leader. We did as we were told and four miles later had three flat tyres in the convoy. Excessive deflation causes extreme sidewall flex which raises tyre temperature until the carcase begins to delaminate. And it can also cause the tyre to revolve on the wheel, tearing the valve out of the inner tube. That is what happened here; four times. Life is about detail.

It was getting so dark I could barely see the pressure gauge but with a head torch and the pressures set correctly I dug energetically at the sand behind each of the four wheels. I dug for 10 minutes, probably more.

Rapidly, my body felt mummified, my mouth suddenly parched, my tongue sticking to the roof of my mouth. I had never been so thirsty in all my life. So quickly. So very, very thirsty. The lightning-quick onset of this savage thirst shocked me and, physical aspects aside, brought to mind like folders clicking open on a computer all my previous data bank on water consumption. Clearly, as with the incident at Tininirt, a skinny, low-mass body such as mine, possibly influenced by involuntary physiological adaptation, got by very economically in normal circumstances but had meagre reserves, quickly used up in bouts of vigorous activity. Where Tininirt had been gradual, this with the burst of energy was very sudden. As I went for my water bottle it was now also clear that the light had beaten me. I couldn't see to jack the axles nor had enough peripheral vision to put the sand tracks in properly. This was going to be 'an overnighter' – bad news. However, despite the effect on morale, it would also have some advantages. Overnight the sand would cool, the surface contract and flotation improve marginally. The ambient temperature would be more favourable in the morning from the workload point of view. And I'd be able to see the lie of the land.

The wheel claw lifts the wheel to allow insertion of the sand tracks. The top picture shows how quickly the wheels sink after even minimal spin.

My minimal supper wasn't good, cooked with the vehicle over at an awkward angle. I slept on a rocky plinth away from my usual position by the rear wheel, my mind churning at the thought of the problems facing me. I was aware, unusually, of how alone I was. I got up early, drank water and got to work quickly before the sun broke the horizon. Pink light from the impending sunrise reflecting off the white flanks of the wagon, I could see the extent of the desolation, the sea of rolling windblown, feather-soft dunes to the south and the high rocky ridges to the north and west. There was a savage, slightly frightening beauty about the scene, its bleakness exacerbated somehow by the knowledge, drawn from my study of the satellite images, that I was on the wrong side, the totally isolated side, of a seemingly impenetrable barrier separating me from the Tanezrouft. Though achingly beautiful in low-angle light, I always had, and never lost, a deep-seated fear of dunes and what could happen when you got it wrong. It was dunes, now, that seemed to be crowding me from the south and west. Where I needed to go.

It wasn't till much later that I realised, on balance, how lucky I had been with the Merc bogging here. If it hadn't stopped where it did, if my tug to the left had worked, I could have finished up, in the badly fading light, deep in the hollow maw between two of these evil close-packed dunes that the daylight now showed me. It was probably the worst bogging I had ever had but it could have been the last.

If internal warning lights were flashing, the well-tried routine of recovery went on methodically. With the sand scooped out from behind each wheel as much as was possible, the temptation to try a quick reverse-out was, as usual, high. To try it and fail with even the smallest amount of wheel spin would drop the vehicle even further into the sand. What now had to be done was to lift each axle so that the sand tracks – loosely connected aluminium plank section in an industrial stair-tread pattern – could be physically put beneath each tyre. To do this meant raising the axle further from the ground. Doing so by digging under the vehicle to insert the jack was a hideous prospect with a serious price to pay in fatigue and water consumption. To avoid this I had evolved, as far back as the 2003 trip, a strong metal claw that, applied to the face of each wheel in turn, enabled me to jack at the wheel itself.

I only had two sand tracks, a practical compromise with regard to space and weight; normally two was enough, one to put behind each rear wheel on a reverse-out giving the front wheels the chance to exert meaningful traction in turn as they passed over them. Here the vehicle was leaning over to the left putting most weight on the left-side wheels. These would require the most help with flotation and traction so I put both sand tracks on that side, one aft of the left front wheel and the other behind the left rear wheel. Bless Mercedes Benz design engineers for providing them, (wasn't that one of the principal reasons for buying a G-Wagen?); I engaged the cross-axle differential locks that effectively locked the left and right wheels together so there would be no risk of the more lightly laden right-hand wheels spinning when power was applied. Multiplied by the low-range gears and a pearl of an automatic transmission, the engine torque would channel down the massive propeller shafts and into the equally robust axle drive-shafts, finding most resistance to get its teeth into on the left-side set of wheels.

It was time to see if any of it was going to work. Getting stiffly into the driving seat, I started the engine and let it idle. I let the engine and transmission oils circulate and warm for a few minutes before giving them their task. With some apprehension I selected reverse and gave the engine its head. With my heart in my mouth, and desperate for the feeling of some kind of movement, I felt the Merc edge back the length of the sand tracks. When it got to the end and the tyres hit the soft churned sand there was a nanosecond of spin before, realising it still needed help, I cut the throttle to prevent further sinkage. So far so good. There was 50 to 100 yards more to go; back up the gentle slope to the firmer ground just beyond the point where the sinkage last evening had started. Hopefully it would get easier but if I had to repeat this process a dozen or 15 times then so be it. The method was

working; I was seven feet nearer to firm ground.

The Merc had had to work hard for those seven feet
and in the process buried the sand tracks in the billion
billion spherical sand grains, like tiny ball bearings, that
I hoped would yield enough traction to effect a recovery.
Despite the promise of a lot more hard work ahead,
optimism welled up and I could have cried out for joy.
There was progress; progress that the previous night
seemed beyond achievement and it was only a matter of taking it steady and time would
see me back where the tyre tread left a clear imprint on the ground rather than a churned
channel with sand grains cascading in on the long groove left by the wheel. More digging
behind the wheels, another session with the jack and the claw to lift each wheel; and re-
laying the tracks once they had been extracted from beneath the surface.

*By dawn, the
cooler sand had
fractionally more
bearing strength.*

47

The sun had now risen, casting long crisp shadows over the sand and highlighting the soft curves and knife-sharp edges of the dunes not more than 100 yards away. Again I got into the cab, started the engine, checked the mirrors to ensure I could see and steer back towards the ruts and tyre marks that had led me into the bogging. I selected reverse and, with a firm progressive press of the accelerator, handed over to the engine, transmission and three locked differentials to work their magic. A hint of hesitation, the wheels gripped the sand tracks, slowed as they left them behind. Now on sand alone without the sand tracks, I eased the throttle fractionally to avoid wheel spin, praying it would keep going and, joy of joys, after a micro-second's pause the G-Wagen regained momentum and sped backwards onto firm ground.

A wave of relief and emotion had my head resting on the steering wheel; the engine idled a rhythmic guttural purr as if nothing had happened.

It was time for breakfast.

4. The Reggan bypass. Part 2

'Cordon bleughh!' would best describe my culinary prowess, especially in the desert. But breakfast – at three spoons of muesli/bran mix, powdered milk and a cup of coffee, similarly powdered, not a trencherman's feast – never tasted better. Actually that's a nice jokey pun of sorts but isn't really true; my *cordon*, if not *bleu* was more probably beige and I ate as well here as I did at home, almost. OK, that still isn't necessarily an accolade. I found on a trip I ate somewhat more frugally and lacked the fresh stuff of course but, except for bread which was beyond preservation by day six – it had developed a kind of creeping black fungus redolent of science fiction films – there were no real problems. The tinned provender obtainable in any high street supermarket does you very well on a trip like this. And, as ever, it usually tastes a lot better out in the fresh air.

Limp with relief still but refreshed, I collected the kit – the sand tracks buried in the sand by the thrusting wheels, the shovel, the jack, the wood blocks, the wheel claw, my bed kit up on the rocky ledge – and stowed them where they all belonged in the wagon. Back on firm sand, with my electric pump I reinflated the tyres to 1.8 bar, the best-compromise (though 30mph speed-limited) setting that coped admirably with both sand and stones.

If my, in retrospect, ill-judged decision to press on in bad light to find a solution's-in-sight spot to camp the previous night had allowed the sand to catch me out seriously, the weather at least had been kind – once it had administered its sharp reminder about thirst. There was virtually no wind and thus no blowing sand. The temperature had dipped no lower than a comfortable 18°C overnight – the altitude here, so close to the *sebkha*, I was surprised to discover later, was only 160m above sea level this far inland. The morning light was clear and clean, the deep-to-pale-blue colour gradient in the sky crisp as it neared the white-out disc of the sun soaring skyward from the horizon. Shouldering the camera rucksack, I walked up onto the first rock ridge, a low one, to survey the scene – a landscape of severe grandeur in the sharp backlighting, implacably challenging to vehicular movement. Wild and untamed, its structure unknowably ancient, wind and weather its sculptor, it stretched a huge distance to the south over the tops of the menacing low dunes – peaks, outcrops, ridges and the hint of further white dune lines rising far off to drive home the set of this difficult place. I had recovered from a very serious bogging but I still had to find a way out to the Tanezrouft.

The temptation to continue on the previous night's heading was fleeting. The lie of the dunes showed the wind that had laid them was from the north-east and would in all probability have piled more sand obstacles on the apparently promising distant declining ridge to the south-west that looked as if it could yield a way onto the Tanezrouft.

It pays to be a nit-picker. To notice things, as with 'Graded rd S' in 2003, however short-lived had been its dividend. And though I would not claim prescience in where I did so, the randomly prodded GPS route-marker waypoints the day before had recorded my route this far with three positions to which I could return. Heading anxiously south at that time I had noticed, registered but dismissed as irrelevant what could have been a gap in the ridge some way off to my right. Then, I had still been convinced the ridges would very soon

Following spread: 'The Terminus' - the view from the ridge after extraction from the overnight bogging.

head south-west onto my required heading and that any gap would simply lead to the foot of the plateau. Now I was not so sure; the ridges appeared to point resolutely south and any gap – like the one I had dismissed yesterday – could be a means of escape. I even plotted, on my ridiculous tourist map which mercifully had the tiny marks of latitude and longitude every three degrees (that's every 207 statute miles!), what could have been a goal waypoint – I called it 'Reg S' (Reggan south) – just far enough to the east of the Tanezrouft track to get close to it without being seen. It gave me a target general direction to aim at. I was glad to have remembered the possible gap, though, and resolved to go back and see what it had to offer. I could retrace my route through at least two of the three waypoints I had laid down as route markers the previous afternoon.

I first headed back north-east to waypoint 4, through the low undulations until the way north was clear, paralleling the high rocky spines, now on my left. The terrain at their foot stepped down like terraces on the eastern side where I now was until it hit the level of the dark brown *sebkha* to my right. This time, northbound, I attempted to drive farther up the steps until forced to a lower level by buttresses and smaller ridges. Thinking ahead, what if the gap I recalled seeing was no good? Impassable or leading to a dead end? What were the alternatives? If I went back to where I had left the road-stone site would I be able to climb back onto the plateau? Discretion and caution, turning back from where the bogging had occurred was, I felt, the right thing to do but I was pinning quite a lot on the expectation of there being a solution further north at The Gap.

Following the next to lowest step at the foot of the great north-south ridge, I reached a point abeam and slightly to the west of waypoint 3. Southbound the day before I had been (and waypoint 3 was) about a mile farther east than I was now. Looking to my 11 o'clock position I could see the beginning of a dip in the rocky spine. I was now seven miles north of the bogging – a place I was later to name The Terminus. I moved cautiously on along the lateral slope. Another mile and I was at the gap. It looked promising. A low dip in the ridge, its crest less than half the height of the main spine dropped a wedge of sky into the otherwise forbidding, rock-fringed western horizon. A dip in a ridge could be a dip without being traversable by wheeled vehicles, a pile of tumbled boulders, a narrow defile. What then? Worse, it could look good and then, in a position from which you could not reverse, present you with an impossible obstacle. A complete on-foot recce would be essential.

But here the prevailing winds funnelling through the cleft and the all-pervasive sand had smoothed it over. The dip was a saddle, a gently curving sand sheet rising to the crest and seeming to fall beyond. It looked good. But I stopped for the foot recce. I wanted to see what the temptingly smooth surface was really like. And what it led to. Was it soft or firm? What was at the crest? A dune edge? A tangle of rock-fall? I walked the course, stamping the ground to check its firmness, a surprisingly valid method of assessing bearing strength given the size and weight of the average human foot compared to a vehicle. I walked all the way to the top, three quarters of a mile, not least because, with the sun high, the glare off the shadowless orange sheet gave no clue as to any sand ridges, dips, soft patches or traps for a speeding vehicle racing for the top. I got to the top and my heart sank as I saw rock ahead. Even as I did so I found the sandy saddle followed the structure of the gap and turned left onto south before descending to a level plain. I could hardly believe my luck.

I allowed myself a surge of excitement. Whatever else this was, it was a way through the tall gaunt rock barrier that had kept me east of my intended course for the last 24 hours; the part of the satellite image I was certain I could remember but got a little bit wrong – or at least my own position on it. Moreover, as far as I could see on the plain beyond there were outcrops but no more ridges. I began to orientate myself on my mental LandSat image of the area. Scale still eluded me, though; it had been a shock to find the previous evening that I was as far as 17 miles south of the tarmac but the picture in my mind now told me I was sufficiently clear south of the Reggan plateau even to try west rather than south west to get to the vast flatness traversed by the long, 500-mile Mali-bound Tanezrouft track.

Returning to the wagon, I eased the Mercedes down off the stony step that had brought me here and faced the slope of the saddle. I pressed the Wpt button on the GPS to establish waypoint 5 – Gap Gate. High range, 4x4 and rear diff lock selected, I gave the throttle robust encouragement, speed in case there were soft spots I had not found. The light was so bright from the near-overhead sun that I could barely see the footprints of my on-foot recce that I hoped would be a guide. The sand sped by, the speed and lack of visible texture making it a plain orange blur, I breasted the top of the slope and swung smoothly left at the crest of the saddle and down the other side, momentarily south, onto the flat ground ahead. Another half mile on south-west and another press for waypoint 6 – Gap Gate South, a good IP (initial point) for anyone seeking the gap from the south. The bearing and distance to my notional target waypoint alongside the Tanezrouft track was 226° and a little over 15 miles.

I found – where did you not in the Sahara – some old wheel tracks heading 246°. I wasn't the first to have taken advantage of The Gap, it seemed. How recent? Unless you could see the actual tyre-tread pattern there was virtually no way of telling. Tyre tracks that have broken the surface crust take a very very long time to disappear. In that there was a structure – the crust – to break, they probably never would. I found a tragic indicator just two miles farther on. Mummified, much of the skeleton visible, neck pulled back and mouth opened as the ligaments shrank, a dead camel lay pathetically on the ground. I hoped it would have died as humans would, lapsing into unconsciousness early. Its body lay on top of the old wheel tracks. They were clearly very old indeed.

My problems were not over. Heading south-west at last I was suddenly confronted with more crusty *sebkha*. Dried out. Dried out? Was it? As well as being very treacherous, *sebkha* has some extraordinary properties, seemingly consolidating from beneath as traffic rolls over it. The first vehicle will create ruts in the pie-crust surface. Subsequent vehicles will compact the new track further, sometimes seeming to raise it above its original level. Later rainfall will soften the surrounding salt marsh but little affect the defined, beaten 'track'. Driving even a couple of feet off the track, however, will result in serious sinkage into the mush. Water will seep up and eventually form salty fringing round the pool.

Another fine mess ... . Sebkha east of Jaghbub in Libya. The 'self-raising' track is well used and consolidated, but one inattentive driver put a wheel off it and suffered the consequences.

This was inland *sebkha*. Inland by about 800 miles yet not too far away it lay at only 140 metres above sea level – here it was 170 – ripe to take the run-off from the surrounding ridges when it rained and store it on the low-lying flats not far below the surface.

I had experience of other sebkha, nourished by the pellucid waters of the Persian Gulf – the vast and unpredictable Sebkhat Mutti at the south-east corner of the Qatar Peninsular where the coastline can't make up its mind whether it is land or sea. Long before the days of

Coastal sebkha – land or sea? It depended on wind and tide. Inland (right), it's different. A dozen vehicles' passage can beat the crusty stuff down like this but if you're number one you're in deep and very dodgy.

the present highway joining Abu Dhabi and Doha, the way west was a track over the sand just inland from the coast. If the tides were high the *sebkha*, and the track along with it, flooded. Yet the same consolidation-from-beneath had taken place with the passage of traffic and, so long as a vehicle did not stray off the wheel marks indicating the 'rails', it would usually be safe, even when sea water covered the track. It seemed to work. Mostly. At the time, on a solo journey from Dubai to Bahrain, a route that even within Abu Dhabi state had taken its toll of life through vehicles getting lost or stranded, I wrote:

> 'Sebkhat Mutti loomed and in its vast, harsh, blinding size, the sheer square mileage and uncertainty of its salt crust was as menacing as ever. The track, looking so innocuously firm, ran over the brown-white surface with no hint of the hazard that lay just a foot or two off it. Every now and then I encountered signs of turmoil where a vehicle had strayed just fractionally off the track and sunk. The awesome size of the dug recovery pits, now filled with salt water, where a vehicle and crew had fought for their lives in the ever-receptive morass were sobering and frightening. I was tingling and on edge. Sometimes the sea water covered the track, usually still and clear enough to see through. One such khor was about 20-feet wide with fresh tyre tracks entering it and nothing to indicate anything untoward.
>
> 'But it was one of those moments that I would encounter again in future years, rarely, but selectively when it really mattered, in which – it was hard not to label it this way – some divine intervention came into play. As I prepared to cross cautiously, some fish broke the surface of the water. Fish! Hardly believing my eyes I stopped and got out to wade through on foot before taking the vehicle any further. To my horror, just slightly to the right of the track centre-line under the water was a gigantic hole about three-feet deep where something

very large and heavy had gone in. Keeping to the left, and it would be very tight if I was not to go off-track into the soft sebkha on that side too, the water was only six to nine inches deep. I stood in silence for a while. If those playful fish had not come up when they did ... .

'I don't know when I have concentrated so hard, before or since. I followed the track for another 30 miles and it slowly gained altitude – if that is not too grand a term to use for the few vital inches above the water table that it climbed. And as if to catch me on the rebound when relief rather than navigation skills prevailed, the track began surreptitiously easing round to some unknown destination in the south-west. It seemed to be a test of attention and conviction but I spotted it quickly enough to take a less well-used set of wheel tracks heading more in the north-westerly direction I needed to get to the Saudi Arabian border post at Salwah.'

At that time there was no GPS, no waypoints to set, no satellite images and no track at all across the bottom of the peninsula into Saudi Arabia. I navigated by sun compass, odometer and dead reckoning plots.

•   •   •

So my anxiety here south-east of Reggan when confronted with more *sebkha* stemmed from previous experience. Dry *sebkha*? Was it? It was a nail-biting two miles. Here I was the first. There were no previous tracks to pack down the crust and I had to hope my assessment of its dryness was accurate. Later, after the trip and consulting maps and images, I would see that there would have been a way round it – a long detour – but here on the ground the crust stretched as far as the eye could see to left and right.

Was it dry? Would it take the Merc's weight? It was and it did. But only just. Willing more flotation, I was using the absolute maximum torque the Merc had to offer, foot flat on the floor, 4x4 and diff locks selected. The further I got the more vulnerable I would be if I suffered a sinkage. The wagon progressed in a series of bounds – paroxysms, half sinking, regaining flotation, rising again, slowing with the drag then making it. I was a nervous wreck by the time I got to the other side. The margin had been zero.

Sebkha being essentially low level, it was surrounded, unsurprisingly, by rising ground. Here it took the form, to the west, of a minor plateau maybe 25 metres high. Again there seemed to be no clear way round and it had to be tackled head-on. I selected a long gully partially filled with sand, but I reasoned that with nothing to break the top layer it should be fairly firm. I charged the Merc at it, foot flat on the floor, and once again the huge torque and the elegance of the automatic transmission's delivery and smoothly undetectable gear changes got the G-Wagen to the top – by its fingernails. I stayed there for a few minutes, engine idling to circulate and cool the transmission and engine oils, and stabbed the GPS to get a position fix plus a bearing and distance to 'Reg S' my notional waypoint south of Reggan just to one side of the Tanezrouft track. Looking ahead I saw a very welcome sight: an undulating gravel plateau. Not very smooth, not all that level but something you could take at a steady, grateful, straightforward, undramatic 15-20mph. That suited me just fine. 'Reg S' was 225°T, 12.5 miles: south-east for half an hour or so.

I pottered on, glad to be able to give the Merc a break after its exertions and soon took back some of the scorn I poured on the 'ridiculous' tourist map I had. For all its inevitable lack of detail in regard to terrain, the target waypoint I had hopefully plopped down to the east of the cartographer's idea of where to draw the Tanezrouft track proved to be a useful goal. As the remaining 12 miles ticked off I scanned the western horizon avidly in my two o'clock position for signs of the road. The latest Michelin map (1:4m or 1cm = 40km) now shows some tarmac south of Reggan extending for 50 kilometres or so and I felt there was a good chance a checkpoint might be located at the end of the sealed road. I didn't want to be spied, a tiny white dot out in the desert, and have them mounting their green and white chargers in case I was a smuggler. I sometimes got the impression, so varied had it been over the years, that the alignment of the track to Mali on maps depended on where the map maker had put his coffee cup. Even Google Earth couldn't do everything at once and, using LandSat of a given vintage, some of its roads overlay information in the better known parts of the Sahara were forehead-thumpingly out of date. (A year later they had got the more current images and the actual tarmac was visible, so fine was the detail. It almost brought tears to my eyes, thinking back to those days of sun compass, odometer and DR.)

Soon a tiny crawling speck off to my half-past-one indicated a truck cruising south. Good old tourist map; my friend for life! It was time to turn left 45° and head south to parallel the main track. The grubby scribble in my notebook, the coordinates of the waypoint to aim for, west of Ouallen but still out of sight of the main track, now became my target. My Koh-i-noor – the means of aiming for it – was, and would remain, the ever reliable, apparently bomb-proof Lowrance 3500c GPS calmly monitoring things with a clear, high-definition, colour read-out on the dash of the Merc.

Even here I was in debt to technological progress, thanks, did they but know it, to some junior scumbag thieves who took a midnight brick to the window of the G-Wagen as it awaited a service in the yard at Mercedes Bedford six months earlier. For some years now I had used hard-wired GPS in the desert – first Libya then five trips in Algeria. It had been as impressive as only GPS (with my background) could be. But the old equipment had a monochrome read-out – a low-contrast LCD, grey on grey, that at high temperatures when the contrast reduced even more became all but illegible. To get an idea of what it was trying to tell you it was necessary to stop, shield your eyes and squint at the display.

One dark night, the Merc was broken into, the thieves zeroing-in on what looked like a cool piece of satnav gear – the vogue item to be stealing at that time. The specially film-strengthened windows baffled them at first but they summoned something more robust to see their dastardly plan through, not noticing that the roof antenna made the display on its own useless. If the breakage and loss of the equipment was not enough, the database of nearly 300 waypoints that it held, records of desert routes and fixes over the previous five years, was a major catastrophe and irreplaceable – on a par with what was later to be the loss of all my maps, carefully annotated over the years. Then, as they say in all the best crime stories, the criminals made their fatal mistake. The local police, seeing a car that did not deign to stop at traffic lights, accosted the occupants and found their haul, my GPS included, in the boot. By now having ordered the replacement, the damaged head unit and its associated

Lowrance's GlobalMap 1600 was easy and intuitive to use and seemingly bulletproof against heat, dust and vibration, but the low contrast mono LCD display was hard to see. This is a rare picture with the sun just right! And 11 feet from my waypoint.

dangling wires was delivered to me a week later. How to recover the data? With the help of Ian Henderson at Silva, the UK agents – immeasurable assistance for which they made no charge. Now dazzled by the new 3500c and its crisp display, three weeks later I also had a list of the stored waypoints from the old unit.

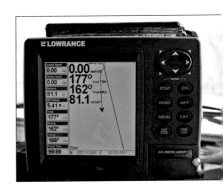

•   •   •

The tarmac feeder out of Reggan would doubtless funnel traffic into more predictable paths as they faced the vast 400-mile flat featureless wilderness that lay before them, but the skein of different tracks that had evolved over the decades remained and though I was careful to stay five miles or more to the east of the principal southbound route where the tiny mobile specks moved far off to my right, it was not long before I came upon one of the old tracks.

GlobalMap 3500 showed and did more – with admirable clarity. Here my heading was 177° and bearing and distance to the Ouallen turnoff was 162° and 81.1 miles. The unit accepted SD card road mapping – for Europe, not the Sahara!

There was something like 150 miles to go on a heading, the GPS informed me, of 178° – just about due south – before I intersected the line that indicated a once-used track to the old fort at Ouallen. There, if a trace of it still existed, I would turn east and head for what I termed the Ouallen gap – a narrow defile that squeezed you through the ridge that faced the Tanezrouft to the west. This was aerial navigation. It is hard to grasp the equivalent of getting into your car and speeding southward in an unwavering straight line, off-road, from Manchester to Reading, Seattle to Portland or Calais to Paris. And this leg equated to well under half the distance to Algeria's southern border post at Bordj Mokhtar.

Just as inevitable as finding an old track was that it should disappear. Odd tracks precisely at right angles to my heading indicated that some kind of survey had been carried out – some time in the past. A geological survey by the oil companies? Something to do with *Gerboise Bleue*, the first French atomic bomb test hereabouts in 1960, 70 kilotons on a 100-metre tower? The track was less a proper route than the path of a single scraper, the little telltale ridges at each side of the narrow path indicating the path of the machine and its doubtless hypnotised driver, told to head south and just keep going. After 15 miles this highway stopped abruptly, presumably the point where the hypnosis wore off or the driver went mad and ran away. Having the courage of your convictions (whilst being, of course, flexible enough to admit when you might be wrong!) is the name of the game in desert navigation of this kind. The most famous of famous last words must be 'Ah! This looks like the right track!' So plentiful are the straws at which to grasp, so many the previous travellers equally uncertain of their position, so prolific the trails left by oil exploration projects leaving skeins of tracks as of a vast army behind them – so many the traps that preplanning must be thorough and a no less thorough regime of caveats and provisos put in place before deviating from it.

I had been this way before, of course, on the 1979 trip (map p32) – also southbound from Reggan to Tamanrasset. Then, as now – but with a great deal less difficulty and hazard – I had had to exercise a certain sleight of hand regarding my chosen route. On that occasion I checked in with the police post but when I told them my destination they said the Aoulef road was the way to Tam, not south over the Tanezrouft. I carefully didn't argue myself into a corner from which an edict would prevent escape. There had been an alternative way down from the plateau and, as now establishing the 'more scenic' Reggan bypass, I had deemed it best not to present myself initially on the regular route. I had proceeded parallel to the main track and a good bit to the east of it and camped among low undulations, taking an astro shot during the dark hours and comparing it with the DR plot-out to be sure of just where I had got to.

Late in the afternoon of the second southbound day of that trip, by then in among the usual muddle of tracks, two dark blobs in my eleven o'clock gradually materialised into a couple of big articulated trucks parked together two or three hundred yards or so on the left. A tall black man clad in Touareg garb walked out slowly to hail me and as I slowed to a halt he came to the window and asked if I had any pills for a headache.

I leant over the seat back to reach for the little box of medical kit. 'Ah, oui. D'accord, j'ai ....' Headache! Headache, for Pete's sake! I looked across at the trucks behind him and froze as I saw the front end of the first one was smashed in and lurid skid marks from a full-lock fast turn led to the second in a similar state. There'd obviously been a major head-on collision between the two monster vehicles. I sat in astonishment for a second or two taking in the scene. Then a blur of activity with my first aid kit, a bucket of water and antiseptic to cleanse wounds, one dead, one unconscious, 10 walking wounded, dressings, pills, tweezering-out huge chips of dashboard paint from the deep gash in the unconscious man's head, the solemn miraculous little group of survivors, all Touareg in dark blue headcloths, squatting stoically by one of the trailers and making tea. Stoicism beyond belief.

The language and communication thing again. The collision had taken place the night before, the two trucks approaching each other in the dark, headlights ablaze, neither one aware of which set of wheel tracks the other was following. Still distant, one edged right, the other edged left. The closing speed must have been not less than 65mph. Again they edged over trying to clear the approaching lights, then with a hideous inevitability and a frantic tug on the huge steering wheel the enormous tractor units met, corner to corner. Those who were to survive must have been in the trailers lying among the soft cargo of grain sacks and free of the cab hardware that would take its toll on the others.

The unimaginable. In all the vastness of the Tanezrouft – a head-on collision.

58

I patched them up as best I could with my limited knowledge of first aid and limited equipment. They said a vehicle going north that morning had undertaken to tell the police at Reggan and they would be on their way. There was nothing more I could do but it seemed inconceivable not to await their arrival and see if I could be of further assistance. I U-turned the Range Rover till it pointed north up the tracks so I could flash my headlights and if necessary fire a flare when I saw signs of approaching vehicles – dust clouds or dark specks on the horizon. As I waited with the binoculars an uncomfortable realisation came over me that with the arrival of the police could well come the end of my journey to Tamanrasset. 'Who are you? Where are you going?' I could imagine them saying.

As the late afternoon light faded, the three little specks on the horizon appeared, billowing dust behind them. I flashed my lights. They homed-in, arrived, went about their business, helping the shaken passengers into the pickups, loading the bodies and disappeared to the north, the big trucks, grotesquely bent and damaged, a gaunt silent monument to a sad and extraordinary desert tragedy. I shook my head in disbelief. Headache!

●　　　●　　　●

Perhaps, I thought, bowling southward in the Merc, eyeing the sudden finish of the track and the little ridges the scraper had left behind it, this was the first alien abduction: whoosh, demented driver, scraper and all, for there was no sign of it having turned round. Of course he could have just raised the blade, as these amazing machines did, and turned around but then again an alien who'd just come to have a sniff around might well have been severely pissed off by that atomic bomb and decided to get his own back. I stopped too. Out of respect for the departed scraper? No, actually, to poke the GPS again for a track alignment waypoint and review the situation. Sixty-five miles on from my 45° turn onto 178° and 71 miles to go to 'Abeam *Balise* 250'.

A *balise* is a marker or beacon, often a cairn of stones with which the French with typical thoroughness in the wake of their truly epic mapping of the Sahara marked the routes connecting wells, outposts, villages and forts. Driving the old routes, agape not only at the size of this task and how well it was done, you are also suddenly struck by the fact that in many areas stone cairns have been built where there is not a stone or rock within 20 miles! The logistic immensity – and the sheer tedium – of the task leaves you open mouthed. Who did it? How many trucks and men on the working parties? How long, in heaven's name, did it all take? I had a sneaky feeling the job must have been given to the new-arrival officers. 'Welcome to Amguid, Pierre!' they'd have said. 'OK, you're on *balises* for the first four months. That track west to Hassi el Khenig. *Bonne chance!*' And the new *légionnaire* would have been eager to do a good job. On the other hand, there were some routes *baliséed,* maybe, by old-hand sergeants in the *merde* for excessive consumption of the *vin rouge* who had said 'Oh the hell with it!' and left navigation to the skilled and attentive; not too many *balises* in sight on those tracks.

Balise 250, though, was a serious marker on the Tanezrouft route – here there were only markers every 50km or so anyway. It was named *Poste Weygand* after Maxime Weygand, Chief of the General Staff in the French army between the wars, and once comprised a fort, now ruined, situated at the turn-off for the track to Ouallen around 70km to the east. Alas I would not get to see the current state of *Poste Weygand*, despite its indication even on the Michelin map as 'ruins', lest there lurked within or alongside it those with that special semi-destructive skill in handling passports, that arrogant, scornful way of snapping pages open with the thumb looking for the visa that you'd already helpfully flagged with a fluorescent tag. Thus 'Abeam *Balise* 250' would indicate time to turn left in the great glaring wilderness and look out for what remained, if anything, of the track to the ancient fort at Ouallen.

As I sat in the cab and pondered my astronaut-scale map and did such sums as I could, I looked up and found that quite suddenly a white pickup had appeared alongside. Its driver was a striking young man in a crisp dark blue shirt and cockaded turban. 'There's a track over there. The main track,' he said, pointing over to the west. He seemed to be in a uniform but not one I recognised. Some sort of company security guard, perhaps. I think he was concerned that I was lost. Him, his uniform and his action in relation to me had me wondering if there was some expat project activity in the area and that he thought maybe I was a newcomer searching for the camp. 'Yes,' I said, 'I'm heading down there,' making a T-shape with my hands and then waving to the east, *'Un piste pour Ouallen!'* A puzzled frown indicated that he'd never heard of Ouallen. *'Pas de problem!'* I trotted out the usual panacea and he zoomed off.

Parallel to the Tanezrouft track wasn't the same as being *on* the Tanezrouft track and after a euphoric 10 mile stretch of billiard table smoothness, low hills, broad wadis and stony going were to exercise the Merc's suspension once more. At one point I encountered the pathetic shell of a little Lada 4x4, stripped, as usual, to the bare metal of anything recoverable, alongside an even sadder pile of personal effects, broken, bleached, now mixed with blown sand, tipped out at some stage of the vultures' scuffle. Driving on, a tongue or two of low dunes sprang up, looked beautiful, got me on edge and then withdrew modestly leaving me on my heading over the once more flat gravel, pebbly plain. My God, I thought, what must this have looked like when it was fertile! Giraffe, antelope, lion, zebra.

All too aware again of my down-sun white-speckiness in the brown infinity as the sun lowered into the horizon to my right, I headed left onto 160° to get farther from the main route in order to camp. An extravagant swirl of high cirrus cloud swished across the deepening indigo of the sky as the sun set, picking an elegant mare's tail of white against the darker colour then to glow orange as the minutes passed. The late afternoon's 36°C gradually subsided. Despite the anxious start and early challenges, I had covered 177 miles since a morning overshadowed by the need to escape the confines of that high implacable rock ridge on 'The Reggan Bypass'.

A 360° horizon like no other; Algeria's Tanezrouft.

5. The phantom fort

How could this planet, in this part, be so flat? So perfectly, utterly flat; this place where each tiny rounded pebble, all billion billion of them, seemed to be *precisely* the same distance from the centre of the Earth – to the nearest centimetre? As far as the eye could see in any direction. Perhaps God was temporarily down to just two when the Tanezrouft spec was written, for it seemed the third dimension had been cancelled and replaced by the perfect hemisphere of sky that was available at the time; vast, exquisitely colour-graded from a deep dark ultramarine overhead to the tender pale peach and orange colours that snuck into the tiny opening of my sleeping bag as the sun prepared, for the landscape, another well-practised cycle of visual transformation magic.

As usual my bed, out in the open – a low-tech, fold-up aluminium-tube Argos garden lounger suitably beefed up with furniture webbing and a built-in sleeping mat to discourage sag, cold and spiders – pointed south. Thus when I awoke by the rear wheel of the Merc the dawn was always on the left throwing rocks, dunes, distant ranges or wide plain into razor-sharp silhouette in the still, cool morning air. Now, the moon, just a few days off full, had done bathing the desert in its gentle blue glow two hours earlier and slipped down west to be ready for an even brighter display tonight.

The legendary Père Charles de Foucauld, priest, founder of the White Fathers, pacifier of the Touareg, politician and adviser to the French colonial government at the start of the 20th century, the man who established the hermitage atop Assekrem in Algeria's Hoggar mountains, wrote:

Charles de Foucauld and the hermitage at the 2585m peak Assekrem in the Hoggar mountains, manned by Brotherhood priests still.

> *'We must pass through the desert and live there for a while to receive God's grace ... We need the silence, the drawing together of all our resources ... .'*

Frère Charles de Jesus

Irrespective of the presence, absence, degree or direction of your spirituality it is rare for anyone who has spent time in the true desert, alone, not to be affected by it. So it was almost unsurprising to find a perfect, healthy,

green, flowering plant and half a dozen others, not 10 yards from where I slept. Just the few. Just here. Why? How? *How?* Despite the chilly air, I felt warmth; sympathy, admiration. And – it sounds silly to say so – emotion; a brave little plant, a miracle of nature or just a random windblown seed that

Tanezrouft miracle. How does your garden grow?

landed there during a rare rain shower. Either way, it was quite simply amazing. Amazing and beautiful.

Balise 250 and what remained, if anything, of *Poste Weygand*, was 50 miles south. Turning directly east when I got abeam of its position could have me parallelling but not seeing the old Ouallen track, a remnant of which I hoped would lead me to the old fort. My recollection of the route was crystal clear. Another 'gap' – this trip would be studded with critical gaps – lay in a thin rock ridge abutting and to the south of a large south-pointing peninsular-shaped massif on the eastern edge of which lay the old Ouallen. The massif was shaped very much like the outline of Malaysia and I would skirt its southern tip at 'Singapore'. To avoid the possibility of missing this eastbound track, if it existed, I would angle obliquely towards it on a south-easterly heading until I was a few minutes of latitude south of the latitude of *Poste Weygand*, thus ensuring that I intercepted it at some point.

The French cartographers of my erstwhile maps that presumably still rested in Captain Rahmouni's dimly lit office had, reflecting the situation prevailing in the '50s and '60s, ascribed a tentative dotted line to a route leading east, and a little south-east, *from* Ouallen, and it was this notional path that I would in due course hope to follow over the next few days once I had found, and was, through 'the gap'. As I did so I would set a GPS waypoint at longitude 2°E, (latitude, er, to be decided (!)) and after that the known, cast-iron, down-in-black-and-white-in-my-2003-trip-log-that-I-had-with-me coordinates of '3 Nov' – the location of my camp on that date, coincidentally, exactly three years before and around 125 miles farther east. Quite a long way, actually, when the terrain is unknown; 125 miles.

Still heading a little east of south, after only five miles I noted, uneasily, a distant blob off to my right in the half-past-one position which could have been some kind of camp. And another suspiciously substantial edifice shimmered through the binoculars' lenses a little later on. Something seemed to be going on and 'something' usually had security overtones and people looking out for oddball vehicles that might have bad guys aboard. I altered heading 12° to the left to put more space between me and the south Saharan Las Vegas or atomic power plant or ice-hockey rink or whatever it was over to the west of the G-Wagen ploughing faithfully on. The flat gave way to undulations and dead ground that I found welcome. It also explained the otherwise puzzling lie of the Ouallen track that, looking at a map, made you wonder why it went out at right angles from *Balise 250* and did not cut the corner – as I apparently was trying to do.

It would have been nice to know exactly where the hell I was. Of course GPS told me that to the nearest two-foot-six, but where I was in relation to a lot of other things was what I really needed to know – and for that you usually needed proper maps. As I reached 'abeam *Balise 250*', virtually the same latitude, I decided I would trust my much-maligned tourist map a little bit more. I had ruled-in interpolated latitude and longitude lines on it since the publishers had committed themselves to dropping in that somewhat loose grid every 3° (that's every 207 miles, remember!) and that had proved to be quite accurate a couple of hundred miles farther north where the track left Reggan's southern environs. Here they had, to fill that blank space again, inserted the name and an actual dot labelled 'Ouallen'. Any port in a storm seemed to justify trusting this to be within, say, five miles of where it should be so I measured its lat/long as well as I could against my drawn-in scale and set up the result – 24° 37'N, 01° 17'E – as a waypoint to aim for. There were no other relevant 'dots' or terrain information on the map for the next 250 miles so I may as well use what there was while I could.

Still heading south-east to clear the uneven terrain and intercept the track, and with 'Ouallen' indicating 084° – a little north of east – and 32 miles, I drove hopefully on. Suddenly I encountered a busy maze of old vehicle tracks diagonally crossing my path. I got clear of the wagon to check their heading with my magnetic compass and, at 108°, it was tempting to think they represented the track to Ouallen. Then again there were so many wheel marks it seemed more likely to be the route to a long since vacated oil or other survey camp. The wheel marks were not so far off my own heading by that time as I sought the diagonal intercept so I followed them cautiously for a couple of miles. Then I saw a route marker; a French IGN survey benchmark cairn, that small squat concrete harbinger of order and security, and knew, to my quiet relief, I was actually on the right track. Way in the distance to the east I saw a rock ridge or maybe some hills; it was hard to tell. But I felt I had, you might say, turned the corner on the way to my immediate goals and was heading for the next 'gap' – 'Singapore'.

The IGN survey cairn that confirmed the track. Ouallen, 7.81 miles off, is on the far side of the 'Malaysia' massif on the left. 'The gap' is straight ahead.

•   •   •

Russ Middleton was a remarkable chap. After I had sent the routine letter to the British Embassy in Algiers before my trip to let them know I'd be on their patch, I had an e-mail from him expressing interest in my expedition and suggesting a dinner as I passed through Algiers. Russ was Security Manager at the Embassy and, together with Chris Tams, also in a security-related post, had a keen enthusiasm for getting out to see the huge country on the top edge of which they found themselves posted. Russ had even imported his own 4x4 with that in mind. It was hugely refreshing to meet Embassy people imbued with this eagerness. All too often a kind of introverted 'compound malaise' overtakes them, brought on, usually, by the onerous regulations that frequently applied to their free movement. Escaping these was something like swimming in treacle and many gave up.

So it had been Russ who I phoned when I was relieved of my maps and satellite images
– my personal property as a bona fide traveller, irreplaceable for the annotations they bore
and for the simple fact that replacements were now unobtainable. I asked if tactful
representations could be made to the Ministry of Foreign Affairs and that the maps be
released in the next few days at In Salah or be delivered to the British Embassy in Algiers.
Wheels were set in motion but from subsequent calls it became clear that, if anything
happened at all, it would not be quick. I could envisage the case dragging on forever – as
Mohammed had so memorably said. Then it occurred to me that the authorities might be
shamed into taking it seriously if the UK press ran a news item about a Brit 'stranded in
mid-Sahara without maps'. Reference would doubtless be made to the case of Mark
Thatcher, Margaret Thatcher's son, getting lost on a Sahara rally of some kind years earlier.
Before the 2001 incident when the Mercedes had, as an unheralded surprise, gone into
'limp home' mode and compelled me to do just that from 23°N all the way to Munich, I
would have been horrified at the thought of being a few button-pushes away from contact
with the bustling, overpopulated world I had come all this way to escape. But the Thuraya
satellite phone, kept strictly for out-going calls – mainly because I would never hear its
feeble ring and because I kept it locked away anyhow – was earning its keep now.

Geoff Renner, ex-British Antarctic Survey geophysicist, now a regular lecturer on
adventure cruise ships, stalwart companion on a number of my earlier trips and science-
meister on the 1975 Joint Services West-East Sahara Expedition that made the first crossing
of the Sahara from the Atlantic to the Red Sea, was the very embodiment of solid gold
reliability. Stepping away from the Merc to give the Thuraya a chance to see the satellite, I
put through a crackly call to Geoff asking if he could rattle the bars at *The Times* or *The
Daily Telegraph* and get them interested: the last thing I wanted was a lurid tale in the
tabloids about 'lone pensioner lost in Sahara' though I admit smiling at the sort of story
they would concoct; the mind boggled! Not at that time being on a red ship bound for the
south pole, Geoff – predictably – jumped into action and I said I would call him later. In the
meantime, with an eye on what I hoped was a reasonably accurate position for Ouallen, I
would follow the trail that, together with the ancient wheel marks, I was now certain would
lead me to the gap in the ridge and on, after turning north for a few miles, to the old fort.

There was, of course, a minor shock in store. Following the old tyre marks I was
suddenly aware of some that were not the least bit old. A mental klaxon sounded a
warning. I stopped and got out to look closer. I have never found a reliable method of
determining in which direction tyre tracks have been laid down but the general to-or-from
read-out and the recent nature of what I saw left no doubt that there had been four light
4x4s or pickups on this track not very long ago. Old fort? *Old* fort?

There had been Ain Guettara and Chebaba a few years before, hadn't there, I thought.
Yes, there had. I had a fascination about these old outposts. The French maps, which
originated in the pre- and immediately post-WW2 period, showed the tantalising little
icons, way out in the wilderness; the tattered tricolor and sand-blasted wine bottles outside
the crumbling walls image again. Too much Rider Haggard, W. E. Johns and Saint Exupéry
in earlier days, I suppose, but I always wanted to go and see what was there.

Ain Guettara (the mere mention of which at Ain al Hadjadj five days earlier had caused gasps from *le lieutenant*) was quite a step off what was now the tarmac over the Tademait plateau to In Salah – away to the east of Hadjadj some 40 miles along the escarpment and tucked up into the top of a rocky valley. It had seemed to me a nice little adventure to find it from the direction I was coming. Strangely, even on the old maps no specific track was shown but as I had studied them at the planning stage in my room with the rattling air conditioner at In Salah it looked to be a fairly straightforward bit of freelance navigation. A vast smooth sand sheet stretching to the north-east flanked the main road at a point 40-odd miles north of In Salah and gliding over this velvety surface for 30 miles comprised the first half of the quest. It then got a bit complicated with low hills to avoid, *oueds* to tippy-toe across, tracks to find and sneaky junctions with traps and deceptions to wag a finger at and foil. Noting the forbidding distant backdrop of black rock hills, crags and outcrops that faced me I voiced tension and unease in the log. I had to get through there. At last I found a stony track that looked virtually certain to lead to Ain Guettara – and I had set up a lat/long waypoint for the fort to monitor the situation. Getting ever closer to the escarpment and into the jaws of a rocky valley, I finally saw a tattered building a mile away on the ridge; my heart leapt. And as I closed it dropped to my boots when I also saw a group of army against the dark recesses of the cliff. My navigation challenge had worked well, but there'd be no exploring the old ruin today.

A track at last after the nervy sand sheet crossing – but with a sneaky twist in it. Finally Ain Guettara itself.

I'd been unlucky enough to pick a day when a visiting army patrol was calling on exercise but I needn't have worried for, as usual, they were a cheerful bunch, amazed to see a foreign visitor and shaking hands with everyone in sight took up the next five minutes. I was to discover five years later when I acquired a copy of *Crossing the Sands*, by Ariane Audouin-Dubreuil, an account of the epic 1922 Touggourt-Tombouctou crossing by a group of Citroen half-tracks, that Ain Guettara had once been on the main route from Ouargla to In Salah – before the road engineers had stepped away to the west, taken a brave deep breath and cut that astonishing road down the cliffs from Ain al Hadjadj.

I was always buoyed by the splendid sense of humour the Algerian army seemed to have, and their inherent good nature. Some comedians in the past, on patrol at this remote, never-visited spot, had painted a huge welcome sign on the cliff face: *Bienvenue aux touristes à l'Ain Guettara*! I felt honoured!

65

Humour had lightened my ordeal with the 1100km escort from In Amenas to Laghouat the previous year. The French language, would that I could speak it properly, has some lyrical words and constructions – only the French could come with a word that sounded as elegant and mellifluous as *merde* when compared with the ugly four-letter English equivalent. Thus I always smiled at their use of *bouchon*, strictly speaking a stopper or cork, to convey the idea of a traffic hold-up. Algeria's busy, narrow, winding roads in the north carried mainly commercial traffic and mobile tailbacks of impatient vehicles were the norm.

At the head of each queue, invariably, was an archetypal, underpowered, overloaded, dark-blue two-tonner, crawling up a hill or rattling along a country road driven by an equally ancient, stubbly chinned son of the soil. Waiting at the handover between escorts on my never-ending trek from In Amenas, I chatted to the gun-wielding young gendarme as he absently stopped or waved vehicles through the checkpoint. A towering load on a two-tonner shuffled and coughed forward in the line. 'Oh good grief!' I said, '*Un bouchon bleu!*' The gendarme fell about with laughter and clapped me on the shoulder – a wonderful, warming meeting of minds that bridged race, nationality, language and age. I had met a fellow sufferer at the hands of the underpowered, blue two-tonners; who appreciated the alliteration – in a foreign tongue.

Then there was Chebaba, actually 'Chebaba 30'. Who could resist a sign like that, especially when Chebaba was the modern incarnation of what had once been Fort Miribel in the days of the French, originally built in 1894. South of El Golea and teetering on the northern edges of the Tademait plateau, I had again expected to visit a crumbling ex-legion ruin. The sign by the road and a track indicated there might be a village or well down there. Some way down the track, a deserted watchtower told me I was getting close. The track lurched left, then right and over a *oued* with buildings away to my right on rising ground. Ah. Slight problem. Occupation again, it seemed. OK, I thought, I'll not bother them and continued down the route that clearly went on somewhere else as well. Guards did not have a busy time there, I guessed, and these two, seeing the white Mercedes van slowly bypassing their domain set off after me. On foot; at the double. Automatic rifles joggling on their shoulders in the heat. Luckily I saw them in the rear view mirror and stopped.

Chebaba was a fully operational Algerian army post. Soldiers swarmed around, there was busyness everywhere and in an enclosure an impressive line-up of motor transport that included several Mercedes Unimogs, the ultimate, unstoppable, go-really-anywhere vehicle. *Le commandant* was delighted to see me and after the usual politenesses invited me to stay the night. Already clutching my dictionary and seeing what upheaval and disruption I would cause if I stopped, I declined as gracefully as I could. I could imagine a long evening of difficult communication: where to sleep, where to perform one's ablutions. I later felt bad about not accepting and hoped I had not offended.

But that was Algerians and the army for you. Nice people. Human with wonderful hospitality, friendliness and humour.

But standing, looking down at those four vehicle-sets of fresh wheel marks on the track to Ouallen I knew I dared not risk being seen. The fort was without any doubt occupied. When I told them where I was going – way on, 200 miles or more to the east where there was difficult country, demanding navigation and no clear track, a route they themselves were unlikely to have taken – it was certain they would turn me back, probably escort me back to Reggan. It would be their duty to do so and, besides not wanting to put them on the spot, no amount of persuasion on my part would be able to change what they had to do. It was a shame; if I'd been coming the other way, as with Plan 'A' and heading for Reggan anyway, I'd have enjoyed calling in to say hello.

So once again I had to hold my breath and go into low-profile mode. I found myself slowing down as I approached the gap in the rocky ridge which I could now see. I had to smile at the whole 'Head 'em off at the pass!' overtones of the situation. If there was military at Ouallen, how could there not be someone in a lookout box up on the rocks at the gap? With powerful binoculars? And a radio link back to the main fort? I stopped and got out my own binoculars but could see no cause for alarm. When I got closer I saw there were actually two ways through the ridge, the more southerly one, with a rising sand sheet and no signs of traffic, was the one to take rather than the lower-altitude, wider gap where the main track went.

There's no way you can make a 4.5m-long brilliant white Mercedes G-Wagen disappear in a pretty dark brown desert, but as it cantered up the sandy saddle I made sure I turned to starboard as soon as I could – the sun being in my seven o'clock position – to ensure the side that might be seen from the fort was in shadow. Though the terrain was not ideal, it did allow me to continue on that heading. Again, I was careful to moderate my speed in case a dust cloud gave me away. I reckoned, on the basis of that not specially accurate waypoint for Ouallen, that I was about five miles south-east of the fort. But, if my luck would hold, I was on the edge of finishing the hide-and-seek phase, the edge of the transit phase and heading towards the landscapes I had come all this way to explore. Keeping a constant check on my left door mirror to ensure that side was still in shadow I was aware that as I did so, the rear of the vehicle was more in the sunlight. But the back end was smaller, it had the black spare wheel cover in the middle of it and the usual coating of dust to merge with the terrain and mask the shine of the paintwork.

Sociable and unafraid, young camels grazed the seemingly dead vegetation with extraordinary delicacy. Very clever animals; they probably know that's Tikkadouine behind them.

I was essentially on a very wide plain heading a little to the south of east. To my left and now distant, thanks to my chosen heading, was a range of rock hills, variously labelled Asedraj on the large-scale maps or Adrar Tikkadouine on the 1:1m. My recollection from the imprinted study back home of this sector of the route was that the vague, dotted line on one or two of the maps hinting at a track ran on roughly this heading but parallel, nearer the foot of Adrar Tikkadouine and to the north of where I now was. Anxious still not to display a bright white flank to the north-east where I imagined an eagle-eyed soldier glued to the local equivalent of the Hubble telescope

pointed precisely in my direction, I stayed on my heading, intent on crossing the plain a little later on. The miles passed. I breathed a little easier, I edged left, and a little bit left again, hoping to light upon the friendly parallel wheel marks of a long disused track. This was not specially hostile terrain. It wasn't, I thanked heaven, remotely in the same category as the Reggan bypass. So long as you didn't get any big ideas and kept to the south of Asedraj and Tikkadouine, it was head-em-up-move-em-out wide space in which John Wayne would have felt at home and there was a hundred miles of it to good old '3 Nov', way over to the east where I knew precisely the spot I would park the Merc.

Closer to Tikkadouine was stony. Closer still was rocky with irritating gullies. I went right again, spying a conical hill and some fairly benign wadis. There was no track. I was now 22 miles from Ouallen, it was half past four, it was hot, I was knackered. The countdown to a cup of pure nectar began – otherwise known as lemon tea, with limes bought from Waitrose in Hitchin 13 days earlier.

• • •

In the late afternoon light the air was exceptionally clear. Though the temperature was only 36°C it felt scorchingly hot as I unlashed two cans of fuel from the row stowed against the bulkhead immediately behind my seat, meticulously cleaned the dust off the filler neck and poured them carefully into the Merc's tank. Aoulef to here had been 391 miles. The tank gauge registered .3 which meant I'd used .7 of a tank or 66 litres (14.6 imp gal) and that gave a consumption rate of 26.7 mpg – an exceedingly good figure. If it sounds unrealistically precise I should add here that the G-Wagen's fuel gauge was astonishingly and unfailingly accurate. On a service station refuel I would have small bets with myself on how much would go in to brim the filler and was right to within one or two litres most of the time. The forecourt attendants would give me odd looks as I watched the cascading pump counters and then burst out laughing when they stopped at the figure I had had in

mind. With the two cans in I now had .8 of a tank on line and four 20-litre cans still lashed down. Fuel planning and the all-important reserves were working well but a daily check would keep me on top of it.

I prodded the Thuraya into life and sat on a rock to ring Geoff. I got up smartly because the rock was so hot, but Geoff picked up the phone. He'd contacted the news desks with my plight. *The Times* was not interested. The man at *The Telegraph* was, I suspected, a graduate of the George Bush Academy of Geographical Studies and seemed to have no idea of the implications of being in the middle of the Sahara with no maps. If it got serious, he had said, I should give him a call. I made a note to try to do that when the time came. And thanks. Terrific.

A near full moon was well up in the east before the sun sank. A fold-down tray on the inner face of the back door of the Merc was my kitchen table and an MSR Firefly multi-fuel stove running on kerosene served as my super-reliable portable Aga. Though multi-fuel, in tests at home I established that running it on diesel covered everything remotely in contact with the stove with a sticky black goo; the ratio of cleaning time to cooking time was about six to one. Hence the small five-litre can of kerosene strapped securely in the nearside back corner of the wagon.

Lunch usually comprised firstly the soothing, authoritative tones of the BBC World Service with the one o'clock news on my minuscule Sony shortwave radio, hitched to the window so the aerial could drag in the signal. It was accompanied by bread and meat paste followed by bread and marmalade for pudding. The In Salah French bread, delicious when brand new, was still only four days old and, fending off the effects of the heat and dry desert air within several layers of plastic bag, had managed to stay edible, albeit I'd have to think about strain gauges for my denture. After the pre-sundown lemon tea, than which no drink could have been more redolent of paradise after a hottish Sahara day, came the wash.

This had to be done with care – both in selection of the timing and, naturally, in the use of water. Leave it too late so that the ambient temperature had fallen from high-bake and the instantly evaporating water on your skin would simulate the application of liquid nitrogen. Wash too early and you were likely to sweat again and thus replace that which you were trying to eliminate. Quantity of water used probably amounted, with the aid of a small face cloth and a few drops of anti-bacterial liquid soap, to less than 150ml. Things had to be done in the right order of course and, without going into details, there were special cloths for special areas but always using the green goo with added Aloe Vera. In general, because sweat in the desert evaporated so quickly it did not hang around long enough for the bacterial invasion to produce unsavoury effects. At the washing stage I would hang my clothing out round the cab to dry out the sweat – this usually meant the introduction of salt-derived stiffness and decorating the trafficator stalk and gear lever with a sock each. Dressing for dinner consisted of donning a boiler suit – practical, roomy, cool and hugely comfortable.

Five-star meal in the making. Separate, split-charge battery ran the interior fluorescent lights.

Now, though, it was time for the evening meal, the chief skill for which was minimising the use of water for either cooking or subsequent washing up. Tins of everything were usually too big so half would be used and the remainder decanted into a Tupperware type of lidded container for use the next day. Easy-cook days like this one would see a small tin of chicken and white sauce and a full (tiny) tin of peas heated while God's refrigerator would evaporatively chill the pud – the dry desert air and a wet paper towel wrapped around a tin of fruit standing in 5mm of water.

At least, as I made the evening cup of Horlicks preparatory to doing the log, the journal, the checking of the photography and the navigation planning, I wouldn't have to trouble too much about the cab illumination and being seen. I looked up and gulped. I'd been right, it seemed. It was 22 miles away but Ouallen was a blaze of lights.

But that was west. I was heading east now, with three or four hundred miles of exciting, new, magnificent, unpopulated landscape ahead. And freedom. No more ducking and weaving or games of hide and seek. The trip was just starting. I allowed myself a daily ration of music and the last thing the iPod, the excellent iPod, on random mix, had played before I stopped to camp was the song that had become, over the last five years, my expedition projects theme tune: ELO's irresistibly catchy *Hold on Tight to Your Dream*. Strictly speaking, it wasn't the last one but it was the one I remembered.

6. '3 Nov'

It was the first morning of the rest of the trip, the part I had come to the Sahara again for: clear of the human hassle, the bureaucratic barriers, the incomprehensible regulations the gendarmerie donned their blinkers for and tried to administer, the swerving away from any distant vehicle, the apprehension at the sight of a uniform or inhabited building in the wilderness. At last it was just me, the Merc and – my patch – about 300,000 square miles of Algeria's most beautiful, probably least known, real estate; fashioned by time, the elements and nature. Inhabited by an elite clientele of animal, bird and insect life, all immensely clever. And an equally select and no less clever and adapted, tiny handful of human beings, just a very few of whom I would meet later.

With the moon gone, the tag end of the night held sway briefly, a dark velvety blue studded with stars, Orion waving goodbye as it slipped away to the west; a short hour or two of dark preceding the fanfare of dawn. I don't suppose we'll ever know but there's a section of Dvorak's *New World Symphony* where it seems to me the composer had a dawn like this in mind – a swelling crescendo of magnificent sound that quietens once the sun has risen and cast its light over the Earth.

With this much peace of mind it was a pleasure to slot into the methodical predictability of routine minor chores just before the sun broke the eastern horizon. Rummage for the keys, out of the sleeping bag, fumble for my rope-soled deck shoes, upturned on top of the tiny canvas chair against scorpions seeking a cosy night. Shake them out anyway. Check the wake-up thermometer: 16°C. Not really cold and no significant wind but, this skinny and your metabolism shut down for the night, my windproof fleece was the first grab through the G-Wagen's door. Second grab the stuff-bag with my clothes in, drag off the long-johns pyjamas, stuff the sleeping bag into the compression sack. Roll-up the blvvy bag – a Gore-Tex outer-layer, khaki, zipped 'body bag' that had seen me through sand storms, a rain storm in the Atlas mountains that had felt like being sprayed with wet gravel from one of those industrial concrete dispensers, and had later borne layers of ice and hoar frost at Abiodh Sidi Cheikh up north – appropriate, I had thought, since *abiodh* was Arabic for white. My fingers had been so cold I felt they'd drop off like snapped carrots if I hit them too hard.

With the main wash being in the evening, the morning brought only a couple of tablespoons of water in cupped hands to freshen up and take the dust off my face before the electric shaver got it ground into its cutters. The sun was on its way and a lunge for the magnetic compass and a stand-off from the wagon made sure I got the azimuth bearing of its appearance as well as the time. Doing this daily meant that evening's campsite position could be adjusted to take in a peak to the east that would be dead in the sun's path for a photo next morning. Then, with them cooled down overnight and before the sun heated one side and not the other, a check of all the tyre pressures – here the general-purpose 1.8 bar for the sand and stones that would probably comprise today's menu. Such vehicle inspection as was necessary was done the evening before, prior to the wash – oil and coolant check, underbody and engine bay check for any oil leaks, tyres for cuts. Now, I raised the bonnet to access the concealed anti-hijack battery switch and switch it back on.

Despite a cunning large cardboard tube, foam insulated inside and out, in which my Thermos spent virtually all its time, it was only marginally effective in producing a passably warm cup of coffee 12 hours later for my breakfast. Normally I parked the Merc facing due west for camping; my south-facing bed by the back wheel was thus at right angles to it and, unloading or cooking at the back door could be done in the shade at the evening camp. Sometimes, though, there were reasons (like a strong wind) to point it east instead and this had the advantage of giving me warm-up sun in the cab at breakfast time. With yesterday's burning-glass feel to it, I parked west – putting up the folding reflective aluminium-faced windscreen shield to prevent the cab and camera rucksack roasting.

So I sat by the back door this morning on the tiny fold-up canvas chair to savour a brand new 4th of November and enjoyed the time taken to chomp through the muesli and suck coffee through the lid-hole in my insulated mug while the minuscule Sony brought me BBC World Service news on 6195 kHz. As the day wore on you'd have to go to a higher frequency – 9410, 12095, 15485 or even 17640 – but for now the ionosphere was still playing ball on the night-time frequencies. With that, and the view, and the sky and the warming rays of the sun it was going to be a good day, I felt sure. The 'washing up' of the Meissen-grade polyethylene containers was accomplished with half an eggcup of water, swilled from one container to the other in the right order – and then drunk because I didn't like to throw water away. If the resulting soup was a bit thick, like after supper, a deserving-looking micro-plant would get the benefit.

Rose-tinted glasses and a nice calm breakfast was the classic way to set you up for a couple of nasty surprises, so I was, as ever, on my guard. I always set off with a 'Nav to' waypoint destination. In nine out of ten cases this was synthesised – a carefully estimated latitude and longitude some way down the route that, from the map, looked good to avoid known obstacles or difficult terrain. In the absence of maps I was on mental DR, of course, but I could remember clearly that there was from this point a curious northerly loop in the 'track' – if track was the right term. On present showing the word revealed an unwarranted degree of optimism. I remembered when I had the satellite shots wondering why the track alignment traced this northerly diversion since a direct line did seem feasible – detail terrain permitting. Inevitably, no satellite shot could show this – firm sand or soft, clear or a mass of grass tumps to slow you to walking pace and hammer the suspension. Equally, my recollection of the French maps was of the great rocky massif to the north flanked by this intermittent dotted line as though they were trying to say, 'Well, there were a few wheel marks on the aerial shots but don't get too excited about it, *mon brave ...*'. Nor did I.

Clearly this was not the time to go pioneering a new route when I didn't even have a map with me of the old one and couldn't set properly considered waypoints anyway. So it was roll-with-punches day, tag onto bits of track if they popped up, try for a broad brush overview and remember the light (or waypoint) at the end of the tunnel was '3 Nov'. That was the cast-iron 2003 camping spot that definitely existed and was the point at which I could plug into my fragile and, I had to admit it, somewhat widely spaced, skeleton of previous waypoints. Here I could start to 'join the dots' heading east and then south for ... er ... 200 miles? Or maybe ... well, we'd see.

Meantime the 'Nav to' was 2°E and an arbitrarily selected latitude, almost but not quite a pin-on-a-stick selection off the lat/long grid I had drawn on the astronaut-scale tourist map.

This waypoint, now hallowed with the name '2°E', would not, of course, be one I could head directly for. There was this odd north loop to take into consideration for a start and who knew what else would loom in the way of terrain imperatives. But at least it was something to have on the GPS and as I set off, all gear collected, stashed away and lashed down in the back of the G-Wagen, it was, as the crow flew (and, unusually, I hadn't seen any of my sleek black visitors for a few days), a mere 27 miles on 108°T.

Could fate be smiling on me, I wondered? Within two miles of leaving the shortening shadow of the stern-looking conical black hill I had camped near last night, the ground went from horrid stony to better-but-still-take-it-easy stony and for good measure a set of those where-did-they-come-from wheel tracks appeared. (When this happened you not only wondered where they had come from but where, until now, had they been? How come they weren't visible before?) They seemed to be going in the direction of my mental picture of the northern loop so, whilst still monitoring the situation closely, I decided to take advantage of what extra smoothness they had to offer and follow them. That was after just a couple of miles. After another one: camels! On their own.

Vegetation seemed the wrong word at the time but ahead there was a large expanse of what looked like dead twigs that had once been low shrubs only a couple of feet high and widely spaced. The camels, of course, knew better. And selectively too. They might well have turned their soft sensitive noses up at what I had had for breakfast – All Bran and muesli mix probably looked like chicken litter to them – but here they were eating the equivalent. With hypnotising delicacy. I could hardly keep my eyes off the way they selected just the top six inches or so of the plants, gently and precisely before moving slowly and gracefully on to the next. There were eight or ten of them, quite young, all heavily branded on the neck so they belonged to someone – as 'wild' camels always do. And best of all they were quite unafraid and when I moved up closer to say hello they went on grazing as if I was a trusted friend. Wonderful, wonderful animals. The nearest water in any guise was likely back at Ouallen, in a well, by now probably 30 miles back. I would find out later, after I was back in the UK and could plot the GPS position data, that the big rock range of hills to the north was Tikkadouine. How on Earth, I wondered for the hundredth time, did the owners know where their beasts were and how to get them back? Watching animals graze is immensely relaxing. Like staring into a wood fire in the grate at home. Motion. Quiet, seemingly random but calm and natural. And here the camels' skill in selecting their meal was poetry to watch.

Sixty degrees left of the GPS bearing to '2°E', the wheel marks bumbled their way round the 'north loop'. Hmm; 60° was a lot but I reckoned it should turn right before too long. At present the route was heading towards the bastion of Tikkadouine and on this heading, of course, I wasn't closing significantly at all on my 'Nav to' waypoint. '2°E' was still 25 miles and now bore 125° instead of 108°. And just as I was reaffirming my better-keep-a-sharp-eye-on-things the wheel marks disappeared. And reappeared. Par for the course in the Sahara. But it seemed to me that there was 'something up there' to the left, a big wide valley that thrust north into the dark rocky Tikkadouine hills. And 'up there' was where these intermittent tracks were going. It was time to have the courage of my convictions, trust gut feeling and the mental map and I turned onto east. The southward extension of the wide valley seemed to present a natural path – a bit less stony, a shade fewer tumps of widely spaced grasses – that would take me back more on to what the GPS was demanding for '2°E'.

As so often happens the decision to break with what could be diversion tracks is suddenly rewarded by encountering others going more in the direction you want. However many years you have encountered this kind of thing there is something compelling about finding wheel marks on your heading. 'Ah! Someone's been this way before. It must be right!' Fool's gold if you trust it implicitly. Can be helpful, though, if you, so to speak, keep your distance. But now a veritable skein of old tracks on 143° – south-east – was upon me. These were very much in keeping with being on the eastern side of the north loop and heading back to a radial that would be in more open country, farther from the hills, and would enable me to head for '2°E' on an easterly heading.

I was going into sun, or at least it was in about my one o'clock position. The terrain was still easy, allowing 25mph quite often. Patches of smooth sand appeared and on one I stopped as I saw the hoof marks of a pair of gazelle – little more than 35cm between each footprint indicating a slow walk, a leisurely Saturday stroll. It was a time to pause and slowly shake my head in wonder, not for the first time. As I drove on slowly I saw a developing streak of dust in the distance like an earthbound vapour trail and, following it to its head, saw the fleet little animals that made it. Another two gazelle flying like the wind, camouflaged so well you could hardly see them against the desert, leaving only the slowly dispersing dust behind.

Eastern side of the northern loop – note the GPS trail. 143° seemed to have been a popular heading at one time. How long ago was the big party?

It was sad that mortal fear and panicked flight – with such a waste of their hard-earned energy reserves – should be the default reaction of these beautiful and delicate-looking creatures. But I supposed, given the area over which they roamed – certainly within range of army patrols from Ouallen – that generations of humans with fast vehicles and accurate rifles would have instilled this instinct to flee.

But it was not universal, even in the 21st century. Just a few days after the original '3 Nov' – the 3rd of November 2003 camp – heading on south, 20 miles or so beyond the extraordinary *guelta* (rock pool) at In Ziza and looking for a suitable spot to stop for the night, I was driving along a shallow *oued*. The *oued* was

The remote guelta at In Ziza in the Hihaou massif – with the hitching rail for camels thoughtfully installed by the French. (Below) The set-up – trying for the moon. Internet astronomical data gave azimuth, and time of moonrise so I caught it rising behind peak 1331.

studded with vegetation that I guessed would be classified as grass but which grew in metre-high rooting clumps and seemed to have the strength and consistency of welding rods. Going slowly through the chassis-wracking chicane of obstacles, I suddenly saw two gazelle not more than a hundred yards ahead. They were actually eating this vegetation. They heard me coming and paused their grazing to look round calmly at the shiny, growling, white metal box on wheels that was clumsily lurching towards them. It was as though they exchanged views on the situation and, with no more than a irritated flick of their tails they trotted, unhurriedly off as much as to complain the lack of a little peace and quiet in which to have their afternoon snack. There was something magical, a kind of Doctor Dolittle meets Walt Disney in the Garden of Eden, about encounters as rare as this: to find, just for once, that the rapacious, clod-hopping, all-destructive human being was every now and then simply accepted as a co-habitant (albeit slightly annoying), rather than a self-elected head of the food chain.

It could happen either way, of course, with any species, and take you just as much by surprise: kids in Saudi Arabia in the hills in the early 1960s, long before the tarmac – by a track we hoped was a route around Mecca – who saw our Land Rover and fled. A Touareg woman way out in the sticks a day and half north-east of Tombouctou in 1979 grabbed her children and rushed them into her tiny round hut at the sight of my Range Rover and trailer ploughing slowly through the scrub several hundred yards away.

Then there was the occasion of the moon shot – another one. I seemed to spend quite a proportion of any trip setting up a carefully planned moon-rise picture, using my internet-acquired date, time, azimuth and elevation to ensure I got the moon coming up behind a dramatic horizon at the right spot. (It was also my way of saying to the world, 'No, this is a genuine shot, not one of those crass pictures where the moon was Photoshopped-in afterwards, usually at the wrong size.') A large proportion of these efforts were foiled by obstreperous weather – distant clouds hiding in the haze so you didn't see the moon till its elevation put it way above the shrewdly selected landscape foreground. Or dust haze so thick you could barely see it at all. Or an all-out *vente-*

sable that was going to spoil a lot more than just your carefully planned photograph – but for good measure shook the camera on its tripod just the same.

I was waiting, on one such occasion, all set up but, in view of the dust in the air not optimistic. Then I thought I saw him. I'd been singing at the time. Like me, he'd been curious. In a few minutes I saw his head pop up from behind the rocks. He was surprised to see me. I caught a glimpse of the blue, then he climbed onto the huge stone. As a joke, rhetorically – in view of the language problem – but to indicate a friendly disposition, I said, 'Can you fix the moon for me? For the photo. Y'know, the dust haze?' But now that I saw him fully I didn't think he did moons; even on birthdays. Like most lizards.

He was magnificent and I'm sure he had never seen a human being before.

It was indeed my birthday and at the planning stage when I had looked up the data I thought it would be hard, after so many attempts, to imagine a better birthday present than a good full-moon shot on that day – for that was full-moon day too. It would have been handy to have a 600mm lens to get a big-moon in the frame – the kind of shot those cretinous editors of TV wildlife films only used to run the end-credits over instead of holding it for its own value. But 300mm would do quite nicely, enabling me to capture the setting as well as the main subject; and there it was on the tripod, facing in precisely the right direction.

The lizard was around 35 centimetres long with a beautiful colour gradient along its body that ranged from an iridescent blue-green at the front to a rich red-ochre brown at the back. I could almost see the thinks-bubble over his little head: 'What the hell ... is that!' He ducked down to think it over then came up for a second look as if to confirm what he had seen. 'It's enormous! With legs, I suppose they are legs but there's only two of them, like sodding tree trunks ... !' Lizards (you see them in natural history films) have a habit of doing press-ups, kind of flexing at the elbows of their front legs and himself was doing that when he saw me before ducking out of sight again. His curiosity, though, caused him to pop round the rock a third time and take another look at this oddly shaped giant that was now laughing and trying not to do so in a way that would frighten his new neighbour.

'Hello, there, little one!' I said, as quietly as I could. He paused to look again before deciding discretion was the better part of valour and scuttling off to attend to the serious business of getting some flies for supper. I could almost hear him muttering, 'What the bloody hell was that ... '

Later, on the same trip at Tiouiine (pronounced Tee-wy-een) I had left the tripod set up for some shots and looked up to find a small black-and-white bird trying it out as a perch. He took very little notice when I appeared round the back of the wagon but decided anyway that the radio aerial looked more interesting and tried a very competent sideways grip on that. Not specially taken with either, he flew off.

Animals, I thought, as I drove on toward '2°E'; aren't they just something else. Especially when they display traits, habits or decision processes with which we can identify. I guess I anthropomorphised them outrageously but, hell, why not? When you saw them out here it all seemed to fit pretty well.

The Merc was good to drive. At moderate speeds on tarmac it was quieter than an E-Class; with so much unsprung weight, I don't know how they did that. Its real

Avian inspection at Tiouiine. He seemed to think it was OK and flew off without comment.

qualities, of course, shone on a trip like this. Mercedes have a reputation for making supremely good seats. The best thing you could say about a seat, certainly here with long driving days on frequently rough ground, was that you just didn't notice it. I get back-ache at the drop of a hat. Not here. In high temperatures you'd expect to get clammy. These seats seemed to breathe better than most – a robust fabric and underlay, definitely not leather (the incomprehensible choice of many who seemed to regard it as smart and up-market). There was inevitably a wetness in the shirt or vest but not on the seat. Unless there was a shrieking sand storm or cross-wind I drove with one or both the windows down. I had not specified air conditioning when I bought the wagon: weight, cost, complexity and power loss were the consequences of having it. Above all, though, you'd be cocooned in a fool's paradise; cool one minute, hot the next when you got out; and the hot would feel far hotter than it really was due to the contrast. Without aircon you got acclimatised to the environment in which you were operating. Though the G-Wagen is one of the few vehicles where you get ambient – as opposed to heated – air out of dashboard vents (with the heater on in European winters you need fresh air to the face to stop getting drowsy), I did take this a step further and install an overhead air scoop to get further outside air at face level. Nothing complex, no fans, but at anything over 15 mph the air

Dream terrain en route to '2°E'. It's nice to be able to give the suspension a rest every now and then.

coming up the windscreen went into the scoop, through control vents and gave a refreshing waft – or blast – to the face.

I made sure the ride was quiet too. It was standard on every trip that all kit was boxed and lashed down with ratchet straps to prevent rattling and damage to box contents. Items within the boxes were also packed to eliminate rattling and chafing or damage. The floor in the cargo area of the wagon was laid with rubber matting over felt or carpet so even if there was movement there would not be noise. The felt, like a similar treatment to the sides of the van, also kept external heat gain to a minimum. All the noise and heat insulation and the tied-down boxes contributed to what I had long since labelled the Rolls-Royce ethos. Drive a silky-quiet car and you drive it well, and sympathetically. With rattling boxes and things sliding about your nerves soon get frazzled – tension, headaches, backache, impatience are next on the list. It really is worth taking immense trouble at the preparation stages.

I'd felt it was going to be a good day and things were panning out. Just as I remembered on the maps, this looked fairly benign country. The big rock hills were on my left still, to the north, and should remain so all day, even as I came off the 'northern loop' and started to edge south-east. Predictably, the raft of wheel marks on 143° gradually disappeared until I seemed to be on previously untravelled desert. The terrain and the edifice of Tikkadouine's neighbour to the east of the great wide valley was receding to my eight o'clock position enabling me to ease left onto the direct heading towards waypoint '2°E'. Eventually I was on the 108° heading the GPS had decreed at the start and the terrain was open before me.

A scattering of rocks broke the surface ahead, a calm battleship grey, easy to drive between, very fine grained, knife sharp at the edges and with no sign of erosion whatever. I wondered how old they were, how long they'd protruded onto the surface like this defying

Just to show how lucky I was to have all that firm packed sand around, razor-sharp outcrops skim the surface but crack to the sun's relentless heat and resulting expansion.

the gradual grinding-down that affected every other rock in the desert. They looked as if they had emerged last week. If Geoff had been here I think he'd have called them basalt for their obvious hardness albeit they were not very dark in colour. The sand was a reddish orange, reflecting light into the shadows of the rocks, now harsh under the sun that had climbed up to a mid-morning position to my right. It was 34°C, hot but not uncomfortably so. Clear of habitation where in a Muslim country it might give offence, I was able to wear shorts now which seemed to lend your legs double the energy when they weren't pulling against long trousers dragging over your calves. Waypoint '2°E' was just seven miles away and the terrain seemed to be smooth ahead; never smooth enough to go above 25-30mph, though, especially in this light with the sun high and creeping round behind me. Sudden dips or those evil hard sand ridges were hazards for which you always had to be on the look-out. Though the 2°E waypoint was completely arbitrary I always took a childish delight in steering till the GPS told me I was precisely there. 01° 59.999'E at latitude 24° 23.600'N and the GPS telling me I had eight feet to go felt like putting my foot exactly on the top of Everest or on the South Pole.

Much as it meant to me to have reached it according to plan and without undue hazard, on balance I did not think, as I squinted out at the savage glare beyond the windscreen, that 01° 59.999'E, 24° 23.600'N was likely to be crowded with sight-seeing visitors any time in the future. It was exceedingly flat and, in the light of a sun by now close to the midday peak with hills hazy off to the north, was probably a little short on scenic grandeur or artistic light and shade, certainly at this time of day. But in the knowledge that I was well clear of the human hassle zone and on my way to spectacular landscapes, '2°E', just seven feet away (pic, right), will always have a place in my heart.

The next waypoint would be '3 Nov' itself with no complications like northern loops to negotiate and, being essentially on a plain still some way out from the hills, would, even at 073° and 34 miles, be pretty straightforward to get to. And so it was. I creamed down the middle, a sand dune

Not just any old bit of Sahara. '2°E', an arbitrarily chosen waypoint, pulled the elastic band clear of the mountains to put a kink in the route from Ouallene.

complex away at half past one o'clock, the rocky range of hills still at half past ten. A little area of stones, some *touffe-touffe* (small grass tumps), quite a bit of sand and gravel, 20-30 mph most of the way. Fourteen miles from it, I could see Adrar Kra – the site of '3 Nov' – a magnificent single dune with surrounding acolytes, elevated on the maps to the status of 'Adrar,' which strictly speaking meant mountain or hilly massif, rather than mere 'Erg' which a sand dune area would normally have been called. It was uncommonly beautiful and graceful at any time but in the right light brought tears to your eyes. It was, moreover, served by a run-up of firm, velvet-smooth sand of the same warm orange hue as the dune itself.

Kra sat on the northern edge of some small, low, sandy-topped hills as if ruling a rather special domain. To its south by a couple of miles, almost as in a museum to demonstrate the different types of dune, lay a big, complex dune (right) peppered with minor dunes on its northern side. Kra was also one of those structures positioned, I always thought,

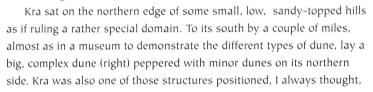

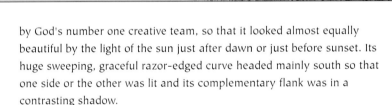

by God's number one creative team, so that it looked almost equally beautiful by the light of the sun just after dawn or just before sunset. Its huge sweeping, graceful razor-edged curve headed mainly south so that one side or the other was lit and its complementary flank was in a contrasting shadow.

It was like coming home. And for once I had time. It was only three o'clock so I had the time to do chores, restock the ready-food box from the main supply boxes, refuel the cooking stove, size up the shots I would take when the sun got a little lower. It was the day before full moon – normally the day I would try for an optimum moonrise shot when there was enough light from the setting sun to give form to the landscape before it. The bearing of its point of appearance over some distant hills was not specially promising but my position near Kra took priority for now. Conditions were perfect. There was no wind. I had time for a cup of lemon tea before the session with the camera began. Parked within 100 feet of my position on 3rd November 2003, I didn't even have to go trekking with the

rucksack and tripod to get what I wanted. It was all here. It was a special day. My first day well clear of potential interference. And to celebrate it – and the promise of a full-moon rise to the east, I groped among my kit for the bottle of Blossom Hill red wine I had brought for just this occasion; with luck and careful recorking it would provide a touch of special refreshment for four or five successive evenings. I wrapped it in paper kitchen towel and set it in a shallow plate of water to start cooling for later.

•   •   •

Pretending I was expecting it, I said, 'Ah, case B,' meaning the moon was not obscured by hidden cloud in the haze but the haze itself was so deep that the moon didn't appear at all until it was well above any kind of meaningful context in terms of foreground landscape.

A suitable foreground to show off its scale and complexity, Adrar Kra's immediate neighbour to the south.

Plus there was actually too much light from the sun still around so that the moon looked pale and unimpressive. If it was like that on the night before full moon, there was a concomitant chance that the following night the boot would be on the other foot – less sun, more moon. I made a mental note that with luck I should get to Idjenoudjane by the following night where there'd be a choice of foregrounds. Maybe.

You can't win 'em all, I thought. But if this, today, was losing I wasn't complaining. I knew that with Foum al Aqbet to come, tomorrow would have challenges but for now some 'soft and fruity' red wine in an insulated plastic cup served at a somewhat elevated 'room temperature' was pretty good. Especially when you are sitting in a tiny canvas chair watching twilight at Adrar Kra. The camels, I thought, would probably be settling down for the night.

Well, OK. Case 'B'. Maybe tomorrow, then.

7. Idj

Idj was short for Idjenoudjane, mainly because I can never remember whether the second 'dj' is a dj or a simple j and also because writing the whole word takes a lot longer, given the time also involved in the decision-making. Idj is a startling hollow triangular shape on the map or satellite shot. Maybe it would be more accurate to liken it to a giant tick mark or Nike swoosh. I had been there twice before. The great, oddly configured outcrop abutted another massif to the north that had a valley running down its axis into Idj. Idjenoudjane's plan outline, being as it were, hollow, included two narrow defiles, one opposite the other where each end of the tick went very close to the neighbouring hills. In the Sahara, strong winds are part of the deal. At Idjenoudjane they are a bit special. Even a fairly ordinary wind will come zipping through the north-eastern gap and scorching out of the south-western one at a very inconvenient speed, raising clouds of dust and causing mayhem. I made a night stop there in 2003 and it was like camping in a wind-tunnel. The scattering of small trees within Idj seemed more than normally hardy and resolved to resist whatever nature threw at them, many leaning into what was clearly the direction of the prevailing gale. I was to find Idj in a playful mood as I passed through.

'Foum', on the other hand, isn't a place name as such but the Arabic word for a narrow pass. Whilst I hoped I might get to Idjenoudjane by the end of the day, Foum al Aqbet was on today's menu first, more scenic than difficult. Again, the map depiction was intriguing. Aqbet consisted of a very narrow, north-pointing spine – a sharp little ridge both in plan view and, when looking south at it, elevation. A traveller was forced to go round the northern tip, squeezing between it and the mountains to the north again. If you held the map a bit further away you could see Foum al Aqbet was quite a useful gap between two large and not very traffic-friendly masses of rock. Coming at it from the south-west as I was, there were quite

Looking south at Foum al Aqbet, the parting of the ways. Right for Ouallene, left for Ahnet and 'Rolex escarpment' – left of Aqbet rocks, far distance. See page 89.

well-defined wheel marks in the final few miles to lead you in – for a while at least.

But Aqbet was closely followed by the difficult bit; with no wheel marks. For good reasons. In the broadest terms Idjenoudjane lay about 70 miles north-east of '3 Nov' Kra where I had camped, but to get there I would have to go through the pinch between two large massifs just after Foum al Aqbet. The wadi that ran immediately alongside had also been pinched – from a wide plain south-west of Idj to a somewhat chaotic affair, randomly changed by the occasional rains tearing down off the rocks and consisting mainly of deep runnels, swirl holes and soft sand – or deep runnels, swirl holes, soft sand and obstructive vegetation.

It was what I called a 'green' wadi. As a (strictly personal) classification, this was probably (next to small dunes) my least favourite type of Saharan terrain. Here, as you followed its transformation from narrow mayhem at Aqbet to wide plain west of Idjenoudjane, the *oued* ran for close on 20 miles and its 'greenness' comprised trees and robust bushes as well as the standard metre-high tumps from which explosions of coarse grass erupted. Inevitably, and characteristically for such terrain, when the water flowed, it swirled round the tough tumps causing erosion and swirl-holes leaving a legacy of hideously uneven and misshapen ground that for chassis-twisting vehicular torture could hardly be better tuned. It was near impassable to normal 4x4s or pickups unless your driving manner consisted of reckless charges and general hooliganism; only with axle diff-locks that prevented a wheel raised off the ground from spinning could you make reliable – as opposed to intermittent – progress. And all this was when it was dry; and that was important.

The wadis hadn't been dry in 2002 when I was en route from In Salah to Amguid – a different route altogether but notable for making a dramatic distinction between dry and not dry. I was trying to trace the old French track that had been heroically hacked over the rocky hills and through the *oued*s that stood in its way for the better part – or maybe that should be the worse part – of 200 miles. The route had always intrigued me; possibly because, though plotted with the standard open-to-interpretation, here-was-once-a-track, dotted line on the old French 1:200k IGN maps, it was mysteriously annotated on generations of Michelin's hallowed Sahara map as *piste interdite*. Around this time the warning disappeared and we were left to discover for ourselves what the problems might have been. It was a fairly challenging route at the best of times, both physically and navigationally, but there were further surprises in store. I did two trips in 2002 and the April one was when I discovered it was the windiest time of year with dust in the air to give the worst photographic conditions imaginable. I set off, savouring the minor navigational triumphs that unfolded as I picked the old track from the desert where it made its presence known only intermittently; the short rain shower I experienced seemed no more than that. I didn't know at the time what was happening farther east.

You went south from In Salah, still on the open plain of the Tidikelt but then branched off the tarmac after around 100km onto the old Arak route – and east off this again at one of those seemingly arbitrary right-angled track junctions in the middle of nowhere that could, you felt, so easily have cut the corner. I headed for Ain Tidjoubar well, 20-odd miles north-east, the northernmost point on a detour round a low range of hills. It wasn't till 18 months later that, ever the glutton for punishment, I took this route again, in the opposite direction, and discovered some old buildings at Tidjoubar just round the corner of the hill.

They were empty, of course. In the silence a spooky, squeaking wind pump still turned eerily in the breeze, the shafting to the pump mechanism long since jammed and broken. It lent a sinister feel to the place. I looked around, half expecting to see a squinting Clint Eastwood strike a match on his trousers and inhale slowly from a thin cheroot or Lee van Cleef flatten himself against the wall of one of the buildings. I turned and they were gone.

East through a small valley and leaving the low hills behind, a narrow plain and then the route re-established itself unambiguously where the French engineers in days gone by had tackled the 850-metre high Adrar Idjerane head-on and bulldozed an epic track over its steep rocky slopes. My gaping astonishment was as much for the logistics of their task as for the resulting route. Getting a huge flat-bed here with a bulldozer on it was a feat in itself. And later, wincing at the brutal rockiness of it – OK, looking less than pristine with 50 years' erosion unchecked – I wondered how many blades the machine had got through.

Recent improvement only at start of Idjerane crossing. Minimalist 'cairn' and fortuitous sun azimuth are sole aids later. Puddles presage problems.

The route on eastward to Amguid put you through the hoop. After Idjerane there was a plain of low hills and scrub three or four miles wide – then another of gravel, so flat and featureless that even Pierre and the cairn builders had given up. Or maybe they left it as some kind of navigational joke to sort the men from the boys. In an orientational vacuum like this my habit of a doing a 'DR ahead' was invaluable. On that occasion my French IGN maps had not been confiscated so I set a GPS waypoint based on a latitude and longitude on the map-marked track some five to ten miles ahead. I was then able to drive on, following what there was of a visible track but, if it disappeared altogether, the GPS waypoint I had generated would guide me to where I might pick it up again. If still no joy I would set another waypoint another five miles ahead along the same track alignment.

The wide, tufty Wadi Habadra followed, the gaunt skeleton of a Honda motorcycle embedded at its edge, enticingly easy to cross except for the fact that in the maze of grassy tumps the track completely disappeared. Further on, where the rain had fallen, shallow puddles still lay on the hard ground but once again the cairns eventually appeared where the *Oued* Habadra entered a rocky valley to confirm the navigation was right. Habadra debouched from between rounded hills onto a wide sandy plain

and went north of the nasty looking Kranguet el Hadid dunes, but it was easy to stay clear and it looked as though things were going well. Swinging round the dunes and breasting some low undulations, the Wadi Askef lay before me. Then I thought I saw the evil glint of water.

Wadi Askef was two miles wide and comprehensively flooded. Yes that was water.

The grass tumps stood in still-flowing knee-deep water running in from the south. The wadi ran across my path as far as the eye could see to north and south. It was not an encouraging sight. It was, in fact, quite seriously discouraging. Now precisely 200 miles from In Salah, a quick retracing of my tracks was not exactly an option to be taken lightly at the best of times. That these were not best of times became clear from the further realisation that I had been lucky in encountering only a transient shower a couple of nights ago. What was before me now was an unambiguous indication that the downpours had been heavy and widespread. Even if I had wanted to, was the way back to In Salah feasible anyway? Why wouldn't it now be as flooded as Wadi Askef?

The pictures of 4x4s wading through 24 inches of water simply did not apply here. First, most of those pictures were of water on a rough but firm riverbed (or, worse, a phoney manufacturer's 'demonstration course'; muddy pools in dips bedded with hard-

Wadi Askef plays hard to get ... and absolutely not for splashing through.

core). Second, the situation here was somewhat different. In rain-storm-stricken wadis, the swirl holes get deeper, yet more uneven and lined with the fine clay some of which for months had blown around as dust. Here, it reverted to what it was best at – being gluey mud. Through the dust-laden haze of the westerly wind I could barely see the other side of the wadi, a low cutaway scarp of red earth where the water had eroded the earlier easy slope of the ground.

To attempt to drive through this was a recipe for a three-week bogging and then a 50:50 chance of recovery: in, wheel spin, sink, stick; wait for the water to go down and dry out. But in spite of myself and to be sure I was not giving up too easily, I took to the water on foot to see if perhaps there might be a way through. Another proverbial 'on-foot recce', the value of which I had written so often about.

The feel of the mud beneath my boots confirmed my worst fears; soft, slimy, deep swirl-holes beside each of the closely spaced grass tumps. Virtually in denial of the situation, I splashed on for half a mile hoping maybe the bad bit was narrow. It wasn't. In fact, there was a deeper channel further on. As I waded laboriously back towards the wagon I scanned to south and north along the axis of the wadi again but the sea of waterlogged tumps stretched to either horizon. A review of the situation was gloomy. Two hundred miles from In Salah, the way forward impossible, the high probability that the rain had cut off the line of retreat anyway. The word that kept coming to mind was 'trapped'. In a manner of speaking, that is; for now. Er ... yes. Trapped.

I tugged off my mud-sodden boots and socks, perched them on the Merc's bumper to dry in the hot wind, and put the kettle on.

• • •

Here, in 2006, I was approaching Foum al Aqbet, 99.9 per cent certain that whatever else the awkward wadi ahead had in store it would not be water. I stopped by the dainty, knee-high green plants with yellow flowers, precisely on the extended centre line of Aqbet's knife-edge ridge just north of where it plunged into the earth like a frightened submarine and admired its architecture. God's traffic island, I thought. Looking south, you'd go left then a dozen miles for the entrance to the Adrar Ahnet massif's well and great hollow amphitheatre core. You'd also see what I called 'Rolex escarpment', where I'd taken a sun compass picture for an ad in 1984. Go right of Aqbet and the edge of the hills guided you onto south-west and, after 20 miles or so, either pretty much due west 120 miles more back to Ouallen where I'd come from or south to the green, pea-soup *guelta* of In Ziza – 136 miles, so my 2003 log informed me.

To make my way northeast to Idjenoudjane I had to cross the wadi at some point. I was somewhat apprehensive as to what condition it would be in but took comfort, as ever, by glancing at the organ-stop controls for the Merc's diff-locks. The crossing I had taken last time was a minor nail biter though fairly straightforward but, swings and roundabouts, the route to and from it was an awful mix of stony hills and other wadis that were almost as bad. The sight of some wheel marks now to the left had me trying something new. In the event, despite the anxiety, the crossing was not too bad. The

'Rolex escarpment', better known as Taghit Adafar, still there after all these years – see page 85.

wadi was deeply undulating and cut up by rains of the previous 12 months or so and you felt as though you were on a huge switchback between the tumps, dips, ridges and patches that looked ... eek ... but weren't too soft after all. Prevention being better than cure I had of course entered with low range and all the diff-locks engaged to be sure there was no wheel spin; a boot-full of extra oomph on call the instant it was required. The cat-and-mouse game with the alignment of the wadi, the beefy vegetation, the dips and holes, the subsequent stony going and general cussedness of it all had me wishing, for the hundred and twenty-seventh time, that I had the maps and especially the satellite shots that presumably still lay in Captain Rahmouni's office. But I seemed to have crossed at quite a narrow spot and, after the diff-locks had earned their keep, was through, after a mile or two, to the almost savannah-like plain that lay just north of Ahnet's foot-hills.

I progressed – through a skein or two of 'green wadi' – out of the now widening 'pinch' between the two massifs into more open country until I thought I could see Idjenoudjane looming through the haze 15 miles or so to the north-east. With a felling of relief I stopped for lunch at 'Idj IP2' – an 'IP' being an 'Initial Point', relic of pilot nav days in the Air Force, meaning a point to reach so you could do a final run-in on a given heading. I'd established the GPS waypoint 'Idj IP2' in 2003 when coming through here in the opposite direction, not realising then that it would be a lot more than a convenience on the next visit. There were other 'IPs' beyond Idjenoudjane I'd use in the next 24 hours but had now no inkling of the alarm that would surround them.

Clear of the 'green wadi' and nearing 'IP2' – smoother going at last.

Before the trip I had bought an infra-red thermometer and brought it with me. My bread from In Salah having some days ago succumbed to the evil dark fungus and rivalled the basalt for hardness, lunch was Ryvita and whatever was spreadable. Ryvita was good even when it was old – in fact it seemed immune to Saharan temperatures and didn't noticeably get old anyway – and if you spread the marmalade on the heavily pitted side you got a bit more and the whole confection was doubly delicious. As I crunched through it and tried not to get marmalade on the infra-red instrument, I found the temperatures choreographed by the laws of physics fascinating as the various surfaces and substances reacted to solar radiation. Ambient shade temperature was 33°C, but the sandy ground under midday full sun was 46°C, rocks 45°C. The rocks felt hotter than the sand but that was due to the more complete surface contact with the skin. The satin-black metal bumper of the Merc registered a blistering 51°C. No wonder it felt hot.

I'd also noted 'Idj W gap' in the 2003 log, another 'IP' and a way through the narrow outer ridge just to the west of Idjenoudjane, and it was that I'd seen in the haze, not the great wind tunnel itself. I luxuriated in the smooth sand-gravel going as I headed towards the gap, the Merc purring along at its customary relaxed 1700rpm or so. As I went through and adjusted to the new landscape that lay ahead I thought I was hallucinating – or certainly having a particularly vivid flashback to that scene in David Lean's film *Lawrence of Arabia*; that mesmerising, achingly long telephoto shot of Omar Sharif, clad in black, emerging from the mirage on his camel.

Here I seemed to see it again. A thin, wavering, animated vertical line. Concentrating on the now uneven ground ahead of the vehicle as I drove, I hadn't realised there was a mirage in the distance at all but the dancing image, dark at the top, light coloured in the lower half, oscillating slowly from side to side in the hot midday air, Idjenoudjane's rocks radiating heat beyond, seemed to say there was. As I got closer, I diverted another glance from my concentration on the ground and the thing seemed to have a life of its own. Left round the runnel, mind the rock, don't run over the small bush. I looked again and it seemed almost two-dimensional, tall with no thickness. Another look and – David Lean would have loved it, I thought – it wasn't Omar Sharif but a Touareg clad in dark blue and shadow high up on a magnificent tall white camel.

I stopped the wagon well short so as not to alarm the animal and so the man could see who I was. He stopped too, threw a leg over the pommel of the saddle, slipped down from the huge beast and we walked towards each other to shake hands. The man was but a boy, probably no more than 17, smooth skin on the part of his face I could see behind the dark head cloth, a fine fuzz of hair on his upper lip. He led his camel by a thin rope attached to a ring in its right nostril. The pair seemed to be one, almost inert, each totally calm, totally at one with their environment. I don't know if the boy had met skinny white men in odd vehicles like this before, wearing shorts, their pale uncovered legs looking curiously out of place. Straight faced, he didn't seem to know what to do. I think he was shy. Signs and gestures indicated that, no he had not come from Arak, he was just on walkabout in the area. I would have given almost anything to be able to converse, to talk to him in Tamachek. How long had he been out? Where was he going; I suspected to the signs of habitation – the bundles hanging from branches, an oil drum – I had noticed after the wadi at Aqbet. How long would it take him to get there? When did the camel eat or drink last? How old was his beautiful relaxed mount?

They both seemed so perfectly adapted. I have huge respect for camels and the way they have moulded to their habitat – nostrils that close perfectly against blowing sand, long eyelashes to protect their eyes, a rough durable coat, pads where they are needed on knees and chest. And feet that should qualify for a design award – thick soles strong enough to envelop stones, a big soft pad area for best flotation in sand. It was then I realised the boy

did not wear sandals either and his feet were equally well able to deal with the harsh desert floor – the heat (that would be 46°C), the gravel, the stones.

I made camera signs to ask permission to take pictures and he seemed to understand, still, I think, slightly at a loss to know the accepted protocols, a serious expression, a frown almost, his arms hanging loosely by his sides. I had seen at

Clever pair.
A privilege to
meet them.

Tabelbalet well, on the old route from Bordj Omar Driss to Illizi five years before, a group of Touareg watering a herd of around 120 camels. One of the men had a badly infected hand, sore and bleeding from rope-pulling to raise the water from the well for so many animals but still stoically carrying on. I bandaged and treated it as best I could but it wasn't till later that I thought I should have given him some gloves, of which I had some spare. Ever since then I carried several sets of industrial gloves around with me. To thank the boy and wish him well I suddenly remembered where they were in the load and brought a pair out. At

first his look became even more puzzled but then I made the actions of pulling on a well rope and pointed to the camel. At last the young man smiled a broad understanding smile. It was wonderfully worth the wait.

As he headed the graceful beast off towards Aqbet and stopped to mount it by stepping on its neck and sweeping in one practised movement up into the saddle as it

rose, I wondered what he would tell his family in the evening when he reached the camp! What an impressive, amazing pair. They lived here. I was just a visitor, with a vehicle, technical adjuncts and carefully chosen supplies that would last me a finite time. They lived here. This was their home.

•   •   •

I drove on a bit further and into the maw of Idjenoudjane, the wind gusting and blowing powdery white dust. As I got into the surrounding hollow of the massif, the wind was not only coming through the north-east portal but roaring down the valley from the north so that the whole enclosure, maybe a mile and a half by two was a roiling turmoil of dust, the silhouettes of the scattering of stunted trees fainter as they receded in the murk. It's happened again; what kind of moonrise shot would I get tonight, I wondered? I had the azimuth and timing and brought out the magnetic compass to choose a suitable peak as foreground. An outlying hill, a sentinel looming beyond the north-east defile seemed ideal and the set-up seemed perfect – had there been no wind. I found a small rise on the south-west side, facing the defile and without much hope climbed to the top to see if the situation improved. Unusually, the dust only rose to about 20 feet. I had a chance.

Tripod set at its lowest and most solid, lens-hood removed to minimise wind turbulence shake, I dragged a large rock over to sit on so I could bear weight down on the tripod when I made the exposures. I waited as the sun went down. A mild blue twilight suffused the sky to the east where the moon would rise. The lens was trained on 071°. I waited, checking my watch against the moonrise information I had. When the first part of the rim showed there would be very little time for readjustment. The very best shot would be if the air was clear enough to get a good image while part of the moon was still behind the hill but I doubted I'd get that. 1718 hours GMT was the appointed hour, albeit the moon was always 'late' because the horizon was never dead flat. After a while – or did I imagine it – a hint of yellow light backed the hill. The moon was shy again, not appearing till it was clear of the hill and rising over the layer of dust that lay to the east. A tentative segment first, then it was there, the disc deep yellow through the distant haze, rising and getting perceptibly brighter as it did so, the moon's well-known surface geography standing out clearly. It rose fast enough that a short exposure was desirable. It was the usual trade-off of exposure and aperture – a small aperture to get the best depth of focus. Even with a 300mm lens this mattered, albeit here the sentinel hill was a good way off so it was not too critical. This being a digital camera – my first after all these years, a full-frame Canon EOS 5D – I could quickly try alternative ISO settings as the ambient light faded, maintaining short exposure, small aperture and hoping that digital noise would not be a problem.

I got around 20 exposures, each saved as a RAW and JPEG and later eventually chose one taken at ISO 200, 1/8th at f13, using the camera's evaluative metering at minus1.3 EV exposure compensation. In the field I revelled in the extraordinary control the digital 5D afforded and the ability to see the shots in the evening when I downloaded onto my GigaVu storage device. The eventual choice was in the end on aesthetic grounds, the half-covered moon just emerging. Close examination on the 23" high-definition screen at home revealed no discernible quality trade-off for using the slightly higher ISO, or even ISO 400 on other shots. What I did notice, and again blessed the flexibility of digital RAW for being able to fix, was the rather muddy blue in the shot. Lulled by how smart the camera's various auto functions were, I had omitted to realise their limitations. Though I'd reduced what would have been an auto-exposure by 1.3 stops to make sure the dark tones came out dark and the face of the moon was not over-exposed, the 'AWB' – auto white balance – had taken a look at the scene and decided it looked altogether too blue and poured in some yellow. At home, later, I was able to select 'daylight' white balance (or tweak by colour temperature) and restore the correct colours. Magic!

I allowed myself to come briefly to the boil, as I often did on this subject, about our superficial, idiot media for a while. Who ever hears about the people who design this stuff?

To anyone who has slaved in a photographic darkroom to get high-quality prints the people who put Photoshop together deserve a Nobel prize for their sheer ingenuity – as much for identifying the problems as for fixing them and making them user-friendly. Who was the algorithms man behind the Canon EOS 5D, I wondered. The lens designer who came up with the conceptually unlikely mechanics of image stabilisation and made it happen? Who made the mind-boggling technology of GPS work? Heroes, all of them! Geniuses!

And what does our technophobic, petty-minded media dish up? Crime news, political scandals, freaks, which football club manager was most recently sacked, tittle-tattle about flash-in-the-pan 'celebrities'; or, worse, tittle-tattle about actors in TV soap operas!

I turned down the heat, calmed down, smiled at the moon serenely and magically going on its way. I had got my picture; not a great shot but a nice one that captured the mood and location.

•   •   •

But four years earlier a number of problems remained as I awoke next morning beside the still flooded Wadi Askef, somewhat trapped, I ventured to think, by what lay ahead – and by 200 miles and a very likely similar situation behind.

One problem at least was resolved, though. My socks and boots were dry. And subtly changed. Arguably a solution waiting for a relevant problem, here, among the hazards of exploring what had until recently been *piste interdite* to Amguid (and I was beginning to see why), I seemed to have invented the ceramic sock. Wading through Askef's muddy waters searching in vain for a way through, the sediment-laden flow had deposited fine particles of clay among the fibres and interstices of my socks. Twelve hours on the Merc's stalwart bumper in the teeth of a fairly strong, hot and very dry westerly wind had wrought a wondrous change. The socks were rigid, a skeleton for some rather unusual pottery. Hose for the terracotta army. Battering my new invention against the front right tyre to crack and dislodge the delicate framework, I attended to the business at hand which, overnight, had taken more of my time than had the healing balm of sleep.

If the water was flowing north – right to left – the main rainfall had clearly been among the hills and minor canyons to the south. Here, before me where I stood, the water spread out over a huge area of soft uneven ground and it seemed to me there was a chance that, south, it flowed over a narrower, possibly smoother rock surface that I could drive through to get to the eastern side. To the north, who knew how far this flood plain extended and how treacherous it would be even when the water was not on the surface? I had often classed myself as what used to be termed 'a woolly liberal', possibly too ready to hear both sides of a case, and it led to a sometimes chronic doubt and indecision.

But the fact was, I simply didn't know what the terrain was like in either direction and, additional to the possible hazards of bad going, roaming around exploring this or that option would be using fuel of which I had a finite quantity. Not much gain getting through here and running out of fuel 150 miles farther on.

On balance and reconsideration, however – and based on what I had seen on the 850-metre high Idjerane whaleback mountain where that amazing track has been carved by the French – rain in these parts was not particularly benign when it fell in large quantities. Especially over thousands of years and without, at any time, the delicate touch of a bulldozer to level the results of its excesses, the chances of there being a smooth rock crossing to the south with water running evenly over it at a handy narrow point were remote. Going north, I thought after looking at the map's far less craggy depiction (2002, remember, I did have maps then; wonderful things, maps!), it seemed to me the water would soak into the ground. Somewhere at least. That's what flood plains did, after all. Using what my maths teacher at school used to call *reductio ad absurdum*, I thought, OK what if the water just kept going north? Could I escape on this, its western side?

What was there, *way* up north? It looked just possible to join up eventually with the In Salah to Bordj Omar Driss route. It was hard to tell. It was also a long way. The learning factor through years of looking at these otherwise excellent IGN maps cemented the realisation that the cartographers did get a bit carried away indicating watercourses. To look at the maps, you could be forgiven, so prolific seemed the network of streams and rivers, into thinking you could come here and start a string of trout fisheries. Some factoring was necessary.

Coming to me inexorably was the decision that north, after all, was the way to go, keeping well clear of the water until it looked safe to cross east on the – sand, gravel? – into which it would have sunk. I prayed it would not be blighted with those tumps of steel-cored grasses. Again, the map's proliferation of blue dots indicating a vast swamp or *sebkha* was not specially encouraging but at least even the IGN drawing office had to admit it was finite, and if I kept going far enough I should be able to cross the end of it – east towards

the ... . Er, that was something of an unknown too, for this was a high plateau in relation to what was to the east and plateaux had a habit of getting frayed at the edges with rocks and gullies and the like. Maybe I could sneak down the waters' eastern edge as I was proposing to do down, or rather up, the western edge. The more I thought about it, though, south was off the menu and north was the way to be carefully sniffing.

Impatient for an improvement, it was of course farther than I expected before there was any change. But change there was. Three miles, four, six and the grass tumps had mostly gone; now the water stood in lakes a hundred or so metres long. The lakes got smaller; there were even some low undulations of gravel. Nice and porous, I thought. From north I was able to edge round onto 060°, a little to the right of north-east. I stopped frequently to plot the position the GPS gave and see how it related to what was depicted on the map – a comparison of topography with cartography as much as anything. From 060° on to 090°. Due east now. I reckoned another two miles should see me on to hard ground, clear of the wadi's flood plain and in a position to turn south to meet up with the track my pursuit of which had been so rudely interrupted by the flood.

Still heading north (above) hoping for a way round the flood. But swings and roundabouts awaited.

The water was gone but I needed to be sufficiently far east not to then head back in between tributaries of the original wadi – a herring-bone

format that was safe to exit in one direction but could suck you into trouble in the other. South by another six or seven miles should see me back on the track if the way was clear.

'Firm' ground was an understatement. Famine or feast, it seemed. The eastern side of the flood was rocky. Very rocky. And after a mile or so it was clear I was not going to rejoin the track through this terrain. The Merc struggled manfully in low range and I set a very low speed. Any

96

further east and the rocks would be so large as to cause under-belly damage to the wagon. Reluctantly and with rising anxiety I pulled back west – towards the Askef. At least there seemed to be a kind of impossibility gradient and as I did so the rocks got smaller so I was able still to make progress south yet be clear and east of the waters. GPS told me I was only a mile or two from the track but a hill, severely rocky, of course, loomed. Going west of it on smoother going would take me too close to the Wadi Askef so I had no alternative but to crawl through a narrow defile, winding east of the rise. Such a gap, naturally, was a ravine in its own right with the usual complement of tumps, thick vegetation and fallen rocks. Whilst it was at least dry I wondered if it would lead me to a dead-end with the hideous prospect of first having to turn around and then find another route. It was giving the Merc a hard time.

Luck, was with me. Though I couldn't see it, the eastbound track was only 400 yards away. After 30 miles of this tension since the morning it was a welcome sight. 'The yellow brick road', I called it, for the bulldozers had been here all those years ago and scraped away the really rough stuff to show a yellowy-beige underlay of smaller rocks.

It led me down off the plateau into a dusty windswept valley, grey skies giving the landscape a sinister appearance. So glad was I to be free of Askef It did not occur to me until long after I got home that the *Oued* Tirit along which I now had to weave a tump-skirting path could easily have suffered from the rains as well. It was no more than damp. The wind slowly died in the late afternoon but the dust hung in the air. As I looked to the west the sunset seemed like a collage of pastel shades of pink card, cut and hung, the sun painted-on, defying the traveller to believe it was real.

The landscape was certainly real next morning, Monday, the 15th of April 2002. Proud hills, rising from the long flat gravel ridge I'd camped on and the rising sun, a slow explosion of light in the now calm air, looming over the distant range. It couldn't have been more appropriate but as I drove on towards Amguid, the tape came up with Wagner's Tannhauser Overture. It can bring tears to my eyes almost any time but here ... that was something special.

• • •

At Idjenoudjane, 6th of November 2006, another special dawn was breaking; as it can, I felt, only in the Sahara.

Idj sunrise, 6 Nov. Heart-stopping, jaw-dropping. An interesting day ahead.

8. Idj to Wadi 'N'

Let's call it Wadi 'N', 'n' being a favourite notation for a don't-know-what-it-is-yet, 'unknown integer' situation I remember from maths at school. The November 2003 trip – the one that begat the memorable '3 Nov' at Kra and the nav log of which I now, three years later, clutched – had started from the Arak-Tamanrasset road and headed west in a slightly roundabout way towards Idjenoudjane, Aqbet, Kra and then turned south to the green *guelta* at In Ziza. It left the tarmac at a point I had noted the year before; a breathtaking plain 10-miles wide, flanked by jagged hills pale grey in the haze and, at its south-western end back-dropped by a sawtooth row of peaks, their silhouettes just discernible in the palest blue. I resolved to return to explore it some time.

'Some time' was November 2003 and by then a study of the maps hatched the idea that going south-west down this wide valley and beyond the sawtooths, I could then head west to Idjenoudjane. Wadi 'N', for even the IGN maps gave it no name, was one of a number of ways I would be able, I hoped, to weave my way through the fairly substantial barrier of the Tanetfirt range of hills, part of the *Monts du Mouydir*. Tanetfirt ran 30 miles – or 50 miles, depending on how you defined it – SSW from Arak and was the westerly barrier of the wide valley I had so inspirationally viewed as I drove past in 2002.

The general excellence and superb accuracy of the IGN maps was marred by a drawing-office house style that, even aside from the multiple-trout-farm depiction of one-time water courses, had a predilection for vast grey patches purporting to be gravel and shown somewhat too dark. It also indicated peaks as tiny star-shaped icons or shaded, contoured hills. Where they changed from one to the other was not clear and though a big/small divide seemed reasonable, interpreting the results on an actual section of the map was not always intuitive, especially with all that irritating grey around.

Satellite images, though, seemed made for desert mapping – and wouldn't be anything like as good, I thought, for jungles. Rocks were generally dark, sand and gravel generally light so a wholly logical picture of the terrain was presented in deserts. You certainly couldn't take a wagon over the dark bits and the light bits were subject to the usual caveats.

Thus the way west through the Tanetfirt hills – or at least the apparent options – were easier to see from the satellite shots than the IGNs. But between the maps and the LandSat images several alternatives seemed to present themselves, there being no dotted line to indicate any kind of previous route. 'Seemed to' was the right phrase for the first wadi I tried deteriorated quickly into an impenetrable barrier of what appeared to be those thick-stemmed steel-reinforced grasses on monstrous five-foot tumps. I would have to sample another. The next thin wadi, seven or eight miles farther south, whilst clear enough on the satellite shot was cloaked in invisibility. From the wide valley I was in, it just wasn't there. So piqued was I at this that I approached the apparently continuous silhouette of hills way beyond the point when I should have given up to analyse the problem.

'Aha! Ya-bugger!' I exclaimed, as it turned out that the wadi – Wadi 'N' as I would call it – had an entrance nested in the folds of the hills. All but invisible until quite close, you headed west into what appeared to be no more than a dent in the range's plan view only to find overlapping hills; you could turn sharp right and, a mile later, sharp left again. 'Oh, all right then, smart-ass!' Wadi 'N' seemed to say, and the golden road to Idjenoudjane began to unfold. It looked as though this way through Tanetfirt was going to work. I even saw some wheel marks, so unless there was a pile of wrecked vehicles at one end of a huge cul-de-sac there appeared to be some kind of route here. Triumphantly I went on 10 or 12 miles along the wadi's fairly accommodating course, noting GPS RACs – route alignment checks – as I called them in my nav log every now and then. These RACs would be important three years later. But perhaps I'd find them a little gappy.

•   •   •

Now, in 2006, with both the wind and dust subsided, Idjenoudjane had laid on a lyrically beautiful dawn and I was ready to head east to poke back down Wadi 'N', the way through the Tanetfirt range, this time from the west. Idjenoudjane, as well as being a great Nike swoosh, also had a wadi named after it. A wide flat one heading south away from the rocks, that supported some magnificent isolated trees and, from the extent of the debris washed up against their substantial trunks, it clearly ran fast and furious when the rains came. Knee-high in the same wadi were what I called 'the cool plants'. I had seen these before and, feeling their broad, smooth, bright green leaves, had been amazed at how cool they were to the touch. In truth, these plants were what had prompted me to buy the infra-red thermometer before the trip.

The amazing 'cool leaf' plants near Idjenoudjane.

'Ah, there you are!' I said, adding 'It's me again,' feeling sure they would remember my last visit. They felt as cool as ever but this time I was able to actually take some measurements. Here, with an early morning ground temperature of 24°C, the leaves, subject to the same solar radiation, were only 18.6°C. Later, on some similar plants in Wadi 'N', ambient air temperature was 28.5°C, ground temperature due to the sun had reached 43.1°C. Leaf temperature on the sunny side – facing the sun, just like the ground – was: 23.3°C. So, again subject to the same radiation as the ground, it managed to be 19.8°C cooler,

and was also 5.2°C cooler than the ambient air. It was hard to see how it could be other than evaporative cooling – expiration of water from the surface of the leaves – but the mind jibbed. This was going on 24 hours a day, 365 days a year. Where was the water coming from? OK it was in a wide dry wadi bed – dry, at least on the surface – but how far down would the roots have to go to be in continuous contact with that much moisture? And how did such plants get to start? They didn't pop out of the seed with 15-foot roots raring to start pumping water. Smart plant. Very smart plant, I thought. I think they must have done the same course in miracles as that splendid camel the Touareg was riding.

Remembering my last visit to Idj, coming from the east and the distinctly mediocre, rocky, weaving route I had had to take, I was open to suggestions on exactly which way to go in order to find the mouth of the long remembered Wadi 'N', some 30 miles off to the east. As ever, there was a gap to find. The 2003 log had 'Gap in N-S hill', a ridge about five miles from the start of the wadi, and I set the GPS to the lat and long of the position as a 'Nav to' destination. Looking past the small plants and the trees alongside the great wall of rock buttressed with blown sand that formed the south-eastern face of Idjenoudjane, I thought I spied some tracks. They seemed worth a look. They set off in a more southerly direction than I could have wished for but quickly turned east, seeming to have picked a superbly smooth route between the rocky outcrops that littered the uneven surrounding terrain. Whoever made the wheel marks knew the route well (or was a practised opportunist) for I discovered later, when I had maps to plot it on, that it followed what was a main tributary of the Wadi Idjenoudjane. Thankfully it wasn't a 'green' wadi or even a deep one, more a series of connected flat playas. Suddenly I was breezing along at 25-30 mph sweeping through the gentle curves of the one-time water course. Wide flat wadis like this get thinner, naturally, as they get nearer their start. And in country like this that also meant they were on slightly higher ground, still quite smooth and gently rounded.

It was all going to be terribly straightforward, I thought, as the outline of the 'N-S hill' – the ridge of Imeddine-n-Arab – appeared on the skyline with its accommodating gap right

on the nose of the Merc and the GPS winding down and indicating around seven miles. As I headed almost due east, Arak was away to my left, sort of ten o'clock position by about 40 miles, and as I went through the gap, following the intermittent trail, it was clear that this was part of the expert's Arak-Idj expressway. For now the tracks veered NNE towards Arak once they were through the break in the hill. For me, though, it was now the road less travelled – or at least the projected route less travelled – towards the western end of Wadi 'N'. I set the lat-long position to a waypoint from the '03 log and headed south-east.

It wouldn't take long. Suddenly it didn't look very familiar or in the least bit obvious where to go. Now the gap was not in 'N-S hill' but in the sequence of waypoints from the '03 log. It was that herringbone thing again. Going the wrong way into the bones and getting into the wrong passageway. Coming out from the

'Gap in N-S hill'. This was another gap a mile or two to the north, as the GPS indicates, but would do just fine.

Looking for the start of Wadi 'N'. Which way? Ahead and then right? No, actually. Try again.

'spine' it's all quite unambiguous but turn round and look back and the way is by no means clear; a confusion of alternatives present themselves and taking the wrong one can get you lost and into a cul-de-sac. A tingle of anxiety began but I did, after all, have the latitude and longitude of the exit waypoint so what could go wrong?

The too-big gap in the waypoints was what had gone wrong. The profusion of low hills that made up the western fringe of Tanetfirt before me presented a dozen different small valleys to aim for. I could remember from '03 the isolated pointed hill Essidjdjene that was now behind me in my five o'clock position but, where I had expected in front of me the wide sandy wadi that 'N' had been, I saw only a series of disorientating dips. Seeing a prominent hill at one o'clock I made for its western edge hoping this was where Wadi 'N' curved around it, but my bearing and distance to the sole waypoint I had to aim for became extremely unlikely. I made towards it but this took me into the little valleys and gullies by the big hill and that seemed an unlikely solution too. I stopped to study the '03 log again. One of the waypoints looked as if it had been mis-written and corrected.

That wasn't quite what I needed at that time. Getting the latitude minutes figure wrong by one unit meant an error of well over a mile and this wasn't the kind of country to accommodate it. I had to take a gamble that the entry really was correct and worried my way through the outer gullies and dips of the big hill, now more northerly, to where gut feeling said the wadi should be.

Gut feeling was not the best way to navigate in a situation like this but as ever it became the outcome of juggling a dozen different parameters mentally and hoping the rationale was valid. As I weaved my way through a small gulch with tall plants shading patches of sandy soil I felt the situation becoming bizarre: there had absolutely not been a small gulch with tall plants on my 2003 route. But I was heading back onto a radial from the waypoint that I figured would be a more likely position from which to latch onto Wadi 'N'; a kind of impromptu 'IP'. Black humour from Air Force days where 'It's always darkest before the dawn' became 'It's always darkest before the storm' was beginning to surface when I suddenly broke through into a wide sandy wadi that headed a little south of east. A wide sandy wadi heading a little south of east was just what I was looking for. I wasn't leaping to any conclusions too soon but at least the way to the waypoint looked clear and in accord with what I would have expected. With hopes rising faster than I should have allowed them to I continued down the wide space between the small hills and became more and more convinced that I had finally got back onto the right track.

It had all taken not much more than an hour and covered something like five miles on the odometer but in this maze of similar-looking small hills and alternative valleys the fragility of my situation, totally dependent on a previous log and the GPS could not have been more clearly brought home. This was the basis, the microcosm, an encapsulation of the whole trip from the Reggan bypass on – to wherever I would finish up – and it demonstrated how just one flaw could have very serious consequences.

As these thoughts tumbled and roiled through my head I found myself at the next waypoint, now unambiguously in Wadi 'N' and comfortably on my way through Tanetfirt. I stopped for lunch, a sigh of relief and another Ryvita with meat paste and took the opportunity to do as accurate a fuel check as I was able to at this point. I had come 477 miles (good grief, 477 miles!) since my last service station fuelling at Aoulef. The Merc indicated 0.3 of a tank which meant I had used 0.7, plus the two cans I'd put in two days ago. That was 106 litres - 23.34 gallons - and gave an approximation of 20.44 mpg. The calculations were not dead accurate but my past knowledge of how uncannily precise the Merc fuel gauge was lent them a comforting credibility.

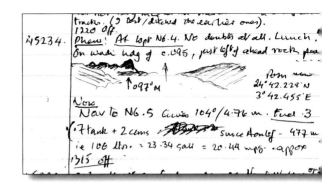

It should only be around seven miles to that sneaky zig-zag entry corner I had congratulated myself on finding when I first discovered the Tanetfirt-splitting route west through Wadi 'N'. And now I was actually eastbound in the wadi – wide, sandy, with space between low hills defining its meandering course – and locked in to the waypoint sequence I had established on that first trip; I was home and dry. I aimed to pop out the other side and sit awhile with the calculator to establish the route from here on.

There would be a choice of three options and I had to be very careful indeed which I chose. The waypoint gaps, certainly in one of the options, were enormous compared with today but at the same time the terrain was far more open and was pretty clearly established in my mind. In the most basic terms, when I emerged from Wadi 'N' I could go left, right or (in broad terms) straight on. Left was a short 35-odd miles north-east to the tarmac out of Arak and on to fuel at In Amenas. Straight on (in a manner of speaking) was tagging on to the 2005 waypoints that took me through the maze of low hills after going around the 12-mile long lozenge-shaped whaleback of Tininirt and on to the same tarmac farther south – still with an In Amguel refuel in mind.

Going right was a lot more critical in terms of gaps between previous waypoints and in the vital consideration of fuel reserves. That way I'd actually be overshooting to the south of In Amguel, would hit the Arak-Tamanrasset tarmac and have to go back north 15 miles or so for the diesel there. Not having maps didn't help. I could deduce a few of the sector distances from the logs I had but others ... hmm, I'd have to think about that. Being reckless or taking undue risks was not on the menu. My calculations, and even the estimates, would have to be accurate, factored for safety, and double-checked.

There was much to think about as I pottered on east down Wadi 'N', savouring the lack of tension, the excellence of my Ryvita and meat paste lunch (everything is relative on a trip like this), the fact that there was no hurry and that I had at last got a grip on and established the validity of the string of waypoints written down three years before. Despite it, though, I

The eureka moment and fuel check in Wadi 'N' (above). 'Idj', Wadi 'N' and camp at '6 Nov'; and the onward route decisions – Options 1, 2 or 3 – that awaited me.

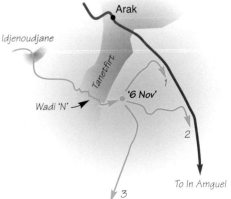

had to admit I was not clear on what had gone wrong this morning, trying to find the entry to the wadi. Problems like this are a lot less worrying if you can find a cause for what had happened, even if it was your own fault. Provisionally I put it down to an error in recording one of the waypoints in the '03 log; later I would conclude that actually they were accurate; there were simply not enough of them. The wadi as I traversed it in 2003 had taken a dog-leg – north and then west – and I had not at the time seen the need to record that much detail. That herringbone thing again – easy in one direction, ambiguous coming the other way.

Sporadic vegetation now dotted the wadi – among it those amazing broad, vivid green leaves that felt so cool. Some small dunes flanked the southern edge with enough soft sand around the edge to have me heaving on the diff locks and edging a little more pressure on the throttle. Quite a prominent hill on the left. My heading was 097°. I made a sketch. After five miles the GPS told me it was exactly 2.1 miles to the eastern entry point – to the hidden zig-zag entrance to the wadi that I had discovered three years before.

I had to smile. Even from the west the zig-zag double-corner out of the wadi was all but invisible, especially with the light slightly behind me as it was now. You looked ahead and there appeared to be a flat cul-de-sac of rocky hills staring back through the windscreen, maybe 200-feet high above the wadi bed. It would have been demoralising seeing it for the first time; without the knowledge that the wadi that appeared to be just finishing would actually take a sharp right turn between two smaller hills and after a mile or so let you out onto the wide plain east of Tanetfirt.

There'd been places in the Gulf, the Emirates as they are now known, like this. Going east from Sharjah (it used to be a little fishing village 10 miles up the coast from Dubai – not any more!) to find the magical freshwater pool in the hills at Shauka was a challenge. A good memory, a log, a compass and odometer were the means of doing a kind of dead-reckoning-in-reverse plot of where you had been. The maps had been a joke so we made our own, albeit later in my tour some excellent 1:100k photo-realistic maps appeared and there was a lot of 'There, told you so!' talk and grubby fingers pointing along wadi paths we had plotted on graph paper.

At last after another mile or so, the implacable barrier of hills ahead, Wadi 'N' revealed the little wadi to the south, the right turn round the bend by a rounded hill. I checked the GPS that had faithfully recorded the weaving path this far and showed in enlarged figures the bearing and distance to the wadi's entry point, now only a mile and a half off.

I raised my eyes from the GPS to look ahead between the narrow walls of the entry wadi and couldn't believe what I saw. Four hundred yards ahead, slip-face towards me, wall-to-wall across the wadi, sat a huge dune, 60-feet high. The wadi was blocked.

9. '6 Nov' to QFAT

Stunned is such an overused word in 21st-century UK as to qualify, darling that it is to our beloved and with-it media, for the status of an eye-rolling cliché. But there are times when the suddenness of a situation and the combination of surprise, bad news and serious implications summons no other, crisper description for the effect on the individual. Three years is, OK, three years and I knew sand dunes moved. But this was beyond the bounds of credibility. How on Earth, with so little evidence of a major sand storm farther down the wadi, could this much sand have moved here in the time since I had first come this way?

My mental hard drive exploded with the implications of the situation. With the way forward so decisively blocked I would have to retrace my steps back down Wadi 'N'; back to its confused western entry point, back to being on the wrong side – the western side – of the Tanetfirt range of hills, back possibly to the gap in the north-south ridge. Then what? I would have to try to head for Arak as the only way round. I had no accurate idea of how far that was: I guessed around 40 miles. I had no previously logged waypoints for that route to latch on to. I had already, that morning, demonstrated how lost and worried you could get in certain types of country within the space of five miles between two known waypoints not more than three miles apart. The best I'd be able to do, in the broadest terms, was to keep the Tanetfirt range on my right and head north, yet I had no idea of how many stand-off ridges Tanetfirt might have or their extent.

And at Arak? 'Where is your guide?' 'Where have you come from?' It all took no more than 30 seconds to scorch through my mind and leave something of a trail of hideous implications. I didn't even get out of the Merc to try and climb the dune. You'd be there all day trying to climb the slip face of a dune that big.

There are moments like this in every trip. Well, maybe not every trip and maybe not so laden with knock-on effects. But enough to make them stand out in your memory. The 1979 trip. Shipped to Dakar with the Range Rover and trailer, destination Tombouctou and then *north-east* to Reggan. Direct, no track. 900 miles without refuelling or external supplies. In southern Mali, still 300 kilometres from the capital Bamako on a rutted bush track long before the currently shown tarmac road was in place, something went seriously odd with the steering. Hardly daring to conjecture what I might find, I got out of the vehicle to see what had gone wrong. I stared, unbelieving, for 15 seconds. That most satisfying of monosyllabic expletives rose quietly to my lips. The track rod – that keeps the front wheels connected to each other – was broken. The Range Rover was comprehensively pigeon-toed, each front wheel pointing in at an angle of around 20 degrees.

'Er, yes!'. A sense of humour helps. Extraordinary care was taken to avoid breaking the fine pilot-hole drills!

The track was remote, the distance from anything resembling a workshop extremely discouraging, and I had seen no other traffic all day. I was, as ever, on my own; and in what seemed like an infinity of that nondescript, post-savannah, small-trees-and-scrub bush that limits visibility to a maximum of 75 yards and is the personification of monotony. But even here ideas come from somewhere; I will never know how. There is a compendium of appropriate sayings about situations like this and the mother of invention soon turned up to get me going. Steel straps hacksawed off the trailer and placed top and bottom to splint the break made a two-inch thick sandwich to drill through – by hand, using a carpenter's brace and bit – and 22 gruelling hours later I was able, very cautiously, to see if the fix would hold.

It did, but not before one of those wonderful instances of human generosity that such occurrences bring to light. A truck had passed late in the afternoon, and I had assured the driver that the plan would work and all would be well. But later, as I pottered around cooking my evening meal by the light of a fluorescent lamp, the job half done, I looked up to see some disembodied eyes and teeth approaching in the dark. Then some more alongside, their black faces and bodies invisible in the night. The crew of the truck had come back, clearly after some discussion as to the best way to fix my problem, bearing a length of heavy chain and several implements to see if they could help. Splendid people. Very kind, very moving. They smiled in the dark and lit up my space. But it was this part of the world, Mali, and typical.

On another occasion on the recce trip for the west-east coast-to-coast Sahara crossing expedition, we weren't even in trouble, just setting up camp for the evening. There were eight of us. We had vehicles. We had supplies. We had water. But over the dune the little Mauritanian boy, no more than six years old, walked carefully towards our camp, concentrating hard on not spilling his precious gift – a bowl of camel's milk. Even as I write, all these years later, I am moved to tears ... .

•   •   •

But at Wadi 'N', a huge dune blocking the exit wall-to-wall, was something else. As ever, if I had my time again I would have climbed the wadi sides to see what aerodynamic phenomenon could have funnelled the sand in this way. Clearly some kind of persistent north-east wind coming down the wide valley east of Tanetfirt squeezing through a gap and picking up the sand from a low-lying stretch just over the hills.

My brain awhirl with fuel states, unknown distances, terrain, lack of maps, the inevitable problems with the gendarmerie and the future of the whole trip, almost like an automaton I turned the Merc around and headed back to the corner that should have pointed me at the zig-zag pass guarding Wadi 'N's eastern end. I paused when I got there again to take in the wall of hills to my right that, flattened by this direct light, comprised an even more implacable looking barrier.

Then I thought I saw what could have been a concave inlet in the southern wall of the wadi a few hundred yards on, a kind of lay-by round the edge of a buttress intruding the wadi's main path. As I pulled out from the mouth of the blocked wadi, the bay revealed itself a bit more so that I pulled over towards it on my right. It began to open up. And a bit more as I moved forward.

There, unfolding before me, was the real zig-zag exit to the wadi. Faced with what the light had shown as its blank end I had turned right through Wadi 'N's southern flank just 400 yards too soon, down a cul-de-sac I hadn't even known was there. Herringbones again. And the flat overhead lighting killing all impression of terrain form. After a minute or two, once in the correct wadi, the GPS trace showed the situation all too clearly: how close the two turn-offs had been to each other and how invisible the right one was from the entry to the wrong one.

I suppose because the media never reports good news, there's no cliché word for anti-stunned, the arrival and relief of things coming wonderfully, ecstatically right after all. But though the whole episode had taken no more than 15 minutes, I was very happy to be in the exit zig-zag. Very happy indeed. Wadi 'N' had had the last laugh but I didn't mind;

'A picture's worth a thousand words,' as they say.

now. My mental hard drive, subjected twice to a certain amount of stress since leaving Idj that morning, began to reassemble itself and straighten its tie. I logged wadi exit waypoints like they were going out of fashion, gradually bearing round from south out of the fold of the hill onto south-east and then a little north of east to keep on the now reassuringly flat firm sand, a sprinkling of trees, widely spaced, off to my right. I guess I kept going a bit, just slowly on the smooth firm sand, to savour the new-found sense of security, the feeling that some quite serious difficulties, or potential difficulties, had passed.

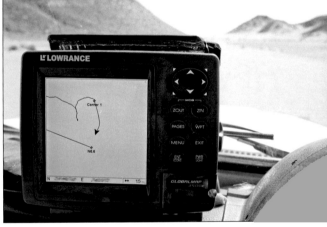

As if to celebrate, the landscape that opened up before me was almost surreal. Before, though Wadi 'N' was wide and flat once I got into it – up to half a kilometre in parts – the flanking backdrop of Tanetfirt had been layer on layer of small rounded hills, and the dips between them, some passable others treacherous dead-ends, had been a real maze. Now, the plain east and clear of Tanetfirt was open and bordered by hills but far off in the distance. And here, like the trumpets that spike out of the calm in Tchaikovsky's *Capriccio Italien*, were spectacular pointed volcanic outcrops, blunted smooth steeples of solid rock surrounded by exfoliated debris. And more of them stretching away to the north; randomly yet somehow lined up loosely to show what had been going on all those millions of years ago. Can the eye gasp? Here, yes.

Next spread: '6 Nov'. Near the camp.

To compare this to Monument Valley would have been odious. This was something of its own. And immeasurably better for the lack of a name or human intrusion of any kind – no tourist access road, no fences, no lay-bys. Some of the peaks had concave sides as though a great hand from the sky had pulled them higher when they were still plastic. The sand was smooth and firm, the light crisp and clear, the sky a rich dark blue laced with flourishes of upper cloud. The air was still.

And even in the harsh overhead light an hour or two either side of noon, it was breathtakingly beautiful. And pristine. Not a grain of sand out of place. A patch of rock-hard micro-dunes lay nearby, those hard little foot-high ridges that were invisible in the wrong light but would get a vehicle airborne off their ramp-like flanks if they were not seen. There was a smooth gently-domed rock opposite the first of the pointed outcrops and, weaving respectfully through the micro-dunes, I slipped the Merc into 4x2 and eased up onto it, circling round to view the panoply of geology that lay before me. I drank in the scene like a thirsty leopard at a pool. This would be '6 Nov', the campsite for the 6th of November 2006. It would be for me also a crossroads – I had some important calculations and decisions to make. I would stay here in this beautiful place for as long as it took.

The effect of the place was almost palpable. As the afternoon progressed and the sun angle decreased, the clear light worked its usual magic. Light and shadow sandwiched the pointed outcrops, the mathematically pure curves of the micro-dunes stood out against the flatter surrounding sand, a gently diffuse shadow edged across the rock dome I had stopped on. There were chores to do before I could start my sums based on accurate

'6 Nov'. Mother Nature was putting on a variety show ...

... and showing off her colour palette with a small flourish.

logistical data. I refuelled the Merc putting two more cans of diesel in giving me 0.75 of a tank and two further cans for the rest of my trip – including reserves – before the pumps at In Amguel or Tamanrasset. Water was not a worry – 51.2 litres in the cans with an astonishingly frugal 2.8 litres consumed for drinking, cooking and washing in the last 24 hours. Nor was food a problem: at my rate of consumption I could probably last another month on what I had. But I topped up the ready-box and checked the lists just the same.

I worked quickly so that I could devote time to the camera in the last half of the afternoon when the light was at its very best. Everywhere you looked, shape, form, purity, light, colour, texture and elegance. The moon, only one day past full, rose to the occasion, as you might say, bathing the fantastical rockscapes in theatrically pale light – white but seemingly blue in deference to the navy-blue sky. Supper was good and accompanied by my penultimate mug of Blossom Hill red from my precious bottle. Firm rock supported my bed for a change instead of shuffling sand that lurched to my every movement, and as ever with a sky like this, it was a crime to shut your eyes to sleep.

•   •   •

I'd had a visitor in the night. Quite close. It wasn't till I wandered 25 yards from the wagon when I got up that I saw the marks. The depression in the sand and shuffle to get comfortable. There were footprints on top of my own made the previous evening; big soft footprints of those incredible feet that nature had crafted so elegantly and functionally to cope with the hardest and softest the desert could muster. I saw them meandering

unhurriedly to the north-east and felt a pang that I had not seen this gentle animal or been able to guess at why she should have lain here and come so near to me and my vehicle. This camel was on her own, unlike the one I'd seen at Idjenoudjane with the young Touareg on board two days before.

But the visual extravaganza was not over. An odd pre-dawn mixture of distant cloud, dust and haze muffled the sunrise into nothingness, until I suddenly realised that a golden-bronze patina was beginning to suffuse the eastern sky and putting a perfect, pointed granite outcrop and closer hills into semi silhouette behind a similarly copper-brown foreground of desert and grasses - 3D theatre on the grandest possible scale.

•   •   •

No maps, a tiptoe past Reggan, the Ouallen fort I had confidently expected to be abandoned, a scribbled guess at a latitude and longitude position at 2°E, the tension negotiating the wadi north of Foum al Aqbet, Idjenoudjane's customary wind-tunnel dust storm and the rising alarm of trying to find the entry to - and out of - Wadi 'N' had led me, safely at last, to this idyllic and extraordinary landscape. The need now was to decide on

one of three options on the direction my route should take from here. Navigation and fuel were the dominant criteria.

Navigation first; and the availability or otherwise of previous waypoints I could join-the-dots with. I did a little sketch – that's a tarted-up version on page 103. Option One was pretty straightforward – left (north-east), back about 40 miles, in principle, along the great wide valley I had seen in 2002 towards a point on the tarmac 30 miles or so south of Arak, using 2003 waypoints to pick my way through the hills. Option Two was more or less straight ahead, the complex but now recorded route round Tininirt to join the same tarmac 35-40 miles further south; 2005 log. There would be no navigation or serious terrain problem with these two alternatives, albeit the 2005 route was fiddly. And fuel would be ample. But ... these were not the routes I had come to do, albeit I was so far now doing things in the opposite direction – Plan 'E' instead of Plan 'A'; and with certain orientational limitations in the cartography department. But before dismissing these as soft options I had to be as sure as I could be that the

third option was practical and as safe as possible. Fuel-wise I'd be back to the only-just-comfortable reserves of Plan 'A' – and without the maps. Navigationally there were potential difficulties with Option Three.

The biggest of the no-waypoint gaps had been accommodated – a pretty huge 200 miles-odd in the Tanezrouft from ('around' – literally, I guess) Reggan to *Poste Weygand* – though the terrain had, apart from the traumatic 'Reggan bypass' itself, been mainly straightforward. And, parallelling the main Tanezrouft track as I was, I'd had an easy 'escape route' close by should it be required. I'd also made it without waypoints from Ouallen, tiptoeing the 125 miles to '3 Nov'. If I now took Option Three on my little sketch, in effect south from '6 Nov' to zero-in on the Arak-Tam tarmac something like another 200 miles away, I would be going from a 2003 fix (the eastern end of Wadi 'N') to using a couple of Nov 2005 waypoints and then leaping a gap of around 50 miles through country I was moderately sure about – or thought I was – and aiming to plug in to other off-piste waypoints I had established in 2001. These I should then be able to follow to the tarmac around 150 miles further on where I could decide if I had enough fuel to make Tam or would need to turn north a bit and take diesel on at In Amguel.

Even my tourist map wasn't any use here, and to get an idea of the spatial set-up and orientate myself I plotted the waypoints I did have on a makeshift graph-paper grid. I spent the whole morning hunched over the graph paper and calculator, working and reworking the sums. Now 490 miles since fuelling at Aoulef my fuel consumption, within the (high) accuracy which the Mercedes fuel gauge indicated, was 21.44 mpg – past experience confirmed this as a credible figure. For a little extra margin I did the sums based on 20 and found I had a theoretical max range of 293 miles. That was 293 miles not to tanks dry but 293 to hitting the notional safety reserve of 25 per cent plus 100 miles. Dry tanks had no place in any Sahara fuel calculations and the reserve quantities had served me well over the past 40 years – prudent to accommodate unforeseen changes to route or difficulties with terrain or boggings.

Having worked out 293 miles as a safe estimated range with the fuel I had, I next tried to establish what the distance to go would be using Tam or In Amguel as destinations. I could get much from the past logs but the '47-mile gap' was the best guess I could get from the graph-paper plot – and it pre-supposed the fairly straightforward terrain from my recollection of the maps. On this basis, Tam would be 260 miles, In Amguel 203. I was pretty sure I'd head for In Amguel and if I did I should arrive there with half a tank, around 10 gallons, still on board. A sensible margin; but I'd get uncomfortable if it went any lower.

For me it was a green light. I didn't know it at the time but the green light would flicker and change to quite a bright red a few times in the next 72 hours but the basic sums looked good. My head had come up with what my heart badly wanted. I thought, as I had thought many times over the previous few days, that there was a dismal likelihood this might be the last trip of this kind that I'd be able to do. There was a strong case for making the best of it.

●   ●   ●

I coaxed the satellite phone into getting through to the Embassy but things had slowed down. They had done what they could and were at the mercy of wheels that ground slow, when they ground at all. The pursuit was worthwhile, however, as with luck I might be able to pick up my maps as I went north again from Tamanrasset through In Salah. Chris Tams was practically drooling when I told him where I was and what I was seeing. With the crackly satellite connection and voice-overlap time lags I couldn't explain the complexities of route and logistics but it was good to talk to a kindred spirit. I promised we should have a debrief dinner when I came back through Algiers.

Though it had given me a heart-meltingly soft and beautiful dawn, the haze and distant cloud visibility of around three to five miles wasn't quite what was required for making 47-mile leaps across unfamiliar terrain in the Sahara. Something that enabled you to size up and aim for any requisite gaps at 10-15 miles was more the ticket. I resolved to set off, however, and make the final decision at the point of leaving the 2005 waypoints 15 miles on. God bless, God bless, God bless, I said for the two-hundredth time, the inventors and facilitators of GPS as the bearing-and-distances to 'Tininirt gate' guided me reliably to my jumping off point irrespective of which way I turned to avoid an intervening hill, outcrop or patch of micro-dunes.

By the time I got there around four o'clock the visibility was significantly better than earlier in the day and the bearing and distance to the 2001 waypoint was almost exactly what I had worked it out to be on the graph paper. My geometry master would have been proud! Now it was dark-side-of-the-moon time: all-new terrain and just my memory of the maps to tell me what to expect. The grey-cells memory chip spelled out pretty open country for most of the way, passing down the east side of Aketeb and through a wide gap to a point where I could turn from the present target heading of 196° onto south-east and through the rather complicated group of hills known as Aghabir.

My memory chip served me well and a blissfully smooth sand sheet rolled out before me as I headed SSW, the occasional rock lending variety to the landscape and giving me something to swerve round. Some long-wave undulations and more rocky sprouts appeared but scarcely slowed the gentle 25mph pace. I didn't really have much idea of how far I would get before camping but was happy to take it as it came. The low-level visibility was now excellent albeit there was upper cloud to the west which was dimming the sun as it got ready to sink. After 20 miles or so a rocky range of hills, dark in my one o'clock position came into view about five miles off. As I drove on down its eastern flank, leaving it to my right, I had a flicker of doubt that it seemed to be too long. Aketeb in my mental map was a blob rather than a streak, something you went round rather than going alongside for some distance. But even in my mind the topography hereabouts was parallel north-east/south-west brush strokes of hills fairly wide apart that you could slot through. I would find, when I got home, that it was not Aketeb to my right after all but a long swathe of hills 10 or 12 miles to the east of it. I veered left onto 160° to avoid some hills and then right again to resume the GPS heading demand as a tall, craggy three-mile-long hill loomed to the left. My 160° steer had been fortuitous as it took me a little east and, now clear of the hills I wanted to avoid, I found myself on something of a plateau and able to look down and right to what appeared to be a long troublesome valley of scrub alongside what I still thought was Aketeb. Though the way ahead here was easy and clear, the going was intermittently soft, almost like fesh-fesh (a fine, powder-like dust) and the Merc lurched and plunged in the soft, yielding ground.

At last I could see a dip in the terrain ahead. 'Aketeb' was still continuing on my right and looked like it was meeting up seven or eight miles ahead with a ridge coming in from the east. Another barrier ridge? Not what I was looking for right now. The apparent dip was thus a welcome sight. After such a good start I didn't want to be tangling with rocky ridge crossings at a time when – just like the bad bogging on the 'Reggan bypass' – I should be stopping for the night. The apparent dip seemed, as I got closer, to be a real dip and providentially profiled to get me through what would have been a fairly demanding escape route from the narrowing space between 'Aketeb' on my right and the encroaching ridge on my left. The shallow valley on my right, immediately alongside 'Aketeb', looked like a good place to keep out of, a typical green-wadi mix of vegetation, sand mounds and tumps. Whilst there might have been a white-knuckle way through at its nearer edge, the low ridge-gap provided a sand-ramp switch-back preferred route. A squeeze with my right foot summoned the requisite additional assistance from the Merc's driveline and we wooshed over the saddle and onto a wide grey plain below. I hit the waypoint button to log the position. An important one. Whilst I had been lucky to be funnelled into the crossing point coming from the north, approaching from the south the gap would have been very hard to find. Even then I thought 'Aketeb' had been a bit odd stretching for more than 20 miles, but the main thing was I was through the conflict of ridges and the 2001 waypoint was a clear-ahead 196°, 12 miles.

It was time for a late camp, the sky to the west grey with blank cloud shading the sunset and twilight supplying such light as was left with which to set up the cooking. The grey gave a sombre and desolate appearance to the landscape, unlike the clear slanting light of the previous evening. I stopped what I was doing and looked out to the south-west, the horizon blurred in a distant soft haze, low ranges of hills rising above the plain far away. As far as the eye could see over this flat landscape, it was still. Not even a pair of ravens. Nothing moved.

Hmm. Quiet, for a Tuesday, I thought. I found myself grinning and went back to the stove and my last half-mug of Blossom Hill.

•   •   •

Option Three was working out and I was 35 miles into the unknown 47-mile join-the-dots gap. But if it was quiet for a Tuesday, Wednesday, I was to discover, would be anything but. Noisy with alarm bells, mainly.

10. QFAT to Issedienne

Most of the cloud had gone by morning but it had hung on long enough to reduce the by now even later moon glow to a bland non-directional spread of dim light and, as it lingered at medium altitude, also prevented the temperature from dropping too much through radiation. GPS told me the ground hereabouts was at an altitude of 2000 feet or so and a clear night would have been a chilly one. As it was, the thermometer registered 14.6°C when I got up; hardly arctic but, as before, low enough (lantern-jawed heroes of the high peaks will find it hilarious to note) to have me rushing for my clothes and fleece. With my economically-clad skeleton I always felt any cold, albeit today there was no wind to reduce me to gibbering hypothermia.

Perhaps something was lost in the translation.

I folded the bed, stowed my stout stick (which, I noted with a cocky smirk, had effectively kept the bandits away for yet another night), packed away all the kit, lashed down the cooking and food boxes; also the camp bed and tiny canvas chair. I was meticulous about litter. Nothing – but *nothing* – was left behind; neither a matchstick nor a teabag, either on the surface or buried. The cooking operation always involved swilling out the empty food tins with a spoonful of hot water, letting them drain and dry overnight and then, in the morning, I would find suitable rocks with which to crush them flat so I could put them into my dry rubbish bag which was 'properly disposed of', ironically, in the waste bins at the next hotel stop – in this case 12 days away. I liked to think that meant what it sounded like but 'taken out to the desert and dumped' was probably the more likely fate. At least it would all be together and not desecrating the really wild places. The little scene just outside In Salah (right) summed it up depressingly well. Here at QFAT, so quiet and Tuesday-ish was it – Wednesday now actually – that, as sometimes happened, I had a job finding suitable crushing rocks for the tins. As part of the general just-don't-have-any-damned-accidents policy I always wore heavy gloves for this operation and was careful to let go of the descending rock a nano-second before it hit the tin target. It was the tin I was trying to crush, not my fingertips.

In the course of the remaining after-breakfast chores and checks I found to my increasing surprise that I had, in the past 24 hours, used a record low of only 2.2 litres of water – drinking, cooking and washing. It pays to be skinny – if not always first thing in the morning when the temperature hasn't yet got going. I had now covered 542 miles since refuelling at Aoulef and fuel state was 0.65 of a tank plus two 20 litre cans of diesel. With any luck there should be around 160 miles to go before rolling up to the pumps beside the tarmac at In Amguel. Tyre pressures checked out again at 1.8 bar; just right for what I expected today – a mix of sand and stones. No praise was too high for the 265/75 BFGoodrich All-Terrain tyres which just ... worked, and kept going, accepting the carefully calculated tyre pressures for each type of terrain I had to tackle and, when treated with the respect they deserved, being apparently immune to what it had to offer.

•   •   •

I wasn't actually going all the way to that 2001 waypoint that had been my 'Nav-to' destination the previous day but I could remember, as I looked out to the south east 12 miles off where it lay, the problems surrounding its establishment. It had been my first trip in the Merc. I had had a challenging and successful first half – the old French track from what had once been Zaouatallaz (now Bordj el Haoues) to Amguid, round the towering Garet el Djenoun, across to Tidikmar and on to a hot shower at Tamanrasset. There – since I had been somewhat involved with them at the planning stage and coincidentally found our paths were destined to cross – I met up with Michael Palin and the film crew making his *Sahara* films for BBC television, a cheering break with an excellent bunch of people. Being short of English-speaking 'encounters', they even persuaded me to put in a brief appearance; a speaking part, no less. 'See me on the telly, then?' I'd be able to ask my friends when I got back; real fame at last!

Michael Palin in person is precisely the same as he is on film: totally unaffected, the quintessential nice-guy, interesting and interested. I often railed that these days there is rarely a conversation. It is more usually a collision of monologues. Few people actually respond to what you say, ask questions or manifest indications that your words have not simply bounced off their skull as they prepare to resume. Michael is a listener and has a response and curiosity about everything which I guess is why his films work so well.

It was an ethos that seemed to include director Roger Mills and his film crew. And here there was hard-nosed, quick-thinking professionalism nearer the surface. On a normal film there is a story board, shooting script and everything is planned ahead, but on a travel documentary like this you have to be creative on the hoof – forever having to make up a script and shooting sequence as each new situation presents itself. Never knowing what the circumstances are going to be, what light there'll be, who will do what or what impromptu situations will arise, you have to think like lightning and much is left up to the fleetness of the man actually wielding the camera if he is not to resort to excessive 'Would you mind doing that again?' requests. Nigel Meakin and his son Peter (who hefted the tripods for the long shots) and their sound man, John Pritchard, were poetry to watch as a team and main footage, cutaways, close-ups, and distant shots were obtained almost quicker than you could envisage the need for them. Rather like flocks of birds that with a kind of collective consciousness miraculously all turn at the same time, there seemed to be a shared, network intelligence in the way they went about their business.

Buoyed by the ambience of the whole episode and the new wagon's capabilities, the IGN maps spread before me in my room at Tamanrasset's Tahat Hotel began to spell out an equally impromptu new route back to Arak in the north: not on the tarmac or even an old French piste but off-pistes altogether, around 80 miles west of the black-top. At that stage, it being a first trip in the G-Wagen and unsure of the fuel and water consumptions I would be getting, I carried eight jerry cans of diesel. The 741 miles since fuelling at Zaouatallaz and topping up at Tam had yielded 24.97 mpg – impressive for a 4x4 off-road all the way at close to three tonnes GVW – so range would not be a problem. Careful examination of the route on the large-scale maps indicated generally open country between the usual sprinkling of hill ranges and outcrops. Access to the planned north-pointing route to Arak would be via a large, wide west-bound wadi that I had been 30 miles or so along on a Yamaha in 1984.

Large, high capacity wadis out of regions like the Hoggar mountains are prone to move a lot of water and debouch onto flood plains; the bit I had not got as far as on the bike 16 years earlier. The flood plain was a pig – a hazy infinity of classic 'green wadi' dried swirl-holes, and huge grass-topped tumps with no obvious consistency of direction or easy way through. But I eventually escaped from it north and, once over a token, awkward little sod of a dune barrier, was out into a valley and the hills of Aghabir. I was through the difficult bit and heading on through much more open country – little thinking then that I would be within a few miles of the spot, mapless – on Braille, as you might say – five years later.

When I bought the Merc I had taken comfort from the simplicity of the Type 461 design; the manual selection of 4x4 and axle diff locks, the lack of air conditioning, the absence of gimmicky electronics. I'd had no option but to accept 'drive-by-wire' electronic throttle control where the throttle position merely indicated a demand to a black box which then, at the behest of more than a dozen sensors clocking up various temperatures, pressures and other quantifiable parameters, relayed the information to an ECU (electronic control unit) which then arranged for the fuel pump and injectors to react appropriately. It was all in the pursuit of Euro emissions standards. If it was Mercedes-Benz, I thought, it'll be OK; they don't fool around with things like this – or any others.

Three miles before what would, in 2006, be waypoint 'Cmp 21/10', the Merc's dashboard 'EDC' warning light came on. That meant a fault in the Electronic Diesel Control – the drive-by-wire throttle. The owner's manual was written for eight-year-olds. It concluded, of course, by enjoining you to take the vehicle to your nearest dealer. Not a helpful suggestion at around 23°N, 3°E.

With no more than the faintest clue in the manual that the fuel injectors might be involved, there was almost immediate confirmation that whatever else was happening under the bonnet, there was a significant drop in power. This was quickly manifested in a down-to-the-axles bogging in otherwise innocent-looking level sand from which the Merc was reluctant to be free. It was a singularly ill-timed coincidence though interestingly, examination of the pictures when I got home revealed a strange sand-type layer formation in the sand the Merc had sunk through. The sand mats, quite a bit of digging

A slight but sudden descent at the behest of an unusual sand structure and the EDC warning light. 'Worse in reverse', as you might say; note how the diff casing is dragging as I try to get out backwards.

Fighting for the cause. Or at least trying to find one – at 23°N and in Munich. After four days' no joy I said, 'EDC light on? Let's just take the bulb out!' They very nearly did.

and a mounting appreciation of what the engine was lacking occupied the next half hour but, in the absence of the high-gear torque that such situations usually demanded, low range and the incapacitated engine together finally got the wagon onto firmer ground. What now?

All I had to go on was the cryptic comment in the manual about the injectors. The fuel stations at Tamanrasset, as is so often the case, had been waiting for a fresh delivery. When it arrived the long queue of customers, including myself, had been taking on diesel almost before the tankers were out of the yard. I wondered if the lack of the customary settling period had perhaps led to some kind of fuel contamination. This, I thought, may have affected the injectors. I changed the fuel filter but the next 24 hours was taken up with draining the tank and all the jerry cans, one by one, into the spare cans and filtering the diesel through cloths and an improvised funnel. I found no sand in the fuel. It was five days before I could get to a telephone to find out what might have happened. The engine had gone into 'limp home' mode, they said, 'Around 50 per cent power,' they jauntily assured me – and in the end I 'limped home' all the way to Munich a couple of weeks later. (But not without taking in the old Arak-In Salah piste along the way.)

In what walk of life are we free from the rule of 'the computer'? The Mercedes professionals were informed by their test gear that all was well. And indeed, during the examination process, the light had gone out. Mercifully, and to quench my apoplexy, the light came on again as I drove back to my hotel. The computer again showed all was well. The servicing people might have been little green men from another planet; totally content to accept that after the computer's verdict there was no more to be said. They simply did not understand. 'Would you', I growled through gritted teeth, 'take this vehicle back to the middle of the Sahara without knowing what the problem is?'

It took three months, an expensive return trip from the UK to Germany and intervention from the highest level at Graz (where G-Wagens are made) to conclude – or conjecture with a hopeful shrug – that it must have been an intermittent wiring harness fault. A short-circuit somewhere was blowing a fuse and the ECU was, correctly, taking that as a fault indication and shutting down the engine to a protective 'limp-home' mode. The computer was right; there was nothing wrong with the ECU. But that wasn't the whole picture. On the instructions of the head electrical whizz from Graz they cut four possibly suspect wires between the left and right sides of the vehicle, hot-wired a new section of harness into position, installed four tell-tale extra fuses and all that, now, on the 7th of November 2006, was keeping things afloat. And had done for four previous trips.

Waypoint 'Cmp 21/10' (2001) – and the ensuing battle – would stick in my memory for some time. It also ensured, for the next trip in April 2002 and thereafter, that I had a Thuraya satellite phone on board so I could elicit informed expansion on what the owner's manual had to say, or didn't have to say, on any further problems arising.

• • •

But now, the dotted-about scattering of separate low hills at Aghabir was the target, there to try to retrace my path through them between the entry and exit waypoints recorded in 2001 on the Merc's first desert trip.

In the back of my mind I was somewhat worried about the Aghabir hills and how confusing they had been to get through in 2001 even with the maps. And then further south there would be that flood plain to try to avoid – again without the benefit of maps. I headed on south, after a few miles leaving the big group of hills I had seen at the start on my left. It was now a bright morning with plenty of visibility. 'Aghabir N(orth)' was on my waypoint 'Nav to' box but I had wondered about there possibly being a way to bypass the hills and zero in on the waypoint two sectors farther down the 2001 route. The usual distraction of random tracks had already manifested itself and I found myself on this heading following some previous wheel marks that appeared to have come out of the north end of Aghabir.

Suddenly a further set, to echo my wishful thinking, appeared branching left and seeming to go round the eastern edge of Aghabir just as I had conjectured. Looking ahead I could see, with Aghabir to my one o'clock, a gap in the hills heading a wonderfully convenient 122°.

The terrain was open enough and it seemed an opportunity not to be missed; something to simplify the navigation. Later, with a map and the wisdom of hindsight, what happened next was as clear as it was inevitable: the old wheel marks veered off up a wide wadi to the north-east. At the time, even if I had known the other vehicle

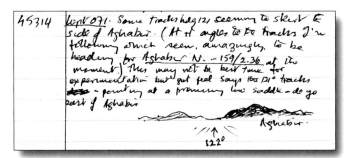

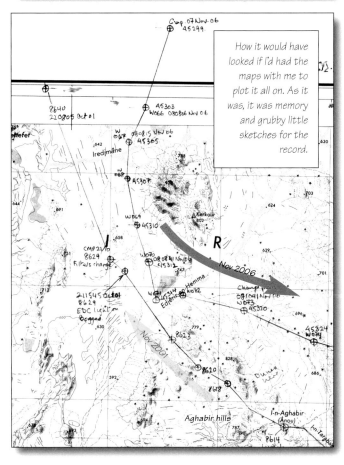

How it would have looked if I'd had the maps with me to plot it all on. As it was, it was memory and grubby little sketches for the record.

would be following the wadi it did, the route would have been no use to me. I stopped on the brow of a rise and pondered the situation. All I had was my graph paper positioning of the main waypoints I was aiming for.

Slowly it occurred to me that to avoid both Aghabir's hills and the tricky flood-plain fringe to the south of them by 30 miles or so, there was an elegance about trying to get to Issedienne and 'Ramotswe' direct from here. What made the idea not only attractive but appear feasible was the view I had to the south-east from my hill. Issedienne was 39 miles on a bearing of 102° and would be part of a more direct route out to the wadi to eventually head me for In Amguel. Waypoint 'Ramotswe' possibly requires some explanation (probably less necessary now) but it commemorates the place where, short of the wadi flood plain I was trying to avoid in 2003, I sat out a dust storm for some hours reading Alexander McCall-Smith's delightful story about the lady detective of that name in Botswana. It lightened my day, despite the dust.

The decision was made. Go direct. A good idea. Or so I thought at the time.

The new route plan would actually be a little shorter than going through Aghabir and along the northern edge of the east-west wadi flood plain and anything that saved fuel was a welcome spin-off, despite my earlier calculations on margins. In the prevailing circumstances there was no point in taking on doubtful tricky navigation if it could be avoided. OK, going this way was a bit of a gamble since my recollection of this region was not as clear as it was of the 47-mile gap I'd covered the day before. Actually the brutal bottom line was that all I really had was a waypoint 39 miles away and a view over the hills in front of me stretching maybe eight to 10 miles. In my memory I had an image of low hills – and was looking at them from my present rise – and low hills had gaps between them which were usually pretty straightforward to weave your way along.

As I swept down the slope and set off, the way proved to be promising; open stretches alternating with undulations on a generally south-east heading. Issedienne was one of those wide circles of rocks, outcrops and hills best seen on a map or satellite image, for

only those gave you a feel for the overall shape of the formation and had you wondering what had gone on to make it happen. About 15 miles north of the east-west wadi and 'Ramotswe', I had come across Issedienne in 2003, fascinated by its plan view from space. Like the vast Richat crater in Mauritania, its size and layout was almost impossible to appreciate from ground level and when I came through a hill gap into the huge arena and looked for a place to camp – there was plenty of choice – I found myself staring at sky through a huge hole in a rock 400 yards ahead. The surrounding rocks were full

of blow-holes and spherical cavities and it was not hard to imagine the geological upheaval taking place when it all rose from the centre of the Earth.

Now, a helpful little valley gave me easy ground to cover and then the sides became steeper and rocky before it swooped up onto a low hill. From here I could see the hills were increasingly covered with small rock outcrops like pins on a pin cushion, boulders and stones too big to drive over and too close to drive around. I was forced to follow the wadis, the space between the hills. The first one, down to my left was not a good start; partially blocked by a small dune of sand but luckily there was space – smooth enough too – to arc up the wadi side round the edge of the sand ridge and back onto the wadi floor. The hills around had taken on an aggressive appearance, the rocks lay thick and impassable on the slopes precluding any thought of leaving the valleys between. It's all in the mind, of course, but the harsh midday overhead light, the glare and a yellowish kind of haze over what seemed like range on range of these small prickly hills did little to sooth the soul. I followed the old watercourses, dotted with trees now but soon the terrain eased out a bit, albeit I was being nudged 30° south of the optimum heading from Issedienne. If this led direct or through a valley chain to Ramotswe then that was fine by me as I could definitely recall the area immediately north of the big east-west wadi being pretty flat. If the wadis appeared to offer an exit in that direction I would go along with it.

Then the country changed again and I was forced to try a sidestep into another wadi slightly to the north that was paralleling my heading and whose alignment was more

Rocky hills definitely for driving between, not over. Looks clear ahead, though. Er, not actually: the deceptive start to an alarming 38-mile maze.

favourable. It worked for a while and then, trying to keep as close as was feasible to my desired heading, I breasted a low saddle between two hills only to be faced with an uncrossable ridge straight in front of me. The way south around it was blocked and I drove up a wide north-easterly valley to get round the tip of the spine. I turned onto a more south-easterly direction but again progress was prevented by a line-hill blocking my path and I had to resort to zigzagging between the hills.

At last a dip in the hill profile appeared ahead, smoothly covered in sand. It would have been a big rolling dune but for the rocky ridges either side, but it looked firm and well packed and the Merc's run at it and the auto transmission's butter-smooth gear changes gave precisely the smooth torque delivery required to sail to the top and over. As I got to the top and eased the wagon over my hopes were again dashed. Not only was there another ridge right up against and facing the one I had just crossed but the valley between the two was, to my right, a cul-de-sac so that my only option was to turn sharp left and exit along the resulting narrow passage. Worst of all, it was heading 297°, almost 180° off the desired steer for Issedienne. I was going in the opposite direction. I had no idea how far this terrain extended. Foot-hills to grand mountain massifs often looked like this but I was pretty certain that did not apply here. The feeling, though, was of being in a true maze, everything conspiring to prevent progress in the direction you wanted to go.

'All looking a bit bloody bleak,' I wrote in the log. Something of an understatement in relation to what I felt at the time. Being 'lost' is not just a question of not knowing where you are but in its truest meaning it incorporates not knowing which way to turn, how best to avoid the obstacles before you. As ever on this trip I knew where I was to the nearest bee's whisker thanks to GPS and I knew exactly where my goal was and how far away it lay, were I a crow flying. What I didn't know was the lie of the land around me.

But the feeling of vulnerability and rising alarm was powerful as I strove, like a pin-ball bouncing off the pins in an attempt to reach the end of the board, finding my way blocked at every turn. Obviously the 39-mile straight-line distance to Issedienne would turn out to be considerably more but being forced onto headings that were now averaging between 60° and 180° off my desired track was not a good feeling. Trying to go back was already not an option for I had now covered about 24 miles since deciding the new route and even if I could find my way back along precisely the same tracks I would have lobbed 48 miles off my fuel reserves and then had to start another route out.

The next obstacle allowed me forward on 058°. After a short distance again the way was blocked and I was forced left along another claustrophobic minor valley heading on the wrong side of north: by now I was needing 125° for Issedienne. After a few hundred yards it debouched like a T-junction into a wide wadi – soft in patches but big, clear, level and open, the hills either side seeming to have less height than before. My spirits dared to rise. The effect on morale of that wide clear wadi and the lower flanking hills was remarkable. The problem was that it headed 055°, still 60-odd degrees north of the heading I needed. But the lower wadi-fringe terrain was what really gave me encouragement. I hoped that the wadi was taking me to higher ground, that the flanking hills would continue to diminish and that I could possibly turn onto the heading I needed.

Three miles in a single straight line was cause to summon a brass band and skyrockets.

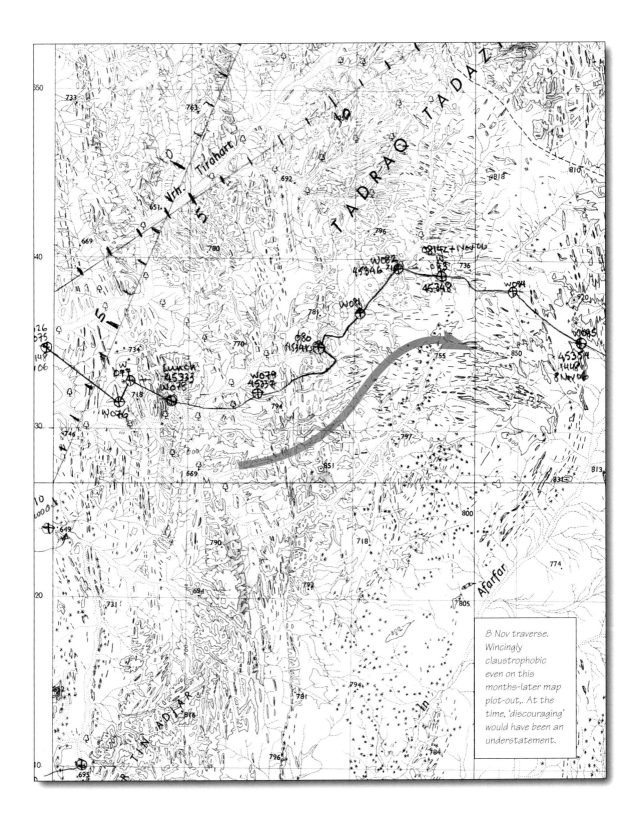

8 Nov traverse. Wincingly claustrophobic even on this months-later map plot-out,. At the time, 'discouraging' would have been an understatement.

The second brass band was mentally ordered when an *embranchement* to the right between the now less aggressive hills permitted me to leave the main wadi and turn onto 094°. The side wadi was shallow and mild, weaving gently but rising to higher ground, what seemed like a plateau that became almost open on top. After another two miles I was able to do another sidestep, again to the right, following the shallowest of wadis until I was virtually at its end, on fairly even going, and able to turn direct onto Issedienne's heading.

It was still quite cautious going but I did seem, irrefutably, to be out of the spiky, rock-covered, aggressive hills and now had some control over the direction in which I was able to travel. There was still a sprinkling of small three-foot rocky outcrops but they were widely spaced and easy enough to weave between on the high ground.

Suddenly I seemed to have come to the end of the rock-strewn ground and could barely believe my eyes. Before me spread a huge plain, 10-miles wide or more, its far end blurred in haze, smooth and even, sloping easily away from where I now was, high up and overlooking it.

There are wadis and there are wadis – anything from a small, awkward, tangled mass of vegetation, rocky edges, swirl-holes and half-dried mud ready to bog you on a semi-permanent basis to a broad smooth plain the centre of which was a touch lower than the edges. This, I would discover when I came to plot my agonising trail on a map at home a few months later, was one of the latter and was

called Afarfar. I could almost have wept with relief. I had covered 38 excruciating miles since setting off from my hill-top perch that morning and the GPS told me there was a further 16.7 miles, if I flew directly and did not pass Go, to my hole-in-the-rock 2003 campsite at Issedienne.

It proved to be almost exactly that, so straight was my path and so easy and shallow the wadi-off-a-wadi that Afarfar had for tributaries. The Merc swept gently through it all, the wide sweep of the ultra-shallow wadis, the firm sand at Issedienne's edges, round the low domes at its centre, over the perfectly level surface-rock until, as I looked ahead through the giant, rounded rock's huge smooth hole at the western sky, the GPS told me I was within 10 feet of my 2003 campsite. As the crow flew – one came to say hello – it would have been 39 miles. Doing it the hard way it was 56. I always thought crows were pretty smart.

Issedienne and smart crow. Showing off, I thought, under the circumstances.

And, the crows, like the other wildlife round these parts, were the objects of my admiration and respect. It never ceased to amaze me how they were somehow always there. I had only to stop for five minute to have my frugal lunch or to read the GPS or write the log and, as though they had all seen the Hitchcock films, they flew over. Always a pair, always their shadow would cross the bonnet of the Merc as if to announce their presence. Maybe, I thought, they could see best down-sun, or like Battle of Britain fighter pilots they preferred to come out of the sun to surprise their prey. Whatever it was, they would fly over, circle and land gently just about 75 yards away, walking up and down neatly and pretending they weren't the least bit interested in the big white thing that had just stopped in their territory.

I suspected, darkly, that their school for smart crows taught that if anything moving stopped (even if it's a Mercedes G-Wagen Type 461), hang around; it might have died and this could be your big feast of the day.

60-mile screen shows vehicle-position arrow at Issedienne and the track required to 'Ramotswe'. Intervening recorded positions are indicated ... 'for next time'.

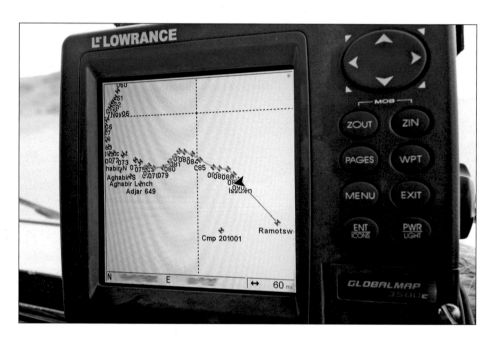

11. Issedienne to Guantanamo

They had survived three weeks – it seemed like three months (or was it years?) – in the passenger-side foot well of the Merc as it fought its way nobly over the burning wastes. I wasn't yet sure if 'survived' was the right word and couldn't remember what I did with them when I sat over on that side to do the log and admin chores in the evenings or had my sumptuous suppers. But the box I now expected to contain nothing more than crumbs or desiccated raisins was now ripe for opening – if only to consign its contents, as part of a general clear-up, to the rubbish bag. The principal trigger for this new-broom urge, however, was that wave of relief and peace and well-being that sweeps over you when you have just been through, and out the other side of, something causing a high degree of worry and foreboding.

I often wondered if maybe I was a worry-guts – and I worried about it. Possibly a touch too anxious: getting so uptight about bad boggings (Lord knows I'd had enough in my time), difficulties finding wadi openings and exits, heading into rocky mazes such as the one '8 Nov' had waggishly dumped on my plate. The endless fuel checks, water checks meticulous tyre care – life is about detail; that bit was fair enough and eminently sensible, though I said it myself, in circumstances such as these. But the challenges against which all that planning was pitted; hmm. Then again, I thought, sod it. In the Air Force there was a saying that there are bold pilots and there are old pilots but there are no old, bold pilots. Take silly risks and you die. Fail to appreciate the consequences of getting it wrong and the same thing could happen. Solo in the Sahara without maps you're already pushing your luck a smidge. And if getting worried is being chicken then so be it. Being a perfectionist is not a universal recipe for popularity, but you've got to be who you are. I recall there's a song that starts that way. My lousy hearing never gets me beyond the first couple of lines.

But serious and prolonged worry had been lifted and it was time to see if the mince pies had, all unaware, weathered the storm. Incredibly, they had. They were delicious and outstanding despite the long bake at Saharan ambients. And the beauty, space and spectacle of Issedienne was the place to enjoy them. Waitrose would have been proud.

Christmas was 11 months late – or six weeks early – but nowhere and on no other occasion could a gastronomic treat such as this have been more welcome.

I didn't know, as I enjoyed the culinary treat and homecoming to Issedienne freed of my problems, that new ones – bureaucratic this time, almost as serious and probably more fundamental – were just around the corner. 'Gitmo', as a naval Tom Cruise termed it in that taut film he starred in against Jack Nicolson's gritty general, was the nick-name (Guantanamo) I would give, in a few days' time, to the place where I would sit, trapped, actually within sight of the tarmac that could lead me to the magical fuel pump at In Amguel. For now, though, ignorance was bliss.

I fought, without too much success over the years, to prevent my trips becoming mile-eating marathons where each day is a race to cover ground, to get to a certain goal before evening and then be off again, your tail in the air, to the next hurry-hurry destination. I was getting better at it, though. The sea ferry to and from Algiers was probably the worst part of any trip, not least because of the random customs and arrival procedures and the chaotic pushing, shoving and elbowing at the port on entry and exit, but I tackled 'schedule-itis' by always buying an open return ticket so that I could take however long I wanted along the way rather than be forever back-calculating from ship departure times.

My record so far for least distance travelled in a day, was in the Hoggar mountains on the 1979 trip – 12 kilometres. There every turn in the track was a photographic feast, every view a heart-stopper of wild Wagnerian peaks dramatically clawing the sky, in every rock nested tiny spring flowers. I was forever stopping to admire, to scramble around for a better view, to take pictures.

At Issedienne I would break the record again, make it a two-night stop and do just four miles. There were thoughts to think, pictures to take, plans to make, more mince pies to savour and, if the satellite permitted, a phone call to try. I made time to run the Merc the short distance to some of the outlying hills in the formation, to regard the minutiae as well as the grandeur. Always, it seemed, there was life or signs of it. A tiny shrub making its way upwards against the climate and all the odds; tracks of lizards, beetles, sudden scuffle marks in the sand where a bird had landed briefly before taking off again. Signs where it had swooped on prey. The succulents and the grasses, in clumps as ever, sand ramped around the bases; bases where the lizards liked to burrow, stiff stems thrust upwards, some still showing unlikely shades of pale green. On the flat areas that universal fine, beautiful, delicate, fluffy-topped grass bent to the permanent wind, the blast of a thousand hair driers. Back in the UK I eventually found a botanist who could tell me what it was. 'Stipagrostis plumosa,' came the disinterested reply. And I thought, what's the point being an expert if you've lost your sense of wonder?

Quite a bit going on with the neighbours in the night.

130

What could be more intriguing than the near miracle of how these plants survive in isolation under desert conditions. And to me the isolation itself is part of the mystery. One plant, bursting with vitality, healthy, green, strong – alone on the wide sand and gravel of Issedienne. How come? Why just one? Why here? How old was it? What combination of coincidences – the

A small everyday miracle at Issedienne.

timing of the last rainfall, the seed landing where it did, the season of the year – brought about this amazing little plant? I would find, 48 hours later, that the big east-west wadi that lay 15 or 20 miles to the south held surface water at one place so perhaps there had been rain here recently. I wondered how fine the balance was between survival and withering away for these young plants; were their roots yet long enough to get among the deeper sand that held the moisture? Clearly the grasses, judging by the size of the clumps from which they sprang, had been there a long time and had considerable resilience.

Being hog-tied in terms of fundamental navigational accoutrements was not the only first for this trip. Going digital photographically after years of shooting 36 shots at a time on film brought an assortment of other firsts in its wake. A thorough investigation of the implications of doing so without – in mid-Sahara – mains electricity or a computer demanded some attention to detail. With Canon's EOS 5D bearing the burden of the task and received wisdom indicating – how right it was – that shooting RAW files was a very sensible approach, the question of image storage arose; to say nothing of battery charging. A 4x4 out in the sticks for anything up to three weeks on its own was the principal parameter in the calculations and demanded that whatever was needed to meet these two requirements should be 12-volt savvy and not too hungry in terms of amps. Drawing the inevitable blanks initially, the obvious solution seemed to be a 12v DC to 240v AC inverter that you plugged into the dashboard and ran everything off as you would at home.

Though it was many years ago, I had encountered this problem before, making the TV movie on the coast-to-coast west-east Sahara crossing trip. Then, the 16mm Beaulieu cine camera had a similar preference for 240v AC power to recharge its battery. AC off the mains is perfect sine wave; the 'alternating current' thing changes smoothly from positive to negative in a nice, curvy, even sine wave. Many inverters available then (and now) do a 'square wave' AC output; cheaper to make. The Beaulieu would have none of it and I had had to scour the Earth to find an inverter that would produce the right kind of AC. When I found one it was enormous, heavy, expensive and ran hot at an efficiency of not much better than 60 per cent.

Did the same problems apply, I wondered? In this, the age of 'the Call Centre Syndrome' in which young, untrained and usually ignorant slave labour is herded into large aircraft hangars to be allocated a headset, a computer screen and one among many rows of desks, there could only be trouble ahead. Given the lo-fi screeching, overmodulating audio system and an almost incomprehensible foreign accent, my query about sine wave vs square wave AC got the predictable response – the Belarus, Romanian or Outer Mongolian equivalent of 'Yer-wha'?'. Deciding to play it safe I got through to the manufacturers of inverters only to discover that yes sine wave devices were available at more than twice the price of square-wave or pseudo-sine-wave inverters and, while the latter would usually run a lap-top (note the cautious 'usually'), lithium-ion battery chargers were a bit picky and there was a chance, my pessimistic consultant informed me with what I thought was a degree of satisfaction, that the charging device and indeed the inverter itself may well 'explode' (sic!).

Having found out from another source, I informed Canon's 'Help line' call-centre that there was reputed to be a 12-volt native charger for the EOS 5D batteries and only two to three weeks later I actually ran one to earth; at Canon. Likewise storage devices into which you down-loaded your Compact Flash memory card containing 2 Gb of pictures seemed to have a preference for mains voltage. (The need for a storage device if one had mains voltage and thus a computer to download into seemed to me marginal. Why did they make them like that?) But at that time I zeroed-in on the available-only-in-the-nick-of-time Jobo GigaVu Pro Evolution – its functionality being considerably more elegant than its name.

An iPod and drying socks share the evening cab console with the GigaVu slurping down the day's photography off the CF card. A second, back-up download was carried out also.

It ran off 12v DC and enabled a lot of post-exposure selection and examination of pictures to be done in the cab in the evenings. 'Evenings' was the operative word since trying even to see, much less judge, a shot on the camera's LCD screen was hopeless in bright Sahara sunlight. A dark cloth over the head as used by the maestros of those huge wooden view cameras in days of yore was marginally helpful but shook more dust onto the camera than the previous four days' use of polythene bags kept off. Later, at home, I butchered an old hold-up-to-the-light slide viewer which, held over the LCD screen, effected both clarity and magnification at any time.

So the break at Issedienne was not only restful but also constructive and neither the GigaVu nor the EOS 5D battery charger took measurable energy out of the massive 100 amp-hour auxiliary battery which, split-charged off the Merc's electrical system, ran all the auxiliaries such as cab lighting, GPS and radio – an early modification soon after buying the wagon late in 1999. The auxiliary battery was that big because it was identical to the main Mercedes battery under the bonnet; I had done the modification that way so that in the event of problems with the main battery I could do a direct swop in the field and the engine starting and heater plugs would not be affected.

The satellite phone joined the queue for battery charging and, though fearful of what the news might be, I had nevertheless to get through to the Embassy and find out the situation regarding the location and recovery of my maps. The Thuraya crackled into action. What they had to say struck me dumb. Russ had received a letter from the authorities.

•   •   •

From the log, 9 Nov 06:

'Bloody hell! "Must be removed from the country ..." says a letter delivered to the British Embassy and thought to have come from the Gendarmerie HQ at Hassi Messaoud or Tamanrasset. The wheels have been grinding. Got through to Russ eventually at the Embassy and the crap has hit the fan. They (ie, Su Sheppard who is Consular) are sending a Note Verbale to the Ministry of Foreign Affairs to explain things.

'I spoke at length to her on the satellite (Lord knows what my SatCom bill will be) emphasising that all the maps and satellite shots were available to anyone who has the interest – map shops, internet etc. I'm sure she'll make every effort on my behalf but it is all more than a little worrying.

'It validates my plan for making the most of the Reggan-Tam leg in the virtual certainty that I'll not be allowed to move freely thereafter. Present plan therefore is to go to Tam on Saturday, check in at the Tahat and contact Su to see what progress has been made. The various outcomes are not pleasant to contemplate. The gendarmerie will have to be handled with delicacy, as being made to look the idiots they are will not help. I can expect, at best, a delay at the expensive Tahat for a number of days, at worst incarceration and further searches and confiscations – or certainly a mile-for-mile escort all the way north.

'I'd had a gut feel this might be my last trip but I sure as hell can't see me getting a visa again – or wanting to after this pantomime.'

It was hard to concentrate on much else after getting this. And it was hard to imagine that the gendarmerie at In Salah and Ain el Hadjadj could have been so wrong-headed as to label as 'Military maps' the sheets bought anything up to 30 years before, some in Paris, some in London and many – the IGN 1:200k ones dated 1960-72 – in the Algerian Government's own map shop down by the harbour in Algiers in 1979. I even bought a complete spare set of these to present to the Royal Geographical Society in London the same year.

It seemed to confirm an impression I got when I was in Captain Rahoumi's office that the troops on the ground, at places like the In Salah gendarmerie, just never got issued with maps and the only ones they ever saw were maybe with high-powered army units passing through. But even there I doubted it. I once came across a three-truck army patrol way out in the sticks, 50 miles or so east of In Salah; 20 or more armed soldiers who sprang from the trucks on encountering the solitary foreign vehicle and formed a wide-spaced defensive circle. Not a map or a compass to be seen; just a bearded patriarch in the front vehicle – the guide. (In passing – as it were – it transpired the 'defensive circle' and its wide spacing was 20 soldiers desperate for a pee and a modesty separation from the next man.)

I had asked Captain Rahmouni at In Salah how they would navigate if they had to go to rescue someone stranded out in the desert. He pointed half-heartedly to a solitary rolled up map (I presumed) on the top of a locker but the whole response got pretty lost in the translation and the conclusions were fairly obvious.

There was little I could do now until I heard more from the Embassy so I tried to enjoy the subsequent sections of the journey. I had to admit after the tensions of the last 48 hours that the feeling of being safely back on the track to Ramotswe, zeroing in on a succession of waypoints recorded in 2003 brought me fairly rapidly back up to par.

So much so, in fact – and to my surprise – that I found myself getting ideas about another small off-piste (not that there was any piste) diversion of a minor nature that I could make once I got to the big east-west wadi that would lead me to In Amguel. As long as I was out in the sticks, in 'Scarlet Pimpernel mode' as I termed it at the time, I was OK to enjoy the landscapes and perspectives I had come to see. The escorts and other nausea could come later and I would choose the time when I was going to face the, I didn't doubt it, somewhat discordant music. In fact, the longer I allowed it, the more chance there was of the MFA (Ministry of Foreign Affairs) responding positively to the *Note Verbale* from the British Embassy.

Nineteen eighty-five, pre silly regulations and illogical edicts about 'guides' in certain directions on certain routes, I had been to these parts on a 600cc Yamaha Ténéré motorcycle. Amadel-in-Anir is an extraordinary circular formation about six kilometres in diameter. Not only is it circular but the outcrops that comprise its rim are spectacularly spiky and jagged. They are also visible from the main road up from Tamanrasset; which is how I came to be aware of them in the first place returning north from the Christmas 1983/84 trip. Looking at the maps later and the grubby little nine-inch square black-and-white prints that passed for satellite images in those days, Amadel

became the focus of a gotta-go-there plan. It wasn't too far from the main road but, solo off-piste on a bike, the amber warning lights were flashing fairly vividly at the planning stage. Great care would be required. The route was basically down the main east-west wadi that was 12 miles from In Amguel, along the wadi to Tin Felki well, and then at SBH (spiky-backed-hill) turn south for a few miles and it should open up before you.

At Tin Felki well some clean little goats trotting around the wadi indicated that there were some visitors in the vicinity. Parking the noisy bike well away from them, the Touareg I met, by that unaccountable communication mystique and after expressing surprise and approval that I knew the name of Amadel-n-Anir, pointed to SBH and said that if I climbed it I would see the route through the scattering of hills that lay ahead.

As is so often the case when you look at a hill from some distance away, climbing SBH's somewhat unwelcoming rocks proved to be an exhausting two hour slog in the midday heat – I later discovered it was about 500 feet above the level of the wadi – but it did indeed afford a view of which route to take. I had the small unscaled satellite shot and a map with me so all was now clear. Especially so after returning from the climb to be greeted by the Touareg holding out a cup of sweet mint tea. I was not an expert enduro or Paris-Dakar type motorcyclist by any means

'... more proficient by the time I finished ... ' A knuckle-crushing tyre repair kept me on my toes. Hospitality for goats and bikers at Tin Felki.

albeit I learnt a lot on that trip and was considerably more proficient by the time I finished than I had been when I started. I travelled very light indeed. I was skinny then, too, and heaving monstrously heavy capsized bikes up off the sand was not something I wanted to do a lot of. I had had the idea of the bike trip after encountering – on that same 1983/84 Land Rover trip with Geoff Renner, a young French lad on a stonking great bike with practically no kit at all. That, I thought, is the way to go.

I made it to Amadel with its huge ring of jagged peaks that made me feel as though I was on the moon in one of those astonishing circular craters with which its poor old battered surface is pock-marked. As I camped there with my micro-inventory and 'space-blanket' covering and minuscule tablet-stove, to my surprise a couple of trucks rolled

through, coming from another entrance and heading off to the south-west – a short cut to the Mali road, no doubt. The crew shook their heads at the stupid foreigner risking his neck alone in these parts but were more understanding when they realised the single bottle of water they replenished for me was one of eight I had on the bike. And they didn't know I had a minutely calibrated fuel tank dipstick that I used every hour or thereabouts. Or that *in extremis*, at around 17 miles, I could walk back to the main road.

Now, 22 years later, I had left Issedienne with the previous 48 hours' dangers predicating a policy of 'I don't care what the route is so long as it's tried, logged and safe'; but then, on reflection, the temptation to take in a return trip to Amadel flickered like a distant light in the night. I thought hitting the wadi and turning south at SBH should be simple enough and would give me a little more of this beautiful country; a little more to feast my eyes on, photograph and be at peace with before returning to the big bad world of gendarmeries and people who had jumped to the wrong conclusions.

Amadel's huge 10-km circle of peaks clearly visible on maps and satellite pictures.

The track that I picked up a few miles out of Issedienne, for track of a kind it still was, was the result, entirely, of the waypoints I had recorded northbound in 2003 and had with me in the log for that journey. It had been, in 2003, another of those occasions when I had been amazingly lucky. 'Ramotswe', as I again recalled, was the spot in the great east-west wadi that I was now aiming for where I had sat out a severe dust storm that limited visibility to around 200 yards and got its name from that of Alexander McCall-Smith's Mma Ramotswe in the book I was reading to pass the time. I had got to the northern edge of the wadi, till then fringed with rocky hills and small dunes, preparatory to breaking out towards Issedienne and the dust storm was the fine clay that floated to the surface of swirl holes among the huge clumps of vegetation during flood times and, when it dried out, became the airborne stuff of inconveniences such as I was now experiencing.

Finally tiring of the mist-like blow I had put my book away and decided to try to move a little despite my misgivings in terms of air filtration for the engine. To my surprise, within a quarter of a mile I had found myself not only out of the wadi but, now away from its coating of dried fine clays, out of the dust storm as well. More surprising still, I was clearly not the first one to have taken the end of the hills-and-dune fringe as an opportunity to escape the wadi's capriciousness for there, before long, were the tell-tale tracks of one or two earlier voyagers. Heading in the same direction as I required to find Issedienne.

So now I cruised back down my join-the-dots 2003 waypoint string, none more than four miles apart, my sense of adventure and reluctance to return too quickly to 'civilisation' having won me the prospect of a minor treat; a trip down memory lane back to Amadel's circle of sawtooth peaks.

The big east-west wadi appeared on time and a quick survey reassured me that there was no obvious water about to make life difficult. Here it was not much short of a kilometre wide, a major wadi rather than the flood plain it became to the west of here. Accordingly it was wide flat sheets of sand-gravel, small embankments where in the past the water flow had stormed around corners and its inertia caused undercutting and three- to four-foot banks, stepping up to other flat spreads of sand. That the water flow was not always as quiescent as it was now was soon made clear. Mid-wadi a rock hillock, about 20 feet high, protruded from the dry coarse sand and I stopped to climb it and take a shot of the wadi's extent. A dead tree, lying on its side across the craggy brown rock, made a nice compositional element to frame the landscape beyond. Inevitably it was only after the second or third shot that I felt it looked right.

As I climbed down it slowly dawned on me that the tree had not grown on the hillock. It had been washed up there on a raging, foaming tide of water roaring down from the Hoggar, a huge bow-wave breaking over the rock to pitch it sideways onto its crest. Twenty feet! Twenty feet of water, call it 15 without the bow-wave. It was not the first time I'd been agape at the power of the elements in these parts when they got the bit between their teeth but it was certainly the most impressive. I would get another small taste of this – and another subtle but extraordinary stroke of luck – within the next 48 hours.

SBH – Spiky Backed Hill (993m, if you had an IGN 1:200k in front of you) – how could the world not know the name of so elegant a promontory – loomed just where the GPS co-ordinates said it should. As if to welcome me back, a set of wheel marks ran down its eastern side between the big green cool-leafed bushes that dotted the small valley along its edge. I paused, as if kidding myself I had still not decided on the wisdom of going back to Amadel – no map *or* GPS waypoints – and then swung the Merc south along the groove

between the hills, being
sure to double-prod the
WPT button every mile
or so in order, by
recording waypoints as I
went, to get back out
again if confusion
should occur. I set the
'Nav to' back to SBH so I
could monitor my
bearing and distance
from the spot I'd left the
big east-west wadi.

I could not pretend I
recognised the way. I
seemed to recall, in fact,
that I had, on the bike,
run down the *west* side
of SBH but since it was
an isolated hill and I
was here following

*In the great
east-west wadi
evidence of
unimaginable
water flows – a
tree trunk
washed 20 feet
up a mid stream
rock island.*

wheel marks, I reckoned it didn't matter too much. Nor had I a clear recollection of how far
Amadel was from the big wadi – five to 10 miles I supposed – but things were starting to
look familiar. A big conical hill in the 11 o'clock position, closer than I remembered, rang
bells as one I had passed on my exit from Amadel on the bike when I had followed, out of
interest, the tracks of the west-bound trucks who had passed through. I began to think I
was too far south and started looking for a pass to the south-west or west that would lead
me into the great arena. Eventually a gap in the low hills let me through and into a corridor
of rocky outcrops. Expecting by now to have seen some of Amadel's spiky peaks forming
part of the horizon I wondered if perhaps I had got into a low valley that precluded such a
view. A wide rising saddle presented itself and the Merc charged up, my expectations rising
with the altitude. At the top nothing looked familiar and I was starting to get uneasy.

Those peaks, at least, should have been showing by now. I was high enough still to see
the conical hill, took a bearing on it and 103° seemed about right for the eastern exit route
I remembered from the bike trip. But at the back of my mind that little niggle about the hill
being a bit close – and, if I was honest, not quite as high as I recalled – got me wondering.

From the log, 10 Nov 06, c. 1600 hrs:

> '45410. There's something wrong here (which a map would sort out). Fuel is 0.6 and
> it's time to acknowledge this is not the place I thought it was. Turn around and find a nice
> camping/photographing spot!'

Enough already, as they say in those American comedies – though I could never quite
understand the syntax. However you phrased it, it was time to call it a day and admit that
being without maps is bad enough; being without waypoints is pushing it. I'd head back for

the big east-west wadi that would take me to In Amguel. But not just yet. Nature was laying on something of a show. Again. It was a beautiful place, to be sure. Fine sand, a warmly attractive creamy brown, had formed delicate ripples on small dune-buttresses to the rocks that fringed a plain of a grace and spaciousness it was hard to conceive being accidental. Yet it must have been, another extraordinary spin-off of the forces of eons of geomorphology that somehow chimed with something within the human soul and lifted the spirits to heights never attained in the environment it chose to call 'civilisation'.

I stopped the Merc where it was and luxuriated in the scenery, the pure light varying its visual music as the sun went down. How fortunate we are to have cameras; to record instantly the beauty of a scene so that we can love it now and almost forever, to freeze that sliver of time when the light is so perfect, to be able to vary our viewpoint to bring all the

Not reaching Amadel had its compensations.

139

Even the dried plants make their contribution.

What conceivable forces could have shaped these rocks, still razor-sharp and un-weathered – like some huge primaeval electrodes awaiting a cataclysmic spark to flash between their points.

elements of a landscape into balance, harmony or special emphasis. It would take a painter days or weeks, and whilst he could add unique interpretation, this too we can do to a large extent with software to reproduce the subjective feeling, the emotional ingredient, the picture we have – as a painter does – in the mind's eye. To the astonishing performance, versatility and controllability of my EOS 5D I added the contribution of two simple but invaluable accessories.

The first was an 'angle finder', a kind of right-angled, upside-down periscope that clipped over the optical viewfinder and enabled you to get the camera down to ground level and see through the viewfinder without having to bend your neck back to a life-threatening angle or dig a deep hole. The second was a Fuji 'bean bag', a bag about the size of a large fist filled with something that felt like coarse sand. It had the feel and consistency of an uncooked bread roll and was the perfect, damped, dead-beat, no-shake resting place for a camera on the ground, the edge of a rock or anywhere that you'd have liked to use a tripod but its bulk or inability to get low enough would have ruled it out.

There was no buzzing, flapping of wings, whining of mosquitoes, feeling of being stung nor that tiny, just perceptible breeze of a hovering insect, but the beasts were about again and to the previous night's harvest (at Issedienne) of frantic itching on the back of my hands and parts of my face was added (the word must have got out among the nocturnal fraternity) even more by the time I awoke next morning. My wrists were so swollen that my watch, the noble, bomb-proof, desert-sand-resistant Rolex, was as tight as a tourniquet. Swollen weals under my chin, on one eyelid and ear-lobe (that must have been tasty) would take the better (or worse, actually) part of a week to go down. I really couldn't complain, though. Neither on this nor the previous six of seven trips had I encountered anything that remotely came under the heading of hostile wildlife.

The mighty Garet el Djenoun that, at 2300-odd metres, ruled majestically over – indeed overlooked – a circle of the Teffedest range not far short of 40 kilometres radius and whose name translated creepily as 'Mountain of the Spirits', had its own breed of sandflies that seemed to bask in the reflected glory of the great mountain and inflict team-effort assaults on anyone having the audacity to sleep in its shadow. Other than that not much. I couldn't remember when I last saw a scorpion – not that I let down my guard. Not a great fan of spiders, albeit in awe of their cleverness (webs, for heaven's sake! Who ever thought of webs!), I can just about (in a cupped hand) deal with those found in a bath at home and am fascinated by their lightness of touch. In the desert the fearsome looking solifugid, sometimes called 'camel spider', puts the fear of God in me but encounters are very rare. I would find, later in the trip, an elegantly coloured spider hiding in my bed, and the poor thing was as anxious as I was not to make contact. I nevertheless comprehensively dismantled the bed to make sure it hadn't taken a refuge from which it could make exploratory nocturnal forays. More than once I have heard the story about some spiders – the solifugid in particular – that spray a little anaesthetic onto the chosen site to enable it to take a few bites for dinner.

I had to admit looking forward to that hot shower and the opportunity to wash my clothes at Tamanrasset – not that, with reasonable care, anything got dirty in the desert. But salt-stiffened shirts, I felt, were unlikely to catch on as a fashion accessory. Tam's quiet buzz of activity and the feeling you got as a visitor that your presence was no big deal and thus not the trigger for hawkers, bovver-kids and general nuisances, made the place a nice peaceful turn-round point on a journey.

I really didn't like dirty hair, however, and though I had devised a means of taking a decent shampoo in only a little over half a litre of water, I had not felt it wise to indulge myself since leaving In Salah. Thus, with thoughts of impending luxury at Tam on the hover, the sight of clean, static, open water in a long pool at the big east-west wadi when I reached it was very welcome and I was soon on my knees feeling that blissful sensation of cold water on my scalp. No sooner done than I noticed maybe four to five hundred yards away upstream, the masters of the water business at work – a group of Touareg.

Their camels had obviously already been looked after and were making their way over to some thin bushes to nibble, and the men were now filling their own water bags – traditional goatskins and ingeniously converted truck-tyre inner tubes. Being the experts they knew exactly where to get the best water and had dug a two-foot diameter hole that only needed to go down a little over the same dimension in order to fill with crystal clear drinking water. They had obviously seen me long before I'd seen them and had no objection to the usual request to take pictures. Again I longed to be able to really converse.

They were going to Issedienne and I wondered why, how long it would take, where then? Equally inevitable was the request for headache pills - mercifully not in the same context as my encounter in the Tanezrouft all those years ago but again I wondered why there was always this predictable need. I always tailored my medical kit with that in mind and as usual gave them the whole pack, trying in sign language to indicate limitations on dosage. There was no request this time for something to patch up sores on the legs – desert sores, the textbooks call them, with an inexplicable reluctance, here of all places, for sores to dry and heal.

Quiet please. Experts at work. Knowing where to dig is 98% of the battle.

The way up the wadi, wide and not blighted with the usual plague of grass tumps and swirl holes, should have been a straightforward case of following the watercourse for 20-odd miles and popping up at 'The Tree' – a landmark I knew well – on one of the

corners of the tarmac north out of Tam. There I'd turn left for In Amguel's fuel pumps. The fuel calculations had worked reassuringly well and I was almost exactly on the estimated fuel state at the morning's check – one 20-litre can and 0.6 of a tank left. I could have made it to Tam, 70-80 miles after reaching the tarmac but thought it wiser to go north the 15 miles to In Amguel first.

As for the route up the wadi, it turned out to be that herringbone thing again – easy and unambiguous coming down the spine but faced with endless Y-junctions when coming from the edges where broad and similar-looking tributaries joined the main wadi. It was nevertheless a surprise to me and made me uneasy that I was again facing possibly serious problems due to not having maps. Too many mistaken diversions – and I had a few from which I had to turn back – would eat into fuel reserves that did not allow for that many errors; particularly errors which were not recognisable until some miles had been covered.

At length I came to one high-banked sharp bend in the wadi, topped by tall bushes, that I remembered even from the bike trip and knew I was at least part of the way to the right exit point. I'm sure there's a doctorate in it for someone but a dissertation on how memory shortens the length of wadis would be popular with travellers in the Sahara. Here memory was having a field day; I began to wonder if I would ever reach the end – The Tree together with that odd fenced-in electrical box by the roadside and the tell-tale black line of tarmac when viewed from an edge down in a dip.

But as I drove carefully through the sand bed of the wide wadi, wary of soft patches and noting that the usual one or two sets of vehicle tracks that would have been a guide were absent, obliterated by recent light rain, I got to thinking again about the letter the Embassy had received. 'Must be removed from the country ... ' Did they mean extradition? Were they 'coming to get me'? Would they march me to the front of the queue to get on the boat at Algiers? (One way of getting through that shambles at the docks, I thought.)

The letter: 'Thought to have come from ... '? What kind of wording was that? What did it actually say? Who wrote it and who was it sent to? And direct to the Embassy? A bit peculiar. Su was being cagey. What the hell was she up to, playing hard to get? The letter she was writing and which I thought had already gone had still not been sent but she said it would go soon. If there was some kind of warrant out for me – or at least until that aspect was clarified or some degree of understanding was received from the Ministry of Foreign Affairs – I began to think it would be unwise to go to Tam and rock the boat. Appearing in Tamanrasset and being questioned or detained by the gendarmerie would torpedo any effect Su's letter would have at the MFA. Much as I was looking forward to a hot shower, some laundry, a meal and a glass of wine, I needed to assess the risks before I walked into a hornets' nest to be apprehended by the nearest gendarme out to make his name capturing the subversive foreigner who carried military maps.

I resolved that only if the tide turned, that my maps were known to be at Tam and ready for my collection would I go there. I rang Su Sheppard and she agreed the wisdom of the decision and said she would try to get a feel for the situation by noon the following day. Meanwhile, I said, I would hole-up in the wadi and await what she could find out.

This, I thought, is absurd! Sitting here – no, hiding; ducked down behind a low ridge out of sight of the road – like some kind of Scarlet Pimpernel lest I be marched off to a dungeon for using maps in the Sahara when all I had come to Algeria for was to see and photograph desert landscapes. It was so ridiculous I had to laugh.

Humour was a life-saver; a great prop, especially when things were going bizarrely wrong. Sick jokes in outrageously bad taste, black humour, gallows laughs and general joshing and leg-pulling were always a sustaining currency in the armed forces. My eight-man team for the Joint Services West East Sahara Expedition (JSWESEx) that made the first Atlantic to the Red Sea Sahara crossing comprised army and Royal Air Force – plus Geoff Renner, geophysicist from the British Antarctic Survey. Geoff was the scientist and carried out the gravity survey – the first continuous coast-to-coast series of measurements secured across the continent. Kevin, ex SAS, and Nick Jasinski, RAF – known to all as Jablonc – were our chief sources of generally terrible jokes.

Kevin: 'Chap goes into a chemist shop. "Got any strawberry-flavoured suppositories?" "Pardon?" says the bewildered assistant. "Yeah. Didn't like the last ones much. And for all the good they did I might as well have stuffed 'em up my ... "

'Ah!' said Jablonc. 'Reminds me. There were these two nuns ... '. Seven team members groaned in unison as another excruciating ex-Northern Ireland forces joke rolled unstoppably on. Mick Pearce was a natural when I was doing the filming; first take, no problems. Barry Doughty, Royal Signals, our sterling cook, head caterer and back-up radio man, was never quite so good when the Beaulieu was out and preparing for a shot. He was always accompanied by a team countdown: 'OK, after three, Barry. ONE, TWO, THREEE !' And then he would look round at the camera as if to say, 'Now?'

Solifugid at rest – a rare picture. Lest I have to get too close to photograph it, a long-focus predecessor to the Hubble was enlisted to take the shot.

And on the same expedition it seemed my horror of the solifugid camel-spiders was shared by other team members. If routine dislike of spiders wasn't enough, the solifugid looked as if it was the unlikely issue of a scorpion and a tarantula: frightening mandibles thrust out front ready to munch into whomsoever came its way. Possibly aware of its bad PR image, it seemed also to go everywhere at 90 miles an hour. Seeing one darting out of the bush towards us in Chad, Jablonc seized a shovel, swung it high above his head, whammed it down with a ground-trembling thud and obliterated the unfortunate arachnid. Geoff narrowed his eyes. 'Hmm. About seven, maybe eight, on the Richter scale, I'd say.'

And so it went. In 1969, my first trip (Libya) after a lung operation that left a livid 14-inch scar around my right side had Mick Burns, my co-driver, quipping, whenever I had my shirt off, 'Showing off the shark bite again, then?' Geoff had a wonderful sense of humour and came on many trips after the west-east crossing. Once, in northern Algeria, in exceptionally hot weather – around 48°C, I recall – it was time to camp and Geoff pointed at a rounded hill. 'Looks good. Camp up there and we'll catch the breeze.' We did. Twenty minutes later, all our kit laid out and a brew on the way, an ominous approaching brown-black curtain on the northern horizon soon became a raging sand storm, scattering our bedding and kit over the plain below. 'Reckon we caught the breeze, then!' said Geoff.

Geoff Renner (right) and Nick Jasinski on the JSWESEx making the first gravity observation at the Red Sea after crossing from the Atlantic at Dakar.

But for now, and for me twiddling my thumbs in the wadi awaiting whatever Su in Algiers could find out, there was no breezy good news – or even decision – for the time being. I had to be patient and sober consideration concluded that a letter carrying the might and majesty of the British Embassy was almost certain to get some results from the MFA. Su's letter – when it was actually sent – would explain, she said, that I was a bona fide and experienced traveller with an overriding concern for the preservation of the Saharan wilderness regions and was working towards a presentation for the establishment of a Protected Area. The Algerian government had no axe to grind regarding the British and it was very unlikely that any kind of tit-for-tat point-scoring over past tiffs would be on the cards. I felt sure the next day's phone call would clear the way for 24 hours' R&R at Tam and collection of the maps either there or on my way north through In Salah again.

In the meantime I would enjoy R&R of a kind here, hidden behind the low rock rise, trapped in my own little Guantanamo, uncharged, uncertain of my future. A group of wandering donkeys strolled down the wadi's green centre snatching the less ferocious grass tips and casting curious eyes over at the white G-Wagen trespassing on their supper ground. It began to cloud over a bit; a few drops of rain. It felt cooler; then a sudden 4° temperature drop then up again to 26°C. Interesting, that. What was going on, I wondered? With In Amguel now only half a day's *walk* from here I allowed myself the luxury of washing some socks and underclothes – albeit, through force of habit, using only about a litre of water. I used the time also to restock the ready-food boxes for the next few days. In the evening I did the usual chores of the journal, completing the log, checking the photography. And all – again as usual – with the front windscreen covered and lights at the minimum so as not to attract attention; a familiar routine that got to be very wearing after a while. Good guys, bad guys, bandits or police, I didn't specially want visitors in the night.

The next morning seemed to last forever as the minutes dragged into hours waiting for the midday phone call to Su and what I hoped would be good news regarding the reception I would get – or to be more accurate, the reception I hoped I would not get – if I went to Tamanrasset. But were it not for the worry on my mind, the desert, even hiding in this wadi, was always quite a bit better than being anywhere else and there was always something to see – the lie of the rocks, their composition and texture, the tiny scraps of life, be it animal or vegetation that had adapted so well to this environment.

The morning stocktaking of fuel and water were done as usual, even this close to In Amguel. I still had 39.3 litres of water, having thus used only 30.7 litres – a can and a half out of 70 litres since leaving In Salah 12 days before. My consumption for the previous 24 hours was just 3.2 litres, and that included washing socks and underwear. The temperatures at this altitude – near enough 950 metres – and the low workload were in my favour but I was still pleased at the economy I had achieved and what this meant in terms of reserves to cover an immobilising breakdown and rescue call (provided the Thuraya was still working) out in the desert. Fuel, with the vehicle now still, read 0.55 of a tank on the fuel gauge and I had one 20-litre can still lashed in the rack; exactly on target.

At last 12 o'clock came and, daring to be optimistic, I stepped away from the wagon with the Thuraya to phone Su. The response could hardly have been more feeble, or the news worse. The Embassy's contacts had, so far, been 'low key', she said, but her letter would 'soon' go to the MFA. So there was no progress. Nothing seemed to have happened or been pushed as I sat hiding in the wadi. Moreover 'concern for my satellite phone bill' was expressed and I was advised to phone again 'in a few days' time'. Life is doubtless manically busy in an Embassy but I got the hint of an impression I was being a nuisance and getting the bum's rush. Yet from where I was sitting there was not much doubt about the implications of the phrase " ... *must be removed from the country.*" Arrest, custody, extradition, goodness knows what other searches and confiscations: and all for, as a traveller, having a set of maps.

It was not until much later that the oddity of the phrasing struck me. What the hell was 'low key'? But that was to be just the start of another saga.

•   •   •

The tarmac was less than a mile away. Velvet under the wheels. It was all I could do not to close my eyes to enjoy the smoothness. The engine a quiet burble, I let the Mercedes drift along at a dreamy 25 miles an hour. I had to remember which side of the road to drive on. I savoured the peace while I could. The wadi at In Amguel was a part-time river – lots of water most of the time; not one for splashing through. They had a smart new bridge that they'd been working on last time I was here and on the far side had been a gendarmerie checkpoint – one of dozens ahead where the status or continuation of my trip would hang in the balance. There'd be no going around this one.

The road narrowed through a cutting as it wound down towards the outskirts of the village, mud brick houses up on the bank to the left, dark shadows in the midday light. The new bridge came in sight, the fuel station a few hundred yards beyond it, but at first glance there seemed to be nothing on the far side; no sentry box or green uniforms or iron bar. First glance was right. No checkpoint.

Still controlling my breathing I pulled into the fuel station. Last time I visited they were out of diesel but the operation was now smoothly under way. Nice cheerful man at the pump; hearty hand shake. I pulled out five jerry cans to refill, unlocked and removed the Merc's filler cap, carefully wiping dust away from the lip to brim the tank. At 45457 miles on the odometer it had been exactly 700 miles since fuelling at Aoulef. I took on a total of 147.1 litres and the fuel consumption for that long off-piste sector came out at 21.65 mpg. The Merc had done well. Very well; close to a three-tonne GVW all the way and an automatic transmission.

As we filled up a small cloud came over and surprised me by raining raindrops of an extravagant size – soup-spoons of water in widely spaced drops – and I finished the operation holding a cloth over the filler to keep water out. Alongside the filling station was a long high wall with a dusty door in it, half open. I idly scanned its length as the fuel went in and looked up at the top. A flagpole bore a familiar pennant. The flag of the Algerian gendarmerie. Oh shit ... .

12. Death in the desert

If I had worried about being worried at the Reggan bypass, Wadi 'N' and the '8 Nov' rocky hills maze, it seemed to me now, as I batted the argument back and forth hearing both sides in my woolly liberal way, that without much doubt there was good enough cause for taking care – the greatest care – in the desert: thinking detail and taking setbacks and difficulties seriously. Thinking ahead to outcomes and consequences. Like the well-known saying about not getting a second chance to make a first impression, you don't often get a second chance to make a mistake in the desert. Maybe – no, certainly – my attitude was influenced by my pilot training where the same applied. To say history is littered with examples of people dying in the desert is to overglamorise it. History implies grandeur. Deaths in the desert are far more routine. And not very grand: people getting lost, running out of fuel, breaking down because their vehicles were not in good order, driving recklessly, having insufficient water or reserves when things go wrong. 'Guides' getting lost and not having the guts to say so in time to avoid tragedy. Even camels die when there is a weakness in their natural instincts, ability to find forage or physical strength to keep going; like the tragic mummified animal I found coming out of the Reggan bypass.

It's a lot safer now with GPS, satellite imagery, satellite phones and emergency beacons – provided none of them has been damaged. But a satellite phone is a satellite phone; it is not a doctor or a winch to right an overturned vehicle with someone trapped inside – benefits that, when needed, are often needed quickly. Nor is it a drum of fuel, a can of water or, directly, the means of getting them to you. Never be too reliant on outside help. On the west-east Sahara expedition, the 1000-mile Mauritanian Empty Quarter was the real challenge both physically and logistically. I made contingency plans and when the fuel consumption of the heavy laden vehicles in the dunes hit 5.7 mpg I sent warning on the radio that I might have to invoke 'Plan B' – an air drop. Back came the reply: 'Sorry, the aircraft is unserviceable.' No 'But we'll try ... '. So equating a satellite phone or radio with a barrel of diesel is not a good idea; placing reliance on outside help doesn't always work.

But safety and advance planning affects operators over, as well as on, the desert and even greater care is needed in aircraft; there are lessons for us all in that sphere. With aircraft the potential problems are higher profile; they stand out more sharply. You can't stop to check over your sums or navigation in an aeroplane albeit the interplay of constant speed, time and distance should give you potentially more accurate tools to use – provided you keep a log.

There are two examples of mistakes insufficiently monitored, misfortunes and situations not being taken seriously, that are part of the tragic legacy of, but not in themselves related to, the Second World War; and they took place over the Libyan desert and are timeless and valuable to us all. My encounters with both were intertwined with my first expedition – and one other – on attachments with the Royal Air Force desert rescue team from El Adem so made a lasting impression. There were, with humility and respect for those who lost their lives, lessons to be learned by the ground-borne desert traveller.

My very first trip in the desert after that memorable flight in the Beverley seeing dawn break over Jebel Uweinat was through the Great Libyan Sand Sea and on to Kufra. Squadron Leader Mike Burgess's desert rescue team, formed from No 1 Field Squadron, RAF Regiment, and based at RAF El Adem, south of Tobruk, was planning a long-range navigation exercise and part of the aim was to find and recover the bodies of Blenheim bomber aircrew who died in the desert east of Kufra. As part of preparation for a north-south Sahara trip I hoped to mount the following year, I was able to get permission to accompany them. The main party was six Series 1 Land Rovers, stripped down for lightness, each with 12 jerry cans of fuel and a crew of two. I was to learn a lot about what to do; and probably even more about what not to do. In at the deep end, the Libyan Sand Sea was a revelation – huge 600-foot dunes in long lines, valleys between and cross-barriers to negotiate. My introduction to the sun compass, star fixes using the bubble sextant, dead-reckoning traverses just like aircraft navigation. Soft sand, boggings, firm sand, details like tyre pressures, achingly beautiful landscape, cold desert nights – but after 125 miles we were through the top of the great horseshoe sand-sea formation.

Learning what to do, and not do. 'Let the tyres down for the sand!' 'To what?' said I. 'Till they look soft.' Four miles later we had three wheel changes. Over-deflation allowed the tyre to rotate on the rim and pull the valve out.

The freedom of the plain south of the Sand Sea – only small raised patches of gravel being there to disturb the magic carpet of 45 mph drive-on-a-compass-bearing bliss – was all too soon shattered by what the old wartime LRDG-annotated (Long Range Desert Group) maps termed 'low chalky hills'. This innocuous description, redolent of a benign, rolling version of the Sussex downs, turned out to be a nightmare of broken boulders that, in the impression it

made and with my wide-eyed inexperience, I felt must be what the rest of Africa was made of and would surely leave our six puny Land Rovers smoking wrecks in pretty short order.

According to the map, the low valley of Wadi Blita would take us through the bad country but, confirmed by the night's specially careful astro fix, we had missed the mouth. With any luck, steering west for three or four miles should put us right. The earlier inevitability, in my eyes, of doom was now replaced by the equal certainty of salvation when, accompanying Vic Steel in the lead vehicle next morning, the better to learn how the Coles sun compass functioned, I saw the truth of what the astro had foretold. Rich red sand, stark outcrops, conical hills led us through the rocky country and into the region of the Blenheim disaster. We were now roughly 400 miles from Tobruk, 200 miles from Kufra, and had approximately 50 miles of difficult country to enjoy before we could expect to be where the Blenheims landed.

The story of these aircraft was a tragic one, recorded in Air Force documents of the time and greatly expanded in the South African Military History Society's journal (to which I am indebted for new detail here and the picture on the next page). In May 1942 three Blenheims of No 15 Squadron, South African Air Force, each with a crew of four, had been on an area familiarisation sortie and were returning to their base in Kufra. Kufra was an isolated oasis, now a healthy town, some 650 miles south of Benghazi on the Mediterranean coast and is surrounded by desert – dunes, rough rocky country and small areas of flat ground. Some reports say

Exiting the Sand Sea and into firmer going to seek the Blenheim site, SAC Chittem checks the group. Navigation was by Coles sun compass (below) and star shots at night.

151

the Blenheims reached Kufra after their recce (there are reasons to doubt this) but for some reason they did not land at once and flew off to the east for some time. Then one developed engine trouble and all three landed on firm desert about 90 miles north-east of the airstrip. It appears that no proper log had been kept of this extra sector to the flight so that by this time they were not sure of their position. The crews could not agree where they were in relation to base and, taking off again, three search sorties were flown in a south-westerly direction without success. The next morning fuel was drained and transferred from two aircraft so that the third could fly another search to try to locate Kufra – again without success. Worse, this flight was inadequately planned and the Blenheim, now running low on fuel, had to make a forced landing trying to return to the group. There were now two stranded groups – eight men in one, three in the other and, it would be later established, 24 miles apart.

Their searches – south-west, east and then north-west – indicated how disorientated the crews were and how disparate was their navigational grasp. Despite temperatures of over 38°C, the time of year and a strong desiccating wind, the emergency water supply was apparently not rationed and by the second day the crews had drunk 20 gallons. Aircraft fuel was too low to permit further searching and sandstorms now in any case made

A Blenheim Mk IV (above). All that remained of 'the third Blenheim' (Z7513) in Nov 1960 – the wing centre section. Sgt Ballam, SACs Minshell and Brown.

visibility very poor. The water was almost gone. The situation can be imagined; May in those latitudes in the desert, high temperatures, sand blowing and almost no water.

The high winds and sandstorms also affected any search being made from Kufra. A recce Bristol Bombay, unable to find the airfield, had to make a forced landing south-east of Kufra and was marooned by the storm for two days. Other aircraft and personnel summoned to help from Egypt and Sudan suffered similarly. Ground search parties sent out in all directions were hampered by very difficult terrain and the bad visibility.

By the third day the Blenheim aircrews doled out the last of the water. In desperation they broke the compasses to drink the alcohol with catastrophic results; they tried to keep cool using the fire extinguishers which brought them out in terrible rashes and sores. The next day the first man died. Seven more died from thirst in the following four days.

A Wellington bomber was put on the search task but again engine trouble forced a return to base. A second joined and, now the eighth day since the Blenheims' disappearance and the weather at last clearing, a proper navigationally monitored search was at last flown from Kufra. After four sorties the Wellington crew saw the two aircraft and landed nearby. Staggering to his feet among his dead comrades, a sole survivor, Air Mechanic Juul, was found, eight days after they had been lost.

•   •   •

Those involved in this tragic episode, flying personnel and rescuers alike, have been pilloried over the years. There is little doubt that fundamental errors were made by the aircrews and that these – the navigation and lack of desert survival discipline – were pivotal in the inevitability of the outcome. But the planning of a proper search procedure at an earlier stage would also have immeasurably helped achieve location more quickly. Nevertheless a crucifying sequence of bad luck played its part – four days of sandstorms and bad visibility and a succession of engine failure and radio communications and direction-finding problems that crippled the rescue effort. Bad luck can strike any time. For us lucky ones around to read of such things the lesson is not to give it a chance; to be relentlessly thorough in the first place and make the detailed contingency planning sufficiently comprehensive that reliance on outside help is less crucial. In short, to be happy to worry; not worry about it.

Three of the bodies of the doomed South Africans, those of the single aircraft to the north, had been found by Mike Burgess's predecessor the year before and taken back for interment in the Tobruk war cemetery, and we were charged with attempting to locate the other eight graves. But at that time we had no location and logistics did not permit the kind of widespread and methodical search necessary to locate the graves.

Inwardly, I heaved a sigh of relief. But there was another lesson yet to be learned. We had averaged only 12.3 miles per gallon in the Land Rovers since plunging into the Sand Sea nearly 500 miles to the north and, approaching Kufra, the sums indicated we now had 60 empty jerry cans and a whisker over seven gallons in each fuel tank. If that sounds not too uncomfortable, rewind and freeze-frame to 30 miles back, dusk turning to night and no sign of Kufra yet. What were our reserves? A jerry can and a bit, that's all.

Nine years later there were more lessons to come. Again in Libya. With the desert rescue team from RAF El Adem. This time it concerned just one aircraft.

The *Lady Be Good* was a B24 Liberator bomber stationed at the US Soluch Air Base in northern Libya, 30 miles south of Benghazi during the Second World War, part of the 376th Heavy Bombardment Group. On 4th of April 1943, less than a year after the tragic events at Kufra 600 miles to the south, the aircraft with its nine-man crew was part of a 28-plane daylight raid that set out to attack Naples, a planned 11-hour round trip. Taking off in the dust of earlier aircraft in the formation, nine of the 13-aircraft sub-group suffered from sand ingestion on take-off and the *Lady Be Good* was one of only four that made it to the target. The timing was misjudged and by the time they were over the target it was too dark to use their bombsights. On the three-hour return flight, the formation became separated

and out of sight of one another but all – except one – made it back to Soluch by just after 11pm. It is hard to imagine that the crew did not hear the RT exchanges between Soluch and the other aircraft approaching and landing back at base and be aware of when it was taking place – 11pm. But it was gone midnight before the *LBG* crew requested a DF bearing, seeming not to have used their own ADF (Automatic Direction Finding) radio compass. You would have to wonder if any DR position was being maintained by the navigator, but the crew were under the impression they were still over the sea a whole *hour* after the other aircraft had landed. If this were not enough, a shortcoming of the ground DF equipment of the time was that it could not tell whether the aircraft requesting a bearing was inbound or outbound. It gave only the bearing of the aircraft's transmission. Thus both ground station and aircraft had to interpret whether they were flying to or away from the DF facility. The on-board ADF and a well-maintained nav log and DR position would be the means of doing this. With this cataclysmic navigational and operational error on the part of the crew a tragedy was set to unfold.

The pictures on this spread make it easy to guess the rest of the story, but its sad conclusion was to reveal extraordinary endurance and courage on the part of the crew and deserves to be told if only to highlight the almost unbelievable staying power, determination and grit of which the human psyche and body together are capable in pursuit of survival.

Aware that their fuel would soon run out the crew had donned their parachutes and prepared to bale out. Inflated life jackets later discovered indicated they still thought they were over the sea. The captain trimmed the aircraft for straight and level flight and the crew baled out. One had parachute failure and died but the other eight joined up – surprised to

Richard Roxburgh, Rusty Pelling and Derek Smith ponder the position of the Lady Be Good in relation to its base near Benghazi on the coast.

find they were on the ground and not in the Mediterranean. Incredibly, the *Lady Be Good* glided on into the Saharan night and landed itself on firm level desert south of the Libyan Sand Sea, well over 200 miles south-east of its base at Soluch.

The state of mind of the captain, co-pilot and navigator can be imagined at this time. Now well out of sight of the aircraft and surrounded, when dawn broke, by an apparent 360-degree infinity of flat desert, between them they were responsible for the situation in which they now found themselves – one crew member still missing despite what search they could themselves mount and the remaining eight now in perilous danger.

Meanwhile rescue efforts and air-search patrols were being mounted from Soluch – over the sea. But out in the desert the crew clicked meticulously into the tenets of the survival training they had received. They had half a canteen of water between them and it was rationed – in teaspoonsful. They walked north-east, clearly realising by this time what had gone wrong. They walked as a group leaving markers of torn parachute material as they went. Diaries indicated at first 'quite warm' during the day but 'very cold' at night. Astonishingly, after four days on virtually no food and negligible water, they covered 65 miles. By now five could go no further and were to die as a group where they stopped.

Three sergeants in the crew refused to give up and kept going north-west despite by this time having met the southern dunes of the Sand Sea. One would keep on for another 20 miles in this exhausting terrain before falling. Sergeant Guy Shelley, gunner, just 26 years old carried on for another six miles on his own and was found dead after an incredible 90-mile walk from the place the crew parachuted down.

The tragedy was complete. The recovery, however, after formal military boards of inquiry concluded the aircraft had crashed without trace in the sea, would not begin until 16 years later. In 1959 an oil exploration company discovered the *Lady Be Good* lying, with minimal damage, some 158 nautical miles north-east of Kufra. Under media pressure enormous resources were put into finding the bodies of the crew, and eventually eight of the nine were recovered and returned to the United States.

•   •   •

Rather like keeping a yacht at a marina, I positioned my Land Rover at RAF El Adem in 1969 in order to be near the desert. Again with a future major trip in mind I got permission to join the desert rescue team later in the year on one of their exercises led by the legendary Polish airman Flight Lieutenant Zeke Zeleny. Zeke took four-tonners into the Sand Sea for the first time and aimed to visit *Lady Be Good* as a navigational exercise.

While the team swarmed round the old aircraft, now somewhat robbed by souvenir hunters in the oil companies after 26 years, it was a moving and poignant experience to just stand and look at it; to recall the story behind it and the crew whose terrible mistake had led to its being there and to their own deaths in agonising circumstances.

There is no shortage of memorials and museum displays and commemorative plaques for these unfortunate and in the end hugely courageous men caught up with the Blenheim and B24 tragedies, but among the many emotional pulls these episodes make on us we must remember one in the cold hard light of day: the desert can be brutally unforgiving when you get it wrong, especially with navigation. And worrying about worrying helps not one iota.

13. Rainbows

Neither freezing stock-still, sweaty palms, nor turning deathly pale is the same as, or effects, total invisibility. But that, rather than the former is what, as I stood by the fuel pumps at In Amguel seeing that half-open door in the gendarmerie wall casually swinging in the breeze, is what I wished for. In the prevailing circumstances paranoia was entirely appropriate, a good idea even; to keep you on your toes. The British Embassy having been sent a letter to the effect that I *should be removed from the country* implied that they were being forewarned of what could be slightly embarrassing, tiresome and involving events soon to be enacted. If the Embassy had been informed by an official communication it was certain that the gendarmerie network in the Tamanrasset Wilaya (in which district I now was) had also been alerted to apprehend, in the event that he was seen, this white van person who would, for nefarious reasons, carry maps.

I have prayed for silent invisibility once before; actually a number of times. The kind of invisibility I manifest, apparently by default, on the rare occasions I go into a pub and wait to be served. Lunch is a wonderful thing and the break for its consumption can sometimes be exceptionally fortuitous. It saved me at Bordj el Haoues over to the east the previous year. Any more than wandering alone the Scottish Highlands or the wild Welsh hills in the UK is proscribed in the Bible or Koran, I did not feel that there was anything fundamentally wrong with enjoying the wilderness of the Sahara on my own. Yet there were busy-bodies who, at least in some areas, on some routes, in certain directions – due to some well-meaning but very fuzzy regulations – seemed to think otherwise. Thus driving, the previous year, from In Amguel north-east up to Bordj el Haoues (Zaouatallaz, as was), a route totalling around 370 miles, somewhat off-piste and involving a certain amount of 'freelance' navigation, I had stopped to take pictures of some brave little plants battling it out with the heat, the winds and the sand dunes.

I looked up as one eventually does when someone you don't want to meet is approaching and you hope in vain they have not seen you.

'You must come with me!' the man said. Actually about two minutes earlier I had also looked up and my heart sank as I recognised the outline of two bobbing Toyota station wagons trailing dust and coming towards me. The foreboding was the result of noticing that while at least they were not green and white denoting the gendarmerie, they had those enormous overladen roof racks that meant they comprised a tourist group – a dusty three- or foursome of grim-faced, Evian-clutching, inappropriately dressed foreigners in each vehicle peering out of even dustier windows to try to assimilate the landscape as it rushed by at 50 miles an hour.

'No.' I said.

Caravaggio lighting en route to Bordj el Haoues. Photo session interrupted by 'guides' who did not know of the French military insignia on the hillside.

'Ah, yes. We are guides and you must ... '

At this point an excessively-tanned, thin and wrinkly French lady dismounted from the mobile oven and through her accent and verbal effluent I detected the words '... it is forbidden ... '. Another attempt from the guides to get me to race along with them the 110 miles still left before Bordj el Haoues (they would all doubtless pant their way in to Djanet that very evening along the tarmac road from B-e-H with little idea of where they had been). Pulling rank or experience isn't my style but it was time for a final 'No!' accompanied by the information that I had been doing this kind of journey for 45 years and that everything was fine, thanks all the same, and I would be going along at my own pace.

The line of demarcation had been drawn and an exchange of pleasantries ensued. Were they going to see the huge French military insignia outlined in stones on the hills just down the way, I asked? They didn't seem to have heard of them. So much for being guides, I thought; or perhaps they were being tactful for, impressive as they were, one of the hillside insignia was distinctly unmilitary, arguably not suitable for the eyes of elderly French lady tourists and attested the earthy sense of humour of the young *légionnaires* posted to these parts 50 years before. The inhabitants of Cerne Abbas would have regarded it as worthy competition.

We parted on good terms, though, exchanging phone numbers and PO Boxes. They were Tazat Tours, it seemed, a couple of enterprising Algerians who had set up a small business for visitors based in Djanet. Tazat was an impressive mountain 50 miles or so east that I would camp by in a couple of nights' time and seems specifically designed to host spectacular sunrises. As they drove off (in a dodgy direction if they wanted to see the French military insignia only four miles away) I had an uneasy feeling that they might report a lone foreigner out in the sticks to the gendarmes at B-e-H. Were it not for nightmare anxiety over the Merc's ignition/starter lock occasionally sticking and malfunctioning that I was trying to keep at bay at the time (a Laurel and Hardy saga that took six months to sort out with Mercedes when I returned to the UK), the thought of an unscheduled interview at B-e-H would have been uppermost on my mind.

It was sufficiently weighty, however, to have me doing a surreptitious cross-country nip-over two days later to the south-easterly tarmac a mile or two south of B-e-H so that I would pass through the town as though I was coming from Djanet. And here, of course, was where my desperate need and prayer for invisibility manifested itself again. How could there not be a *barrage* on the outside of town, or even in the middle? But B-e-H was an odd place. With the sun this high, Clint Eastwood would have loved it and Sergio Leone could have shot some evocative footage, once he'd built one of those Mexican churches and placed a few dozing sombrero-wearers in its shade. All the buildings had their backs to the road. It was lunchtime that saved me. At an hour after the noon-tide, and the sun that high, there was no-one around.

No-one to demand papers and flick disdainfully through the passport while peering into the wagon to see what was on board. Somewhere there'd have been a fuel station but I was not about to stir the sleepers and go looking with five cans still on board. I held my breath and drove at tippy-toe speed (25 mph, which I was getting good at) north towards the northern fringe of the town that headed over the once-horrendous Fadnoun Plateau to Illizi. Amazingly, on the right, one of the Tazat Tours' Toyotas rested in the shade some way off the road. The guide recognised me and the Merc and we exchanged cheerful waves. I don't think he had reported me after all.

I was through B-e-H but on that occasion would meet my nemesis later after BP at In Amenas and that record-breaking 1185km escort all the way to Laghouat. Meantime I had two more days to myself in the wilderness.

• • •

Now, seeing the ominously swinging door in the gendarmerie wall while I refuelled at In Amguel, I'm sure I momentarily froze stock-still, went pale and experienced sweaty hands but in a way the sight was like – and just about as welcome – as the doctor behind you snapping on a lubricated rubber glove; what was going to happen was going to happen. There was nothing you could do. As if to prolong the tension the diesel pump on what passed for a forecourt, par for the course in these parts, had counters that didn't work too well so the good-hearted chap serving me and filling up my five cans had to do prolonged key-punching on his pocket calculator. Any other time I'd have again revelled in the roughly 10p per litre the precious fuel was costing. That done and the payment made, the cans had then to be threaded back in amongst the cargo and each one lashed down before

I could move off. Furtive glances back at that door confirmed how free its hinges were and how easily it swung to the random call of the breeze. No-one came through. It was lunchtime. Ramadan was long gone. They were all inside. In sleepy In Amguel.

The clouds thickened and it got darker, the sprinkling of huge rain drops became more erratic yet more purposeful on gusts of wind – as they do when the elements are contemplating a rather special downpour. But it never looked better to me. Rain would keep people indoors. I was about to leave. I locked the filler cap, walked round to the driving seat and put the key in the ignition.

Sorting the wonky ignition lock after Tazat the previous year had surpassed belief and upheld my conjecture that my order for the G-Wagen would have caused gales of laughter (or groans of despair) at Graz when the spec came through. They will all have spoken like Germans do in the old war-time films, of course. 'You hef ein order für ein *right hand drive kastenwagen* (van)? Mitt ein heavy duty rear axle? Mein Gott hef ve got ze parts?' As well as the scrabbling around for bits that included the moth-eaten wiring harness that had already made its presence felt with the EDC drive-by-wire failure and limp home episode out in the desert in 2001 (and would cause a different kind of failure later in the UK), there was clearly something of what we would now call 'ein issue' about locks.

What I had expected would be a simple replacement of the ignition lock after the Tazat trip bounced repeatedly off the Mercedes HQ parts computer resulting in no less than *five* attempts at finding the right part. In the end all three door locks needed replacement – three out of a set of five that was sent for the three-door vehicle *and* the engine ECU had to be changed. A few years ago I wouldn't have been too clear what an engine ECU was. I was soon to learn that it seemed to control just about everything on the vehicle. Certainly it interfaced with the drive-by-wire throttle but also with the ignition lock. The answer to 'Hef ve got ze parts?' would probably have been well, yes, but I think there's only one. Eighty per cent of the parts I ever needed for the G-Wagen came out wrong. The fifth set of door and ignition and fuel-filler locks worked; but only after the engine ECU joined the list. To their eventual credit Mercedes took it on the chin and paid for it all. And I learned that the cost of the ECU would have been £1500.

At In Amguel, the ignition lock worked as was now its wont. I waved goodbye to the happy chap who served me diesel and set off north on the tarmac, now brimmed with fuel. North for In Eker, for Arak, for In Salah where my hope for recovering my maps had now slid down to zero, and thereafter – and I had plans for a special route – back to Algiers. But the trip was not over by any means. There was a return off-piste trip to Ezz-Tes to soak up some more astonishing landscape. Ezz-Tes was my shorthand for the awe-inspiring geomorphological extravaganza 'off to the left a bit' from the northbound tarmac between In Eker and Arak; 'rockorama' I was tempted to call it but though invoking what I saw, the term lacked the dignity the place deserved.

But first there was In Eker, site, under the nearby mountain, of French atom-bomb tests back in the 1960s and now home only to a tiny army detachment housed in a tatty group of Portakabins opposite a filling station of meticulously matched tattiness. There would be army passport checkers there for sure. Though army wasn't gendarmerie and in the field they were a happy bunch they could sometimes be a bit po-faced at checkpoints; the one

100km south of In Salah I think must have come top of the class on the Grumpy Demeanour course I felt sure they ran. In Eker was only 25 miles north of In Amguel. It began to rain. Heavily. Very heavily. The Merc got a wonderful wash; the underside got spray from the tyres and road to wash the dust and lodged-in sand off the undercarriage. And my spirits, now in devious mode and ever on the defensive, rose. In rain this heavy the soldiers on duty probably wouldn't even see the number plate much less be eager to come out and check papers. Being waved through would be one less checkpoint on the long list that lay ahead; one chance less of hassle.

The windscreen wipers struggled bravely on fast wipe. The sand at the roadside had first pocked under the heavy raindrops, then darkened, and floated in the streams of pure water that ran over it. The rocks and plants were cleaned of their normal coating of dust and their colour richened even in all the spray and gustiness that abounded. Through the runnels of water that covered the windscreen, the clouds ahead roiled, lightened, darkened again and threatened drama. In Eker was only a few miles away as I drove on north. As I prayed the storm would continue so that I could drive through, instead the sky lightened, bright patches appeared to the north-east. Where only the downpour had filled the sky, In Eker's huge high mountain and surrounding fence emerged clear in the clean air. Then the army post and the little sentry boxes on each side of the road. Eagle-eyed, a green camouflaged uniform stepped out with a raised hand. I wondered if it carried a lubricated rubber glove.

There wasn't a problem. There wasn't much smiling either but they let me go. The different hymn sheets from which the army and the gendarmerie warbled their tune were paying off. But even if they'd never heard of me, there was still no query about guides. The nutty 'guide-southbound-free-northbound' policy seemed still to apply and that was good news. If they didn't smile much I certainly did. And went on my way. Slowly. Marvelling at the dramatic change wrought by the rain. The quantity of water that fell had been immense. Huge areas beside the road were flooded. Small torrents ran in response to only small differences in height, the water a rich brown foam as it swirled round rocks and over sand, eddying ferociously round the plants grown in clumps by the road.

The suddenness of the flood's appearance after heavy rain is astonishing. Fortunately here the rocky hills parallel the road and direct most of the water alongside rather than at it.

I was on the firm tarmac – not high but that vital 18 inches that put me above the water. And, critically, on a firm surface. A firm surface. I thought back to where I was just 48 hours ago in the big east-west wadi.

It suddenly struck me.

What if this rain had fallen 48 hours ago? The thought stopped me in my tracks. It had happened again. Some pretty providential luck. Extraordinary luck. You really had to wonder. I thought about the tree trunk lying

grotesquely on top of the rock island in the great east-west wadi. This was not in the same league but you didn't need 15 feet of water to stop a 4x4 and strand its driver for a very long time in a wadi like that.

I'd been saying it for some time now but looking back over the past 10 to 15 years it occurred to me that, paradoxically, the new hazard in the Sahara is water. Time and again on expeditions both on and off-tracks I had found myself in thrall to its power and effects. Mostly it related to what it could do to the bearing strength of the ground. A little rain caused dry sand to bind more closely and its bearing strength was considerably increased. Sometimes the weight of rain on a dune as it soaked into the upper layers of sand would cause those layers to slip down the dune face, dry sand over dry sand four to six inches down. The result when you encountered it was to see dark patches – the wet sand – some way down the slip face of the dune, backed by the lighter dry sand beneath.

The beneficial or dangerous effects of rain, it seemed to me, depended on the surface upon which it fell. Moderate to heavy rain on pretty flat desert was usually quite good news but the trouble started when it got channelled into streams, small wadis and deep wadis. Any wadi was usually there because it had been a wadi before – no chicken and egg about it; it began small and got bigger with successive downpours. As the underground structure took more water there was

Timing. If this had happened 48 hours earlier ... . The skyscape was dramatic and beautiful; the rainbow an appropriate reminder of my good fortune.

a kind of reversing hydraulic gradient – not self-explanatory until the meaning is explained! When the heavy rain falls there's a lot more water in the upper layers of ground than the lower layers – a wetness gradient: wetter up top, drier down below. As it sinks down, the gradient reverses, wetter down below, drier up top. But these conditions encourage vegetation growth and even as the upper layers dry out over time, longer roots get down to where there is still moisture to be had. Plants become established, successive sand-blows deposit sand and the fine dusts around the base of the plant and the well-known 'green wadi' grass tump formations appear.

Subsequent rain turns the finest dust (often clay) into slime, and water flow evolves swirl holes downstream of every single tump. Thus are formed the really bad wadis so far as vehicles are concerned – very uneven, slimy and sticky mud to bog a 4x4. The smaller wadis just harbour the water a little below the surface. How much and how far down is the big conundrum for drivers. Get it wrong and you'll sink through apparently dry sand into mush. Once again a serious bogging situation.

The really harum-scarum wadis taking huge rainfalls 'skid' round corners due to the momentum of the water, eroding and undercutting the outside of the bends like a racing car that's going too fast to get round the curves. When this happens alongside roads, the tarmac and foundations are undercut, the tarmac collapses and the road is wrecked.

For now, pootling north from In Eker, everything was holding. The flooded areas remained either side of the road with only a little undamaging flow across its surface and I marvelled at the display the elements were laying on. Like an extrovert orator who has forgotten what he wants to say but still keeps going, the thunder rolled ferociously even as the sky began to clear. When I camped I made sure it was with due regard to the hydraulic possibilities for the night. I unrolled the rear door canopy for the first time, tried to remember where I'd put my waterproofs and cooked a rapid meal.

Fine clay, ready to blow into the wadis (top). A 'dry' wadi shows what's in store for the unwary. Rain-flood yahooing round a corner in a wadi incurs 'collateral damage' to the tarmac.

The thunder growled away and I told it, yes, I understood. Eventually it gave up and went away. Later in the evening a 20-truck military convoy passed along the road 100 yards off. Perhaps they've come to get me, I mused, but they rolled noisily on into the night.

14. Ezz-Tes

I had made it through the rock-hills maze where the only passable route headed me sometimes in exactly the opposite direction from where I wanted to go or 60° to the north of it; and before that the labyrinthine wadi N and before that the big 125-mile gap between the oh-so-inhabited Ouallen and Kra, the '3 Nov' camping place. And before that the 200 miles down the Tanezrouft. And before that the frightening 'terminus' bogging on the Reggan bypass. With much of the stress now removed a kind of peace prevailed, a warm comfortable ability to take things gently, to enjoy pottering the Merc at 40mph on a good tarmac road whilst I savoured the scenery rolling past each side-window in the still-scowling bad weather, the great brown rock outcrops newly washed-down after the heavy rain and the rain-flood run-offs freshly sculpted and tidy with the sweep of the departing water. I suddenly realised that in all the years I'd been coming to Algeria I couldn't remember actually coming down this bit of road before, despite it being on the main north-south In Salah-Tamanrasset tarmac. I'd always been off into the sticks east or west of the main road by this time. I didn't know what I'd missed as there was some spectacular scenery through which the road wound its way.

That 'don't hurry it' thing was chiming in again. It had in Libya eight years before. After 5000 miles or so there, an ambitious grab-it-while-you've-got-the-visa, all-four-corners-of-the-country solo run – Tripoli-Ghadames-Ghat in the west, the huge crater of Wau en Namus, the Rebiana Sand Sea, Tazerbo, Kufra, Jebel Uweinat and the Egyptian border in the east; Jalo, the top edge of the Great Sand Sea – I was heading eventually north. From Jaghbub up towards the coast at Tobruk, paralleling, within yards, the Egyptian border to my right and not wanting the wild part of the trip to finish. I found myself doing 30mph on a clear tarmac road with a clear horizon and burst out laughing.

But I had also realised for the first time – and here it was again now – that as much as I loved the desert for what it was – God, how I loved it – I loved it too for what it wasn't.

It wasn't crowds of elbowing, insensitive people bustling around streets and supermarkets, it wasn't me-first traffic jams, tailgaters and numbskulls on mobile phones to whom motorcycles were invisible; it wasn't smoky pubs and noisy restaurants; it wasn't pavements full of stereotypical women bulging out of tight jeans, with untidy hair, grubby bum-freezer mock-suede jackets fringed with straggly mock fur, bulldozing egregious pushchairs full of mewling children and clutching phones to their ears. It wasn't overweight 'Nah-mates' with stubble, cropped hair and no neck not listening to your question in hardware shops. It was blissfully free of dilettante, technophobic, smart-ass, cliché-monger media persons trumpeting that 'suddenly everyone is ... ', or 'blah, blah, blah ... Until now!' It wasn't TV news wallowing in crime, missing teenagers, 'emotional appeals' or salacious rumours about micro-celebrities; rabble-rousing radio-persons cutting off toe-curling vox-pops in mid-sentence or talking at 80 miles an hour to inform you, with an urgency appropriate to announcing WW3, that the M25 ring-road was busy (amazing!) – or that Termsandconditionsapply and that Whatever-it-was was OutNow.

En fin the desert was free of the overwhelming majority of our fellow humans, free of excess of population, of excess in general. And the very few people you did meet, out here, usually made you feel better. It was, if you dwelt on it, a gloomy, shattering pronouncement on the consequences of excess – in the main, of population. Like the setting of competing rats in a cage, it was the proportional rise in hostility, selfishness, greed, territorial hegemony, crime, that goes with increasing numbers. In bleaker moments I often wondered – as I pondered the problems of global warming, looming water and food shortages, polluted rivers, overflowing landfill, urban and rural congestion, increasing energy shortages – if any politician, world leader, media person or head cleric of any faith would ever have the guts to conclude and point out that the spectre of increasing population lurks menacingly and monumentally behind it all. Are *any* of these issues not population-related in some way? Is anyone going to have the vision and courage to hold your gaze and proclaim, in *both* senses of the phrase: 'Too many fucking people'?

Possibly echoing the words in private, the Duke of Edinburgh's media-sanitised view in 1984, as World Wildlife Fund patron, spoke of '*We're just one species. ... enormous increases in human population ... reaching plague proportions.*' When will someone listen? And act?

The human race has to grow up. It is still in classical adolescence – and part-denial: bright, staggeringly awesomely and admirably inventive, creative and clever, hugely ambitious, beautiful. But immature, greedy, selfish, headstrong, undisciplined, lecherous, unable to look ahead, confrontational, aggressive. And often ruled by leaders who are, to a degree, the same. Isn't it a world bereft of humility where the loudest voice wins, where no-one will admit they don't know – where, too often, they don't know they don't know?

And, what with that socking great pot-hole ahead filled with water that looks like level tarmac and which I only just saw in time ... !

Having let off steam, rolled-out my beefs and *bêtes noires*, reaffirmed my credentials for membership of Misanthropes Anonymous and uttered an appropriate expletive or two, I had to – tried to – smile; very much a defensive smile because I knew that despite my cab-temperature-raising, blood-pressure provoking mental tirade, the thread of truth in just about all my concerns wasn't a thread but a hard, won't-go-away stainless steel cable of exceptional strength and validity and there seemed to be little I could do about any of it. Worse, I had a hollow feeling there wasn't anyone else who had the vision or the will to do much about it either; 'Politically tricky, old chap.' But you had to keep trying. And beefing.

• • •

In the meantime my attention, pot-hole aside, was drawn to a mysterious collection of Portakabins (or their north African equivalents) half a mile or so off to the right. You could never tell in these parts whether such agglomerations and their attendant junk were inhabited or not. Dusty somnolent trucks on sagging suspension, oil drums, old tyres, a bulldozer or two, something that could have been, from this distance, a generator surrounded by an oily mess and the whole sprinkled generously with a dusting of plastic bags flapping in the wind or blown against fences, poles or such vegetation as bravely kept going. Did it matter if it was inhabited? For me, almost as always, yes, for I was about to leave the tarmac for a short break at Ezz-Tes – my shorthand name for it. And again as usual, you could expect anyone seeing that to want to know why, to narrow their eyes and flick through your passport. In Libya on one occasion – that same trip – a gun-toting functionary stepped out from a road-side hut and halted me, demanding to see what I had in the vehicle. I opened the back door to display the usual neat stack of lashed-down boxes, cans and soft luggage on top. He pointed to one of the jerry cans. 'Whisky?'

Coming at it this way, Ezz-Tes was not far from the road, logistically challenging, dangerous or difficult. But as a geological *tour de force* it was off the graph. It wasn't a Grand Canyon or even a Fish River Canyon. Canyons, after all, are pretty much fault-derived or soft rock worn down through millennia of erosion by water – lots of water for a very long time; essentially cracks in a plateau for whatever reason. Here, you had the impression it wasn't too different from Day One. Gargantuan chunks of hot plastic rock heaving out of the Earth's crust (now neatly surrounded by flat sand) and just staying there for the next billion or so years. Very hard, smooth, rounded, all of a piece. A little exfoliation from time to time – surface cracking, layers a couple of feet thick sliding down the slope to the bottom in chunks – but not much of that.

While this cap of still plastic, semi-molten rock was solidifying, another erupted beneath it.

I came across Ezz-Tes first in November 2003 from the other direction, the south-west; Leg Two (of three) that had earlier (on the 600-mile Leg One) established '3 Nov'. That time Ezz-Tes was something like 200 miles off the main road, the way I had come via my first hello to Issedienne and its amazing hole-in-the-rock. Having the luxury of maps on that occasion, I had, north of Tamanrasset, come west down the big east-west wadi that I'd now left behind just 48 hours earlier, got held up by the dust storm that bookmarked Waypoint Ramotswe and then weaved my way north, sidestepping west with the maps' able assistance in order to avoid the sneaky snaky dune-lines that the IGN people had so neatly indicated would be there. And so they were. Not huge like the Great Sand Sea in eastern Libya but – a lesson learned many years before – the smaller ones are usually the worst to cross and thus worth taking trouble to avoid. As ever, my careful navigation was tempted by random encounters with previous wheel marks from who knew where or when.

Not for the first time I observed the wheel marks had formed shallow channels in the ground that in turn had caught the rain and here the wispy grass grew in long lines, the dormant seeds, blown there over the years taking advantage of enough water to get them started in life. Nor, of course, was the wildlife slow to see the benefit of the rolled-out thoroughfares and many were the tiny delicate jerbil footmarks I saw that chose to follow the wheel marks rather than hoof it over the stones nearby. The elephants in the Botswana bush are similarly smart enough to appreciate the luxury of leaving footprints down a track rather than shouldering through all that jungle stuff – a bit of a drag, even for an elephant.

Finally (on the 2003 trip) around the most south-westerly extent of the low dunes and through some low hills that needed a little care, I had found myself on a vast wide open plain that the IGN maps called Tahaiek. Actually the 'i' had two little dots above it (like this ï but not available in the Tiepolo Book font in which the rest of this book is set) but the refinement of the attempted Tamachek transliteration was lost on me as I'm not too sure of

the pronunciation implications of umlauts anyway. I turned north-east, aiming to cross the Arak-Tam tarmac 30-odd miles ahead, and thereafter continue on to retrace, now east-to-west, the scary trip that so dramatically introduced me to the flooded Wadi Askef (p88 and 94) in April 2002.

A certain amount of haze can lend an extra dimension to a plain that's already big and Tahaiek was all but intimidating, seeming to go on forever and have no visible end. It was not a thick haze and the sun bored down through it at midday till I thought the only roast item for lunch would be me. A brave little

'What d'you mean, you didn't see it?' Well, it was, the ... er ... light ... . At low speed no real harm done except for one needless extra shock and bruised pride. On inspection, the lateral shear in the sand is interesting.

tree offered what shade it could for my midday snack and I set off again soon after. In due course a rounded hill loomed in my one o'clock about three miles off and out of curiosity I made towards it.

With the sun now behind me and reflecting a beige glare back off the sand, a sudden

sharp bump had me realise the little hard-ridge dunelets had once more caught me out. Again, however, my routinely low speed saved the day and no harm was done, apart from feeling something of a prat for not being more alert. The rounded hill appeared to be on a trolley that was being dragged away as I approached, and three miles turned out to be more than six, as so often happens trying to judge distance in the desert. The hill kept getting bigger; and bigger, eventually enlarging to colossal dimensions and turning out to be solid rock – smooth, rounded, creased in places and with exfoliation slip-down around the foot (that's it opposite, on the left). I had arrived at Ezz-Tes for an introduction and the next 24 hours would be an eye-opener.

Now, three years later, I could not pass by on the road just to the north without peeling off to be there again. I had been back once since 2003 (2005) after Tininirt and meeting the astonished blue lizard, so despite my lack of maps I had the waypoints still and could make for my favourite locations. Ezz-Tes covered a patch probably 15 miles by 10 so favourite locations were just the start and I was still careful to log positions over even the short distance – 20 miles or so – I covered from the road.

Get closer; and when the light is right ... it's breathtaking.

The wonder of this surpasses the imagination. Just the one. A huge strong trunk emerging cleanly from the ground. Not defiled by picnickers' junk. Shade, as the footprints aver, to a few passing gazelle. A tree being as wondrous and extraordinary as it can be. And more so here for its solitude.

Ezz-Tes, looking north: a treat to wake up to on my birthday in 2005 from my privileged parking spot. (Below) Metal-hard bark on one of Ezz-Tes's acacias with pointy-peak beyond (see next spread).

You could drive slowly and reverently among the huge geological megaliths on crisp, crunchy sand. All about was pristine, clean, unmarked; monumentally, emotionally, beautiful almost beyond words in the clean clear light.

The rain had been here too but not enough to cause worry – just firm-up the already strong sand and clean down the outcrops for their portraits to be taken again. The light now was close to perfect. For once, the slightly overdramatic portrayal on the IGN map was entirely appropriate. The Sahara had laid on a bit of a show and it had been well documented by the ever-diligent mappers back in France; people who cared and took pride in what they did.

But first (previous page), doubtless benefiting underground from the rain there had been, a single, lone, amazing tree, a way out from the rocks from which the water ran. The wonder of it, its strength and perfection, the spread of its branches and the small, tight tough foliage they bore, the robustness of its bark, the little ecosystem it hosted – ants,

insects, small birds to prey on them, shade for itinerant gazelle. And what always intrigued me was the one-ness of trees like this. By what involved selective process was there just one tree here? By what criteria was the tree population so minutely matched to the resources? I would have given anything to know what I hope we shall never know – the depth and extent of its roots. And how old it was. How many searing summers it had survived.

There were others dotted around far off, in one of the other valleys between the vast outcrops. If you were (understandably) minded to be a tree hugger the sentiments might be laudable but the practicality dubious. Mostly the bark of the tree was, if you can imagine it, akin to savagely textured, crushed titanium.

Ezz-Tes, the 'Alpine slopes', firm crunchy sand delicately marked by the footprints of a lone gazelle.

At first glance it looked quite soft and pulpy but if you tried to break a piece off to examine it you learned the cragginess was as hard and immovable as cast metal. And if that did not deter an arboreal embrace the putative hugger would, in some cases, finish up with a chest full of thorns. Certain trees, as well as the customary thorn formations on the branches and twigs around the tiny, tough, almost fern-like leaves of the acacia species, had thorns on the trunk too. Even the tiny trees elsewhere, no more than a foot high, came up fighting, thorns ready to deter predators.

Easing the Merc up onto one of the shallow-slope outcrops, I had spent the night here on my last visit. Being there, a present like no other, I awoke next morning – my birthday– to this astonishing primaeval panorama, flanked and bordered by an immaculately rippled

173

sand sheet that ramped up one of the nearby slopes, firm, crunchy and bearing the Merc's tyre tread as a benevolent temporary acknowledgement of its insignificant perpetrator.

I left Ezz-Tes with a heavy heart, wondering if I would ever get back here again. As with Libya in 1998, whatever the rights or wrongs of the case, there'd surely be 'a file' on me by now and the likelihood of getting a visa in the future seemed depressingly remote. I could get blood-boilingly angry if I allowed myself; what possible harm could I be doing driving carefully round this fantastical landscape on my own? Nor was there much encouragement from up north. I rang Su on the satellite phone and she said, rather pointedly, that Russ was now back in the office and he was the one to contact. The provenance of 'the letter' became ever more blurred. I had been left initially with the impression it had been written

by the In Salah gendarmerie to the British Embassy which, on reflection, seemed extremely unlikely. Then Su had mentioned it had been 'passed to them', implying it had been sent from somewhere else. By whom? And again who would write to the Embassy direct? Russ's mention of *'removal from the country'*, that sounded unambiguously like deportation to me, had, apparently, been a 'suggestion'. I dared to hope the situation was perhaps not as dire as I had first thought. It would have helped to be put in the picture.

15. North

It is never a good feeling. Going north; with the major part of the trip behind you. Even the sun was usually behind you, especially at this time of year, mid November; rising in your four o'clock position and setting well south of west – usually on something like 250°. Fortunately the days didn't shorten as dramatically as they did in Europe or the UK and you usually got around 10 or 11 hours of daylight. And again, the light was usually superb – unlike similar day-length in the spring when the winds blew strongly and seemingly without respite to fill the sky with dust, diffusing and dulling it.

By now in a state of almost continuous moderate underlying paranoia, I managed to get back onto the northbound tarmac without being observed by anything that could be taken for an 'official' vehicle whose occupants might have seen me coming from 'down there'. And despite the beautiful and rugged scenery of the Mouydir mountains to the south and east of Arak, my worry was the checkpoint that was positioned there, manned by the gendarmerie. Of course, if In Eker (in the rain) was anything to go by, the wacky no-problem-northbound 'policy' – if that wasn't too flattering a word – might still apply, and my vision of earnest, headphoned operators crouched intently over crackling radios in dark bunkers and 'APBs' (whatever they are) being ordered from Big HQ could possibly have been over the top. Nevertheless, the passport-flickers at Arak lay just 70 miles ahead and even slowing down (as I found myself doing) wouldn't help. Not that it occurred to me at the time, but 'bypassing' Arak would have been totally out of the question (what with the mountains, and all) and would have involved a vast detour west, almost as far as Idjenoudjane.

Rain, shine, dust, tarmac or diversion, the big trucks keep going – here, south from Arak towards Tamanrasset.

The road through the hills south-east of Arak had, as usual, suffered from the rain. The strip of overworked tarmac followed the wadi which in general was accommodating but it had to perch beside it most of the time, sharing the valley, and the trouble arose when it had to cross from one side to the other. By now I knew the routine detours which were quite scenic but dusty and needed care when you encountered an oncoming articulated 42-tonner bravely taking on the rough stretches of non-tarmac as only Algerian and African truckies knew how and needing to maintain its hard-won momentum.

Rain-flood in a hurry has no time for culverts.

After weather like there had just been, gangs with black faces, cheerful white smiles, bulldozers, and long shovels, seemed to appear from nowhere (where did they come from; the distances were huge?) and paths were scraped out around the debris of scattered culvert linings where the water was supposed to go *under* the road and not merely push the whole thing out of its way. I guessed the road engineers and the people that controlled them must have been faced with a continuous head-clutching dilemma. Do you try to engineer the road to withstand *all* weather conditions or do you admit there'll be damage which, to patch up on an as-and-when basis, will be cheaper than the enormous budget required to make the entire route bullet-proof? Again, the sheer length of roadway and the scale of the task compared to piddling Euro-network distances put a perspective on the budget-wracking problem faced by the Algerians year after year.

Having succumbed with my camera to the siren call of Ezz-Tes brought to life that morning by a diamond-sharp sun rising steadily to a mid-morning position, I had been a bit late getting away. I had a leaden feeling that Arak would delay me by not less than three hours – if I was that lucky. How could it be less? I hadn't much idea of where or how I would be spending the night but hoped it wouldn't be listening to a droning generator in the dusty yard behind Arak fort.

As I got within a couple of miles of it, a billowing of road dust seemed to fill the valley and from it emerged a greenorama of gendarmerie vehicles and roof-racked Toyota Land Cruisers; a column so continuous I could not gauge how many or guess who was escorting whom. It was something like 20 vehicles all going at a very purposeful (and unnecessarily high) speed all closed-up and eating each other's dust. If this was, as I suspected, a state visit by the King of Siam, Arak would be *en fête* and knee-deep in rose petals, and they might be favourably disposed towards a lone traveller such as myself. On the other hand it probably wasn't; there might well be no rose petals and they'd take me apart.

Neither of my defensive scenarios, designed to buoy my hopes or cushion them when they were inevitably dashed, proved to be true. First of all I was greeted by the young gendarme in the makeshift wooden shelter like an old friend. Incredibly, he remembered me from the previous year. Then, southbound, I had mentioned that I had first come this way on a Matchless motorcycle in 1961 and, instead of the Arabic equivalent of 'Uh, huh?', I had gained instant hero status. Now, still enthusiastic and with that pink-cheeked Kabylie Berber look that people from that hilly part of coastal Algeria had, he took my passport and the little paper that I always handed out that had details of parents' names and job that they always asked for and which European passports never showed. I was careful that it showed job as *écrivain* – writer. I had learned in the past they seemed to have similar views on '*journalistes*' that I had myself. Indeed *écrivain* often itself got raised eyebrows and something of a nod of approval. He asked if I had had a good trip and I enthused as much as my still-dreadful French allowed.

This was the point where, were it a movie, the soundtrack and visuals would have slowed down and gone into monochrome frame-by-frame flicker. Because he next said he had not seen me when I went through southbound towards Tam. It was probably my fervid imagination and mental state and could have been a perfectly innocent question but I immediately interpreted it as loaded and having official overtones. In my alarm I played for time by pretending not to understand the question and even when he repeated it I feigned difficulty with its meaning. Then, '*Ah! Oui. Là bas. Là bas!*' Over there; waving an expansive arm to the east, carefully not naming any places that could subsequently be construed as a falsehood, hoping desperately he would mistakenly interpret that as my having come south via Amguid or Djanet. I should have waved to the west, strictly speaking, but I could claim mild disorientation later if required; for the moment, his thinking I had really come south by a more westerly route would definitely have sparked deeper enquiry. I hoped the harmless ruse would work, for I really, *really* did not want to get knee deep in going back over the map saga, the different rules applying west of In Salah, the assurances of the cheerful policeman in the Commissariat at In Salah, the er, 'unusual' route I had taken (not against any instructions), or – if only I knew – what was going on with oddball letters from mysterious sources to the British Embassy.

My friend seemed to take it all in his stride. And then he said, 'I will have to go and speak to the captain.' I prayed my face did not show the further alarm I felt – not that it really mattered; what was to follow would follow. He said I could go over and get refuelled in the meantime and walked across in the direction of the fort, a hundred yards or so away.

It was not a happy few minutes. Was there a notice out to apprehend me? How long was this ludicrous cat-and-mouse, Scarlet Pimpernel pantomime going to go on? In Eker had taken no notice; but then they were army, not gendarmerie. I concentrated on the job in hand and took on 28.72 litres of diesel, and the Merc, having covered a whisker under 200 miles since in Amguel turned in a very respectable 31.06mpg. For nearly 29 litres I handed over the equivalent of £2.89. That, at least, made me smile.

I looked over to the fort and at last the creaky door opened and my Kabylie friend came out. Accompanied by the captain. My heart sank. Was that a bad-news walk? Or ... they both looked cheerful enough; but so had Captain Rahmouni when he announced that he was keeping my maps. They seemed to take forever to come over and be within earshot.

'I have phoned In Salah,' the captain began, 'and it is ... ' the soundtrack slowed again, '... OK. *Bonne route!*' I don't go around hugging gendarmes but, suppressing the urge, I certainly found myself thanking him with a very warm handshake, an even warmer smile and an optimistic, if not very realistic, '*À bientôt!*'

•   •   •

I suppose it's like that corny old saying about hitting your head against a brick wall just to enjoy the wonderful feeling when you stop. But tension like this certainly accentuates the sensation of freedom when it is lifted. I positively glowed with relief as I got back into the Merc, turned the key and drove off what the filling station concessionaire would doubtless have called the forecourt, a rough, stony area of dust and diesel spills.

The gorge at Arak is narrow, running north between spectacular cliffs, and the road there crossed the wadi on the wadi floor so always took a beating when the rain floods came. The worst bit was about 400 yards from the filling station and just about every time I had visited over the years some minor reconstruction drama was being played out. When the road went down, impromptu diversions were the order of the day and the volume and sheer weight of the traffic ground the sand into powder-fine dust that lay in ever-deepening ruts.

On one occasion I had been creeping through the dust cloud left by the truck ahead and saw some unfortunate man bogged to the axles in a two-wheel-drive Peugeot 404, having misread the road, and desperately trying to dig himself out without even a proper shovel. It took only a few minutes for me to stop the Merc, reverse back, get out the tow-rope and pull the car free, but the man's gratitude was most moving. He hastened to get a paper and pencil, write down his address at In Salah and invite me to have a meal with him when I went through. Certainly, for me, it was nice to be able to

The Merc unfurls its longest tow-rope and Superman cape – but knows its limitations.

utilise the wagon's capability in this way. Another time, about 60 miles south of In Salah on the wide plain, flood water had breached the road and a spontaneous *bouchon* of bogged vehicles had arisen due to a couple of overloaded six- or seven-tonners getting stuck in the breach and blocking it to other traffic. I was able to get by at the edge and again, the Merc's longest tow-rope, low-range gears and all the diff-locks had managed to 'un-cork' the *bouchon* to applause from the assembled crowd. A huge 42-tonner that had tried to drive round the break in the road and had gone in really deep had, alas, to remain where it was waiting for something a bit bigger to tow it out.

Farther north, on that tedious, featureless bit of nondescript sandy beigeness between El Golea and Ghardaia I was driving along fighting off boredom and saw a car parked at right angles to, and just off, the road. Only after I had passed I noticed in the mirror the two occupants were out of the car and scraping away sand with their hands at the back. They'd stopped for a snack, I think, and bogged down. Here, the driver and passenger were pretty casual about my help. Snappily dressed young men, rather well fed, they clearly thought it a bit infradig (as it were) to accept assistance from a passing tourist of vintage years. Or maybe it was sensitivity about their Korean car. I couldn't help humming

'*Daewoo! Daewoo! Daylight come and I wanna go home ... !*' but I don't think they got the joke, as sometimes happens with snappily dressed young men.

It was nearly four o'clock and the sun was beginning to get lower in the sky, moving Arak's northern cliffs into deep shadow. Despite the rain, the approach road at the top corner of the *oued*, just as it turned west, was not damaged, only flooded, but the sun shining off the flowing water made a good picture and I tiptoed over the rocks to get a picture. Bang on cue a Toyota pickup splashed through, its cargo of soldiers waving cheerfully at the camera-wielding visitor trying not to get his boots wet.

181

Looking west at the old French fort at Arak – fallen into disrepair since 1961. The current fort and filling station are half a mile down the wadi (left).

Just opposite, the old French fort – where we had called on the, for me, memorable trip in 1961 – lay in ruins, the wooden beams long since cannibalised for other uses. When I clambered up the hillside to take a picture on a previous visit there had been, below, the identifiable wreckage of an old Dodge Power Wagon. If ever a vehicle type made an era its own it was the Power Wagon. It was a shame the fort had fallen into disuse – a fine, well-planned building – but it needed more altitude and was too near the level of the wadi when it flooded. Nor, in that position, could pits for fuel tanks have been dug for the filling-station-to-be without them being flooded. The present one, half a mile south down the gorge, was about 30 feet higher and well clear of the flood-line.

As for the wadi, in a dry year when it was barely a trickle as I went through, I stopped, unable to believe my eyes. For there, strutting about in the shallow water in that deliberate way they have when intent on the business of gathering their lunch, was a heron. The mind boggled. A heron in the middle of the Sahara!

It was time to move on after the photos of the artistically-splashing, backlit Toyota, to wrap the Canon EOS 5D in its plastic bag, put it back in the camera rucksack, cover it with a cloth to shield it from the sun that now streamed in through the windscreen, and head up the tarmac that would lead, tomorrow – or maybe I could stretch it to the day after – to In

Salah. This was the new road. The old road, through the rock hills and gorges, the one we had come down in 1961, was clearly based on an old camel route, for it took in wells, *gueltas* (rock pools), and villages based on watering points such as Tadjemout. It lay 15-30 miles east of the new tarmac where logistical resupply and the needs of animals like the noble camel were not deciding factors in its alignment and engineering. The space between the two routes had been of interest to me in the past and was stirring memories.

The Erg Mehedjebat dunes are on this new westerly route that, in more open desert, must have made life a lot easier for the road-builders. As dunes go, the Mehedjebat patch, something like 30km north-south and 20 east-west, probably sets some kind of record for sheer mass: height, bulk, complexity, and – if you are in a vehicle at their base – sheer bloody-mindedness. For the sand is incredibly fine and something of a pig to get out of if you have carelessly got bogged in it. I was, on an earlier trip – those nicely illustrative shots on page 45 were taken on that occasion. And careless is probably the right word.

Trying to select a spot to camp, I had been thinking to myself that – just off the tarmac, with the tyres at road pressures and hot to boot (so the pressures must have been up around three bar) – I was pushing my luck a little in some rather iffy sand with the tyres that hard. Then, of course, the Merc sank to the axles. Despite the wheel claw (its first outing) and the sand mats, my lemon tea was considerably delayed that evening.

Now I hoped to make it a smidge north of that treacherous little plain alongside the dunes just west of the road, to camp for the night. A 26-mile chunk of road that sat in the middle of the 53-mile stretch north of Arak had other ideas for it was an example of Saharan road-building at its worst – broken-up, deeply potholed, and badly frayed at the edges. I wondered if they ever nailed the contractor. To a tree?

There was no speed that (as with regular corrugations) smoothed the jolting and, wincing for the Merc's suspension and underpinnings and general bodily integrity, I had no alternative but to weave between the jagged holes as best I could at 20-25mph. I bled for

The vast Mehedjebat dunes on the new route from Arak to In Salah. Huge, complex and forbidding.

the big trucks coming towards me and gave way where I could; the ride for them must have been even more excruciating.

Born to be awkward, the Mehedjebat dunes faced west and were very difficult to photograph in terms of form-defining light unless, around midday or mid-afternoon, you were trying to show how enormous and intimidating they were. Come to think of it, on that basis their orientation was near-enough spot-on.

183

A little later than ideal, I made it to a reasonable camping spot and unpacked the kit, looking forward, after a somewhat tension-filled day, to a refreshing cup of sweetened lemon tea. My Waitrose limes had at last been either consumed or reduced to hard green dried-up bullets and I was now into 'Lift', a powdered equivalent. After my encounters with – and received wisdom and tales of – solifugid camel-spiders I was uneasy about coming across any new species of arachnid. Thus, as I unfolded my bed and a bright red spider with a spherical body like that of a ripe cherry-tomato scuttled out in that lightning-fast way they have of moving, I was keen to find out precisely where he had scuttled to. I could imagine him, already exhausted from his 26-mile joggle over the broken road, wishing for nothing more than a hidey-hole in my bed from which, during the night he could emerge, should he feel the need, and take a nibble at the incumbent upstairs. My tea had to wait while I dismantled every possible component of my camp bed without a successful outcome. I hoped he had made off and burrowed into the sand. And I wondered how many nights he had already spent soaking up the warmth of his neighbour. And if, perhaps he had been responsible for my long-lasting, frantically-itchy lumps and tourniquet Rolex watch-strap on my absurdly swollen wrist. If so, no wonder he was plump and spherical.

•   •   •

It was the satellite pictures that did it, of course. And what got me thinking about it now, after a night's sleep (without the attentions of the colourful spider), was being where I was and seeing 'Ridge A', 'Ridge B' and so on, away in the haze. They brought October 2002 flooding back like seeing an IMAX movie of it. Even five years before Google Earth lent the genre a special and unique magic and unprecedented precision, there was LandSat raw – or pretty much raw – to be downloaded from Maryland University. The images were addictive to study, dwell on, examine, compare minutely with the IGN map and make your own overlay of latitude and longitude. Just as Mauritania's Richat crater in the early 1970s and Amadel's 10km-diameter spiky circular rim in the mid-1980s had grabbed my imagination with an irresistible urge to see and explore these amazing formations, I had zeroed-in on the possibility of crossing between the new and the old Arak-In Salah routes. The space between them probably didn't amount to more than 25 miles but looked fascinating with some challenging terrain and promising geological features.

Most of the space was filled with mountains that would have been out of the question to cross but there seemed to be a kind of cummerbund of less forbidding ground. If you could get through the western boundary of ridges there appeared to be sandy areas and a wadi and then a possibly clear way through to meet up with the historical route on the far side. How wonderful satellite images are but they can never tell you what the actual going is like!

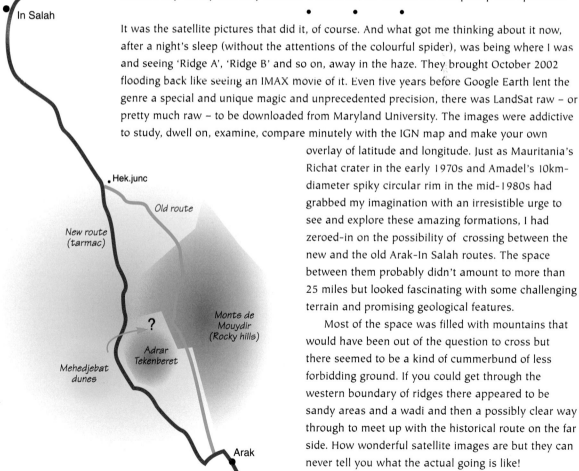

Relationship of the new and old routes between Arak and In Salah. (See also map on page 32.)

In Salah

Hek.junc

Old route

New route (tarmac)

Monts de Mouydir (Rocky hills)

?

Adrar Tekenberet

Mehedjebat dunes

Arak

Truth to tell, snaking south from this still-to-be-tested cummerbund, and no less irresistible than Richat and Amadel to see on this moon's-eye view of the Earth, was a sinuously curved split in the otherwise implacable mass of dark rock – not only fascinating in itself, but seeming to cut through the whole massif and emerge on the gravel plain opening out towards Arak again in the south. It was, of course, left to the old French IGN maps to put a name to it – *Gorges de Tekenberet*. And who could not hack jungle, beat off dragons and pterodactyls, conquer tropical diseases and hostile tribes to see what that was all about? On the IGN it even looked as though it might be a passage you could get a vehicle down.

Carefully planned in advance, there would be no resupply problem. I had refuelled at Arak. The next fuel stop was In Salah, 170 miles to the north and, even with this road-to-track lateral diversion, I could do that on less than half a tank. With six full jerry cans as well I could have made it to some place north of Marseilles after the ferry. I had a similarly abundant water capacity on board. No, the only real imponderable was the terrain. Two imponderables, really: was there a feasible route across the cummerbund at all and, if there was and if I could access it, could I get down the gorge that cleft the Adrar Tekenberet massif. If I did, I should be able to turn left at the southern end and join the old Arak-In Salah track a little to the south of the straight-across cummerbund route.

If I was uncertain of the terrain and the chances of getting through, another thing I didn't know was that I was to make, within 48 hours of leaving the tarmac, one of the most electrifying discoveries of my entire expeditioning career. At least I would find it so.

It was the end of October 2002 and, after a trip way off to the east to see an intriguingly-marked dry sebkha called Hahoumered shown on a vast plain of oddly coloured sand where salt had been harvested by caravans in years gone by, I had been – as now – heading north after a stop at Arak to top-up with diesel. The first challenge of the Tekenberet trip was getting through the long undulating north-south ridge that ran a mile or two off, parallel to the tarmac. The ridge undulations dipped beneath the sand in a number of places so appeared to be a series of smaller ridges with gaps between them – Ridge, A, B, C, etc, as I romantically called them. Though it was clear enough in principle from the satellite shot, I could not know which gap would afford access to the main stretch of 'the cummerbund'. Nothing like starting at the beginning, I thought, especially as it was access to interesting all-new terrain, and tippy-toed off the road south of Ridge A.

Beautiful it certainly was, with the big brown rocky ridge capped with rippled dunes of sand, caught in the low sunlight, but no sooner was I through than I was hemmed in to the north (where I needed to go) by a low wadi cliff up which there appeared to be no path. The wadi bed seemed to be climbing slightly so I followed it, albeit in an unpromising direction as I went north-east towards the main massif of Adrar Tekenberet. A shallow cliff – no more than three metres high – is still a cliff and eventually I stopped, scrambled up it and viewed what it was I was trying to get up onto. At least the terrain looked acceptable but there was no apparent access to it. Then off to the east a bit seemed to be a small ramp. It was steep and stony but I thought my luck was in. Going to it, I turned the Merc in the narrow wadi, selected low range and rear diff-lock in case the loose stones should allow spin and, with no fuss at all, went up in the world by approximately three metres.

I was now on the eastern side of the main ridge chain but it remained to be seen if I could stay there – since I would have to go north quite a bit before being able to turn east around Adrar Tekenberet's north-western edge into the band of terrain comprising the cummerbund. The careful probe began the next morning. North a bit to the first ridge gap; OK. North a bit more; still OK. North a bit ... ah, no; not over the big rocky hill that now presented itself, for once understated on the IGN map and unquestionably something of a no-go region for even the most able 4x4. I would have to break out west again through the ridge line and try the next gap. It was rather like going down a long corridor with a series of doors until you found the one that accessed the big hall heading east into the grounds.

186

The wind loves hill-gaps and usually indulges in a little sand sculpture – rather like that gap back at the early stages of the Reggan bypass. The great sand sheet between the two whaleback rocky ridges was, with the mid-morning sun right behind me, a smooth, untrodden tawny reflector with no texture, shadow or form to betray its surface plane. It was time for a walk; and adjustment of the DIBS-mirror with which I could reflect the sun as a bright light-spot onto the sand and thus, noting its movement when I drove forward, get an indication of any sudden change in the surface – hard small ridges or indeed the edge of the sand itself as a dune-lip. All appeared to be well and driving carefully I was soon out on the western side of the ridge line again within sight of the road – not quite back to square-one but certainly at a place I realised I could have reached direct from the road without the little problem with the wadi cliff. But I'd seen a little of a new world I would not otherwise have seen so the detour had been worth it for some more of that first-man-on-the-planet feeling that the Sahara is quite good at providing.

I'd got out; now I had to move along and try to get back in again – the next door in the corridor, to get back to the east side of the ridge line. Even looking at the map I had thought this might be the one and indeed it was. A neat little gap between the two huge rocky whalebacks, sand-overlaid and topped like icing on the cake, yes, but not difficult and, once through, a turn to the left and a few kilometres had me finally looking out east over a smooth sandy plain, bordered to the north by the dark, 'no-entry' stony hills that the IGN called Adrar Tibaradine. This was a name I would curse later in – and throughout – the day for it nailed the awful wadi I would spend agonising hours trying to negotiate. Hugely encouraging – at least for the time being – however, was the sight of (God bless them again) a tall, neatly-built

*Getting out.
Bouncing the sun
back onto the
ochre wall and ...
getting back in
again at the gap
between the last
two whalebacks.*

hilltop cairn obviously constructed by Pierre and his team of cairn builders in the 1950s.

If the French had been here – presumably coming east-to-west in those days – then it boded well for a broadly feasible route over to the old Arak-In Salah track that still lay 20 miles or so to the east of where I now was; albeit over country the characteristics of which I had yet to discover. The cairn's boost to morale and the effect of the smooth sandy plain I cruised over briefly did not last long. The midday harsh-light now upon me that lent a forbidding look to just about everything it landed on found me scanning ahead to a haughty stand of dunes to the south and a wadi of a kind to the north. Perhaps the dunes, or at least their flatter fringes, might have looked less hostile if the light had been a little more welcoming but in the circumstances I opted for the wadi, despite, even from here, its obvious predilection for the usual bad-wadi accoutrements of big, strong-grass tumps, dips, and the inevitable steep stony wall on the northern edge (as at *Oued* Tirit en route to Amguid and the flooded Askef earlier on). When I got closer I would realise that what I had seen was just a taster, and giant swirl-holes, real-time mud and soft patches (to be avoided like the very plague) was what I was in for.

The next four unrelenting hours' chassis-wracking, torque-burst-demanding, diff-lock-dependent, low-range-predicating, nanosecond-path-picking torture was fraught with constant tension; the real danger that the next swirl hole, coming on you suddenly as you recovered from the last and which you had no option but to tackle with vigour, might be the terminal soft one underlaid with sticky slime. Progress of any kind would have been impossible without the diff-locks; where the suspension's articulation ran out and a wheel lifted off the uneven ground the diff-locks would keep drive to the wheels still in contact and avoid that heart-sinking lurch to a standstill that would otherwise have happened – the precursor to back-breaking digging to get the machine back on an even keel so that traction could do its job. But the Mercedes' robust, sensible, commonsense driveline handled the job it was designed for – competently and without drama. Nor, in the cold objective light of day, was it rocket science, quantum physics or advanced neurobiology; it was a straightforward approach to an obvious problem, properly executed. And why other 4x4 manufacturers seemed incapable of grasping either the challenge or the solution was beyond me; Toyota's outback-friendly Land Cruiser 70 Series, with the options, was a notable exception and as good an expedition vehicle as you could want.

But even such drivelines have their limitations when flotation goes down. Encounter soft mud in such conditions – and softer underneath – and you have a major problem. So as good as the driveline was, the driver was on exhausting tenterhooks.

But once again Providence and my physical and mental limits were in elegant harmony and at the point I said to myself, 'Enough!', so a flat camping area, clear of tufts, presented itself and it was time to put the kettle on and reach for the remaining limes.

I had, I think, simply got it wrong. I should not have gone along the wadi but arced a little to the south around the fringes of the dunes. Moreover I had met, at one stage, a channel which at first seemed to provide a smoother route but then showed it was actually practising to be a river. The Merc had done brilliantly under appalling conditions – heaven knows what murder it would have been without the automatic transmission. Now nosed around into the west, as always when I stopped to camp, and with the rear door open bearing the fold-down 'kitchen' table and the kettle just starting to boil ... I suddenly heard a voice behind me.

Oued Tibaradine taking me for a ride. 'Ah, HA!' it seems to be saying. 'Oh, very amusing ... ', I replied.

A Touareg, alone and on foot, not 10 feet away, greeted me. My surprise was complete but his timing was good and he appreciated the lemon tea. It was not till afterwards I thought that, shirtless at that point and in shorts, I was probably offensively naked to his eyes and should at least have put my shirt back on. He asked if I had seen any camels and I was able to recall, amid my wadi trauma, seeing six or eight of them, a few kilometres back down the way. He seemed pleased but was not given to smiling. Tea over, he took his leave, as I recorded in the log, on a

heading of 145°. It's not often you record people appearing or departing on a particular compass heading; but it was that kind of situation. He said his camp was about 10km away. He had also indicated that the Tekenberet gorge was full of rocks or water and not very suitable for vehicles but as the cool of the evening soothed my frazzled nerves I thought I would have a cautious look the next morning anyway. That snaking channel on the IGN and the LandSat shot was too good not to probe – with due respect and caution.

Certainly there was no question of trying other than the gorge. The surrounding rock hills were cataclysmic in appearance. Not specially high or peaky or having any recognisable silhouette but almost indescribably chaotic, as though a million giant, house-sized, cubiform boulders had been hurled miles into the sky and landed in a Dantean hell of impenetrable grey-brown, scale, roughness and obstruction. If ever a landscape said 'Keep the hell out!', this was it.

But if Nature had demonstrated a fit of past ill-temper, she was not above revealing some more little amazements to make passing travellers slowly shake their heads and smile. Where you have rocky gorges and occasional water – as there had obviously been here – the evidence, pretty unambiguous, stays for a while. Tekenberet had gushed north out onto the plain, smoothing, gouging, routing, swirling, pushing vegetation into a tangle, but succouring it all. And some of the vegetation was more organised than others. Out here, a few kilometres north of the mouth of Tekenberet, the water had rushed headlong onto the flat, respecting a truce with nearby dunes but, in its vigour, exposed along the wadi fringe astonishing lengths of roots that looked for all the world like the fibre-optic cables I'd seen similarly laid bare beside the tarmac to the west. Was there no end to plants' ingenuity and adaptation? How long were these roots? Where were they going to and where from? Which direction was the flow of nutrients to the plant? How long could the roots lie open to the elements?

And you had to wonder how long this adaptation process had taken. How it had chimed in with the changing climates that had taken place over the millennia. I was about to find out, suddenly, about other things from the past.

A spur wadi had aroused my curiosity, three or four kilometres to the north, picked out in the morning light by the shadow of the wadi wall on its eastern edge. Now free of the worst the *Oued* Tibaradine had to offer, that lifting of tension had it's usual exhilarating, expansive effect and I decided to strike out before savouring the exploration of Tekenberet to the south. In spite of the Touareg's warning, that could lead me out of the gorge's southern end and I would not be coming back this way. Though Tibaradine was in more conciliatory mood, it still threw gullies and suddenly alarming soft patches in my path

190

despite my now being in a south-bound feeder to the main watercourse. Wet mud on the tyre sidewalls is not normally something to get uptight about, but here it was different: that lemon-meringue-pie event waiting in the wings again.

The wadi was wild, an exciting mix of near-white sand, rich-green bushes and flanked by the dark-grey rock, all overseen by a vivid blue sky soaring over the wadi walls. But the erstwhile waterway narrowed and petered out against a rock-fall at the northern end where the rain, when it came, tumbled down from the hills above. It was a wonderful place to ponder the geology and geomorphology of it all and I turned the Merc around to head back, towards the campsite and the other wadi that would lead to the Tekenberet gorge. Now, as I returned southerly, still concentrating hard on the lie of the wadi and any unseen traps or signs of soft patches there might be, something – I will never know what – made me look to my right and I caught sight of a small overhang 10 or 15 feet up the wadi bank. Again, an inexplicable impulse made me stop and go back. I halted the wagon and got out to have a closer look.

You hear descriptions of how people's skin crawls when confronted with extraordinary sights, almost a super-emotion that demands more than the usual reactions. The rock art before me had that effect and produced an unstoppable welling of tears in my eyes. I sat back on the ground and just stared almost in disbelief. I reasoned much later that there was every indication that this had not been previously seen by outsiders – what we arrogantly call 'discovery', as though nothing exists until a white man in a pith helmet has clapped eyes on it. The large-scale IGN maps I had were meticulously prepared and if the French survey teams were aware of *gravures rupestres* then the site would be marked on the map with the appropriate icon. On this map in this area there was none.

It seemed almost fantasy that one could drive by, see the overhang from the driver's seat of your wagon, then step out and see the paintings. But then that was precisely the kind of location past inhabitants would have chosen – high enough to be above any water the wadi might hold, a strong reliable shelter where rain would not back-flow down the rock into the cave, a good view of approaching enemies or wildlife. I rather lost track of how long I stayed there and how many photographs I took. And how many back-ups in case something happened to the first film.

My wonderful 15mm fisheye lens came into its own once again to give that sense of location combined with close-up detail that no other lens could achieve – and what subjectively, despite ill-informed carping about 'distortion', the human eye took in (and autocorrected to produce linearity). The light in the recess was good but, to reduce the contrast with the outside illumination without resorting to the soulless flatness of (and possible damage caused by) flash, I used my aluminium-surfaced survival blanket to wash

The figures are almost classical – echoing across the whole of Africa. How? The delicacy of the brushwork is astonishing; the precision of the cow's hooves. And the durability of the paint ... ?

diffuse daylight into the overhang. What I found astonishing about the rock art, when I had calmed down enough to view it objectively, was the fact that the figures seemed almost to be classical, as though they had been taken from an 8000-year-old book of clip-art. The style of the figures was different in detail – probably just reflecting different tribal customs in clothing and hair – but, both in medium and execution, the paintings I had seen at Jebel Uweinat, 1500 miles or more to the east on the border of Libya and Egypt, had a similar look – more obvious still in Hungarian collector András Zborays' encyclopaedic collection of record photographs.

How had peoples separated by that distance – and sometimes a millennium – felt the same creative imperatives and decided to display them in the same way in, and on, the same medium? They focused on their livestock, the wildlife, their ceremonies and often on their weaponry as well – spears, sticks, bows and arrows. All this, of course, was their whole life so their subject matter was not surprising. But what was their 'paint'? How had it lasted so long and so well? And their 'brushes'; capable of rendering such fine detail? To us modern folk, who see inkjets fade within months, there was something almost surreal

Dramatic up close, the Adrar Tekenberet rockscape from afar looked cataclysmic. How had this great rift, now so neatly filled with sand, come about?

about being in the intimate presence of paintings that had been done so long ago.

Eventually I carried on past the campsite, along the wadi with extreme care to be sure of not hitting the dry-wet patches masking soft mud that could lead to a serious bogging. Concentrating so hard I almost didn't see the huge dunes – in truth only a mini-*erg* by Saharan standards but enough to stop a 4x4 – and I soon found the steep rock walls of Tekenberet looming before me like a great grey-black gateway heading south. Mercifully there was not much vegetation in the wadi so there were few swirl-holes. The water had just swept smoothly over the sand and then sunk. It was mostly firm but at times I got out to check its bearing strength on foot. I walked over to where it looked suspicious. I trod on it once; it was soft. I trod on it a second time; it had the consistency of blancmange. The third time, water oozed up and the patch slopped like a bowl of mushy peas. This was not the place to commit 2.9 tonnes of Mercedes, however good the tyres. My Touareg visitor seemed to be right. I went on a little but it was clear that to go farther would be foolhardy.

But I wanted to see more of Tekenberet. And I wanted to right my omission of not making a small gift to my guest into whose territory, however notional, I had strayed. I packed up some tins of food, a small LED torch and some spare batteries in a bag and set off on foot. The big surprise was the relief at not having to worry about the going. On foot there was no problem. With a three-tonne 4x4 there was.

I walked and I walked. I gave myself half an hour but didn't stop till nearly an hour and a half had elapsed. Bend after bend in the great gorge, firm sand, softer sand, vegetation that sprang from the sides of the gorge where the water gathered at flood, water pools clear and clean in which I bathed my feet and washed my hair. Between the high, echoing walls of the gorge I sang, absurdly, the *1492* theme by Vangelis at the top of my voice and hoped that if the Touareg was camped nearby he would come out and I could give him my parcel. I was put in mind of the film again; Lawrence riding his camel down the Wadi Rumm and feeling compelled to sing about *The Man Who Broke the Bank at Monte Carlo*. But I didn't see the Touareg or his camp and, hoping he would be coming north through the gorge again to find his camels, I left my package prominently on a rock in the middle of the wadi, covered in aluminium foil so it would not spoil and so that he would see it.

It was roughly a five-mile walk at 35°C, no big deal but the farthest I had been from the wagon and strangely exhilarating. If I was alone when I was in the Merc, this – on foot, three miles off in the wilderness, with nothing – was solitude-squared. Extraordinary, a feeling of lightness and ethereal freedom. It had been a day among days, and as I trudged

That's the way; straddle the gullies until … oops! Nature's crazy-paving of dried-out clay after the flood – here much larger blocks than usual. Precise gaps and those perfect right-angles. How come?

back along the wadi, picked up the Merc and headed out into the plain again I would find myself camping no more than a couple of miles from the previous night's resting place.

I would be heading north-east now, past the three distinctive flat-top mesas towards the old Arak-In Salah track, something like four miles away. I scanned in that direction, willing myself to see flatter smoother ground than *Oued* Tibaradine had had to offer and it certainly looked better. I thought Tibaradine got its water from the Tekenberet gorge but the truth was the water came from all over. The cummerbund was surrounded by rocky hills and all shed the rain towards the lowest ground. Thus there was a continuance of the wadi where I wanted to go – wider but still sufficiently 'green' to be well-equipped with the standard-issue three-foot steely-grass tumps that would bring a variety of swirl-holes to the party. But whilst I permitted myself some optimism, the wadi still had some surprises – here, for the first time, gullies filled, unaccountably, with powder-fine dust and offering wet mud beneath. A minor heart-stopper when it takes you by surprise but not widespread.

The Arak-In Salah track was still where it should have been and despite probably 40 years of no-maintenance and the consequential rain-flood washouts dotted along its length, it felt like a French autoroute in comparison to the last three days' going. If it was Pierre again, his cairn-builders had done well and what would have been classed as a high-speed bend had cairns on the outside to keep the vehicles from missing the track.

Coming north on this track the year before (2001) with the Merc on 'limp-home', but then trying to follow the old route all the way from Arak past Tadjemout, I had camped a couple of miles back down the track. It was at a place marked on the map as *Oued* Tighatimine and I couldn't resist going back to take a look. It marked a kink in the road as it went through a great rocky pass and I wondered what the rains might have done to it. That earlier time it had been April, so it was very windy. My sleeping mat was snatched from me as I folded my bed and was last seen leaping and cartwheeling south-west over the hills and probably finished up in Mali. The rains had gouged the track a bit but not too

There is beauty even in blowing sand and dust; a gentle gradient of transparency to echo the variability of the wind. Hills and windy plain to the north of Oued Tighatimine.

badly so it boded well for the way north to In Salah.

Irresistibly, the *guelta* of Tiguelgamine lay close beside the route to the east and I felt I should give it an inspection once again. In the quarry-like rock pool last time, the water had been low and it was a sinister black among the dense thicket of tough reeds. 'Giant 40-foot crocodiles and grottosaurs!' I had thought to myself, and wild horses would not have got me to venture into the water. This time the water was pea soup rather than primordial tar and did not look so ominous. A rock tossed timidly into the pool failed to produce an explosion of irritated grottosaurs so I presumed they must be off somewhere on holiday. November: early skiing, perhaps.

In a two-hour walk I ventured to the upper pool beyond what must be a spectacular waterfall when the right conditions prevailed. It was not hard to see why the old route went this way; precious, permanent water for the camels originally. Back near the road the pool looked safer, and my feet and socks both got a treat in the cool water. So cool, I thought, but in this kind of low ambient humidity the evaporative cooling would be vigorous and very effective.

The track met the modern tarmac at what I called Hek.junc – Hassi el Khenig (as already mentioned, not a well any more despite its title). 'Cren-fal' – another in my burgeoning lexicon of DIY waypoint place-names (crenellated *falaise*, of course; what else?) – afforded me camping on the best, crunchiest, firmest sand in the whole of Algeria, and the next morning I drove slowly round its northern end, through the little pass where the well had been, in order to reach the tarmac a couple of miles farther on.

Two things surprised me within a nanosecond of each other. One was what appeared to be a long fence protecting a series of canvassss ... er andtheotherwasasoldierrunningat-me-with-a-gunnn. Then he knelt down so he could point it rather more accurately and 20 others hove into my peripheral vision. Also running. Also with guns. The one at the front wagged his gun left-right indicating, like they do in the films, that I should dismount. Up-and-down wag was put your hands in the air. Yes, why not, I thought. Three minutes later, in true Algerian-Army style it was shift-the-grip-on-your-rifle-to-shake-hands. Nice guys and rightly quick off the mark. It was the time of the baddies and they were on their toes.

•   •   •

Now, four years later, and on the new tarmac road up from Arak, I was again approaching what I now knew to be the camp at Hek.junc, 100km south of In Salah. Even so – with the current regulations – I was no less anxious about getting through. This time there wasn't much bonhomie; it was hot, the flies were maddening and the soldiers at the checkpoint were probably looking forward to their lunch break. But they let me go.

16. *vers* Timimoun

Denied my shower, hotel laundry and meal at Tamanrasset, I put my paranoia on hold as I approached the *barrage* coming back to In Salah, aiming for the Tidikelt Hotel. What would fate have in store for me this time? I needn't have worried because the police greeted me with smiles and a handshake as though I was the one person they'd been hoping would turn up that morning. Among them was the happy policeman who had advised me to go west towards Aoulef so long ago – or so it seemed. Nor was he tactless enough to ask how, having left west on the Reggan road, I had returned now on the road from Tamanrasset. He was such a good chap that if he'd asked I think I would have confided the whole story and I think he would have roared with laughter and clapped me on the back. It was in any case beginning to look as though, coming north, as I suspected in this whole Alice in Wonderland scenario (and as the last two checkpoints appeared to confirm), no-one would now be bothering about trivialities such as guides. Apprehending a marked man to be extradited, though, was another matter – but so far so good.

Nor was the welcome at the Tidikelt any less warm. I think the staff were aware, from the toing and froing of the gendarmerie vehicles and the good Captain Rahmouni when I was last here, that Something Was Going On that wasn't entirely my fault. Indeed they forbore to keep my passport at reception when I checked in: no honour could be higher, I thought. Halliburton, the oil exploration people, were sniffing out a project to the south and it was good to see the hotel actually had a dozen or so guests this time. I was used to being the only one, and the multilingual Ahmed was operating well above cruising rpm in the dining room. It will have been a fillip to the staff to have the place working like a hotel for once. Still state-owned, it was clear that funding for maintenance and the like depended on throughput of guests and it must have been extremely demoralising for them to arrive for work day after day to an empty, echoing establishment. An inevitable spin-off was the state of the utilities – electrics and plumbing. I had long formulated a check-before-unpacking routine – lights, aircon, plumbing, shower, timing of the hot water, etc – knowing that when a room went down they simply moved you to one that ticked more boxes – and that's more, not all. I longed for them to have the funds to get a major refurbishment company in to sort it all out once and for all. If the shower worked you couldn't always be sure the outlet wasn't blocked, so I now underwent the not unusual process of changing rooms with a towel round my waist and leaving wet footprints down the corridor.

The services of the hotel laundry, where, in such a dry climate, everything was returned in miraculously short order, was especially welcome and was a luxury I allowed myself. Without it, the usual sequence on arrival at any hotel was clothes-washing first, rig a clothes-line, then shower but, plugless, of course, the tedium of doing laundry with one hand holding my Universal Traveller's Plug over the drain-hole in the washbasin was nice to be able to avoid. As was the sinking feeling when the water went off before you were able to rinse the washing. Geoff-the-geophysicist-Renner from the west-east Sahara trip and companion on a number of trips since, addressed the no-plug problem by stuffing a sock into the aperture but I sometimes cringed at the thought of what the sock might pick up half way down the drain.

I stayed, as I often did to unwind, two nights and experienced again the extraordinary effects of the Tidikelt's coffee. You hear of people having a caffeine fix – something that had always sounded like pure fiction to me since I have never detected any effects at all from coffee except stimulation of the bladder. In Salah coffee, though, certainly as served at the Tidikelt Hotel, was something different. I suspected this could have been simply due to its sitting in the percolator for days on end. Nevertheless, I had experienced this before and asked Ahmed's young assistant what they put in it but he assured me, straight-faced, that it was just normal coffee. Whatever it was appeared to be directly connected to my creative juices and I was able to write – brilliantly and fluently – as never before. Well, that's what it felt like, anyway.

Time came to leave and, reluctant to risk a trip to the market to get fresh bread (which would have been worth gold bars) because I would have to pass the gendarmerie and Captain Rahmouni's domain, I left without. I planned to target Algiers and my open return Marseilles boat ticket via a great loop to the west taking in Timimoun and making a return visit to Ain Sefra after an absence of over 20 years. But first I would have to continue north, over the Tademait plateau, passing the location of my south-bound nemesis, Ain al Hadjadj, where doubtless *le lieutenant* still lurked waiting to pounce on any remaining maps he might have missed when I first passed that way or execute the *coup de grâce* by having me delivered to the undesirable aliens counter, if there was one, at *Alger port*.

Instead, the experience was – in a perverse way – like a kind of homecoming. The same soldiers were on duty as had been (in their inexperience with foreign travellers, summoning the lieutenant) the instrument of my problems. Again the handshakes were warm and genuine, enquiries as to where I had been were not made. The exchange of addresses had taken place on the original visit. As part of my attempt to establish non-spy credentials I had produced a copy of my latest 4x4 book and, responding to their evident interest, I had promised to send them copies. One of the soldiers' names was Adnan Boumedienne.

'Ah!' I said, *'Monsieur le President!'* – referring to his distinguished surname, that of a past Algerian head of state. We had all conversed as best we could despite the language problem and, at length and with some deliberation, he said, *'Vous êtes très sympathique!'*

I have to say I found that quite moving. There was more to the word in French than the literal translation.

The Tademait plateau was as flat and wide as ever; a 200-mile expanse of grey-black gravel and surface rock. Now, at least, its vast size was subjectively diminished by the fact it was spanned by a well-made tarmac road, not the ever-widening skein of unsealed tracks that had once been its chief characteristic – and the attendant fine, choking dust that billowed behind every heavy truck and 4x4 that embarked on a crossing. I followed the road to the northern end of the plateau where it swooped down to a lower level. At the rim before the descent you could look north and see the road taper away, arrow-straight, almost to infinity but still to a perfectly flat horizon, 80 miles or so before El Golea. It was El Golea I was happy to avoid, where I had been robbed at the filling station (and there were other reasons), so I would head south-west at the Timimoun junction some 40 miles short. Even in the, by European standards, traffic vacuum of Saharan routes, getting off the main north-south route to In Salah and Tamanrasset was like transferring to a quiet country lane and the sense of tranquillity was palpable. In Salah to Reggan, via Aoulef, had been the same. It was a road where you gave other vehicles a friendly wave.

•   •   •

It was beginning to resemble a prolonged family reunion. I'd last been here three years before. Tray held high and leaning into the turn as he swung round the tables as if he was riding a motorcycle, he caught my eye; raised eyebrows and a broad smile announced recognition and when he'd delivered his dishes, Groucho came over to shake hands. I suspect that wasn't his name but the moustache and facial similarity to Groucho Marx so labelled him for me. Last time I'd been here the hotel proprietor's son Mohammed Amine Mekkaoui had offered to escort me out to the nearby village of Oulad Said for the post-Ramadan Eid *fête*. In truth I think he wanted to see it all himself but the decades-old spectacle – drums, dancing, huge banners and old, frighteningly rickety guns – was a privilege to see. Crowds of villagers surrounded the display in the sand dunes and whilst to those untutored in the language or tradition the prolonged chanting, stamping and swaying might have seemed chaotic, it clearly was not. For a precisely synchronised fusillade from the old muskets had me jumping a foot in the air and my eardrums meeting in the middle as blue-grey smoke veiled the scene and the smell of cordite filled the air.

Celebrations at Oulad Said after the Ramadan month of fasting. Those things are all loaded. Bring your earplugs!

What with the jam leaving the festival site, it was some time before Amine had eventually found our complex return route through the now darkened labyrinth of village back-lanes. So I had been late returning to the hotel and had apologised to Groucho, as the only guest then, for keeping him waiting in the dining room. He seemed greatly to appreciate the politeness and, three years later, remembered it.

For this was Timimoun, a delight for its situation on the elevated southern rim of a vast sebkha, for its view to the north of the awesome dunes of the Grand Erg Occidental, for its local collection of indeterminately old mud forts, for its ancient and meticulously-irrigated *palmeries* (see below), for its busy covered market brimming with green produce, for its unique mud-plaster building style, for its delightful people, for its special peace and for its Hotel Gourara.

The Gourara – so named after the region of which Timimoun was the centre – was one of the hotels designed by the charismatic and colourful French architect Fernand Pouillon in the 1950s and '60s. Appointed Chief Architect to the City of Algiers 1953-57, he was later, in 1965, also commissioned to build 30 hotels for the Ministry of Tourism. Prior to this he had been the subject of a furore in France when his company had gone bankrupt, he had been jailed, escaped to Italy, escaped again to appear at his supposedly *in absentia* trial, finally leaving his homeland for Algeria.

Traditional palmerie irrigation is a work of art – and depicted in Cultural Centre Director, Djouiber Mansoor's impressionist painting.

To some these Scarlet Pimpernel escapades and his eventual pardon from Georges Pompidou characterise the man, but his reputation as an architect outshone this – nowhere more clearly than in his Algerian hotels, unique and original, that contrived to be witty, sensitive to, and incorporating, local architectural styles and – as we entered an era of international architectural sameness – all quite different from each other.

Currently run down (El Golea's Boustane would make you weep), the freshness of the designs still shines through – you find yourself wandering round the buildings and breaking into a smile at the originality – and even the most demoralised receptionist in an all-but-empty hotel in the 21st century knows who the architect was.

The Hotel Gourara at Timimoun is surely among his best. Its site on the ridge overlooking to the north the 10 by 20-kilometre palmerie and salt flats that separate it from the dunescape of the Grand Erg Occidental is just the start. Chosen with a sensitive appreciation of its potential, the site was then the motive force in Pouillon's design – a main building in local style and, stepped below it on the hillside, huge curving arms with accommodation set into them in a double layer. Down the middle and looking out of a gap in the pincer-like arms of the accommodation, a double-decked cascade of two swimming pools such that swimmers could look straight out, a millimetre above water level, at the panorama of the Grand Erg's magnificent dunes in the distance.

The whole building was executed in the characteristic style of the Gourara region architecture, design and pattern. The dining room has one huge wall, 30 metres long, covered in panels of Gourara grooved-plasterwork design motif. Each about a metre square, no two panels carry the same pattern and all were executed by local craftsmen without drawings or other references. Even the bedrooms have sunken wall lights mimicking those originally designed for candles or oil lights – and, for good measure, a wall panel of Gourara plasterwork ornamentation.

Crying out for meaningful refurbishment (like the Tidikelt at In Salah), the Gourara was Groucho's stamping ground, and it was good to see 20 or more oil- and gas-exploration people as well as mixed groups of men and women keeping it busy. An Algerian omelette is like no other, coloured and spiced with tomato and other vegetables, browned and firm, wonderfully tasty – not like the underdone Euro-slop you get in the UK. Preceded an hour or so earlier by a hot shower, an unpacking and shaking-out of dust and, at the table,

Timimoun's Hotel Gourara looks north to the Grand Erg Occidental. Guest rooms arc, pincer-like, around central garden and swimming pools. Brilliantly evocative painting (opposite, top) in Timimoun's Centre Culturel is signed 'Moulin'.

201

assisted by some quite acceptable Algerian red and Groucho's welcome and bonhomie, it made an evening of relaxation, warmth and, for once, an absence of the need to keep a low profile, cover the cab lights and wonder if anyone had seen where I was camping.

I usually avoid, if there is an option, rooms with televisions or fridges, but on my last visit to the Gourara I found myself in a room with a fridge. When it was working it made a frightful racket and, unsurprisingly since all fridges are heat-exchangers, raised the temperature of the room. Putting nothing in it, I hoped it would calm down and not operate but it kept cutting in and out at random intervals that usually made you jump. Determined to win the battle for some peace and quiet, I unplugged it and shuffled back to bed. It then deployed its final weapon – expansion in the ice-making compartment: *tnk ... TANK ... tink-tink ... tonk ... ... tk ... zzzng ...*(long pause) *... tnk ... ggzzzzt ... .*

If anyone had been watching at one o'clock in the morning they would probably have wondered what the skinny Brit in his underpants was doing struggling to move a refrigerator out onto the access path that ran alongside the rooms. I went back to bed. On the balcony newly-washed socks, pants, vest, shirt, pinned to my cunningly-rigged clothes line, dried in the cool night air while I slept. (I was getting quite good at rigging my parachute-cord clothes line but over the years concluded that bathroom designers – and balcony designers too, for that matter – had a secret pact with hotel laundries that precluded them providing suitable opposing fitments to which clothes lines could be attached. Next time, perhaps a huge sucker-pad like they use to move plate-glass windows? This would work at least on bathroom tiles.)

Timimoun has a very wide main street with carefully spaced palm trees, whitewashed around their bases, running down the centre, a carriageway on each side. It pointed to what had obviously once been the main road to El Golea, 360km to the north-east, and

Evening stroll, Timimoun. The people are a bit special.

now served only the 'circuit' villages that fringed the huge sebkha. Among the small shops along the main street's south side a singular pinnacled building stands out, a unique example of Gourara mud-plaster work. Now the *Centre Culturel*, the building started life as the Hotel Transatlantique in 1926, patronised by the *Grande Duchesse* of Luxembourg – to whose memory a plaque now adorns the room she occupied. Built before air conditioning, the building is all dark, cool corridors within. Inside, the walls and ceiling buttresses are decorated with expanses of intricate mud-plaster relief designs, done – like those in the Hotel Gourara's dining room – spontaneously to no drawing by the craftsmen of the time.

The name was later changed, so Groucho told me, to *l'Oasis Rouge* before taking on its present role in the mid-1990s. Nor is it some run-down, dusty wreck like so many of the grand ideas of culturally-minded notables.

Djuiber Mansoor, its director, dropped what he was doing to show me around the place and the collection of artefacts in the displays.

The quantity was small but what counted was the care and reverence with which it was all treated. Some of the paintings were a little crude, others exceptionally evocative – like the one on page 200; you could almost hear a soundtrack of the drums, singing and stamping through the rising dust. Mansoor himself was no mean artist and was working on an oil painting when I arrived – a montage of Timimoun life.

Preparing to head on west, I went into a nearby shop to ask for bread, some biscuits and eggs. Not having anything smaller I offered a 1000 Dinar note – worth about £7. But the shopkeeper didn't have any change. Undecided as to what to do, after no more than three or four seconds he said, 'Well take it anyway!' The shop two doors down where I bought oranges had change so I was able to pay in the end. Splendid people.

•   •   •

I got no nearer solving the mystery of the crumbling old mud forts around the Timimoun area. Why were there so many? Was this any indication of the number of fiefdoms or a concerted effort to keep out raiders from neighbouring tribes? How old were they? To even such a basic question I couldn't get a clear answer. 'Maybe 200 years,' was as close as I could get. Another said 300; and that there were over 100 forts in the area. Leaving Timimoun, just 10km south-west, there were a pair of the ruined *ksars*, at the junction of a minor road down to Aougrout and a shortcut to Adrar, not marked on the map. I stopped to have a look.

Much of the mud structure had been eroded away by many decades of weather but a surprising amount still stood tall, overlooking the plain before the escarpment upon which

Timimoun's city gate, a tradition of the small towns in the area, is typically well made and maintained. The accurate history of the many old mud forts is unclear.

it was built. Cunningly, the entrance was close to the edge of the fall and a narrow path along the rim was the only way in – a clever first line of defence against unwelcome guests who could be knocked off to a limb-breaking drop if the politenesses of calling on neighbours were not observed. Horses or donkeys, led with care by the friendly, could have been got into the fort along this path. Inside was an open courtyard surrounded by rooms or shelters and, at the end opposite the main entrance, what had clearly been a two-storey building. The whole complex overlooked a valley in which was now a *palmerie* of probably mediocre yield, but a couple of hundred years ago the climate would likely have been more favourable. Guarding such valuable property could well have been the rationale for these buildings. The similarity to classic medieval castles was notable – certainly to me as a non-historian. Wind moaned quietly through the broken structure, a thin spray of blowing sand nurtured the tiny dune growing within and the mystery remained.

There was something oddly relaxing about driving west – more like south-west actually – out of Timimoun; the mood the place and the quiet traffic-free road conferred upon you, I guessed. This would meet up with the road running north-south between Bechar and Reggan – the map back on page 10 will refresh your burgeoning, and by now possibly confusing, lexicon and orientation of Algerian place-names and places. There I would turn north towards Ain Sefra and take the wiggly route back to Algiers.

I was already slipping into that slow-down mode, unwilling to give in to the fact that the trip was coming to an end, planning a visit here and a visit there to try to spin it out so that my open return ticket on the ferry could slot into the sailing-after-next rather than the first available. The feeling of wanting to make the most of it was even stronger in the light of my current situation and the uncertainty ahead. It was an uncertainty overlaid with pessimism. The Embassy appeared to have reverted to a tick-over and were getting on with other things; understandably, I supposed, since once they had written the letter they had, all they could do was wait till it filtered through the offices at the Ministry of Foreign Affairs. At least it was a letter from the Embassy; I dreaded to think how slow it would all have been if it had been a letter just from me.

But I still had no indication of my status as a visitor. Was I to be extradited? Was I to be stopped and questioned if some kind of directive had reached one of the checkpoints I passed? Was I ever going to get my precious maps back - my personal property, bought legally in map shops that included the Algerian Government's own outlet in Algiers so many years ago? My 'military maps'? Wretched *lieutenant*, I thought. Wretched man. But again, unfamiliar with how widespread was the use of maps and used to seeing this type deployed only by bustling military convoys (if then, what with their reliance on ancient guides), I supposed he was only doing his job as he saw it; in all probability thinking he'd been pretty quick off the mark to nab me. Me, so obviously a scout for a future territorial invasion. If he'd seen other visitors with maps they'd likely only have had concertina fold-up tourist ones – certainly without topographical detail or lines of latitude and longitude.

Then again – I had to smile – hadn't he provided me with a neat little challenge? My most, how can I put it, interesting trip in 40 years? Forty-six, to be more accurate. How clever was a 700-mile off-track-sector solo trip in the Sahara if you actually had maps and satellite images and Google Earth printouts? I'd have been coming the other way too. No hassle about looking for the western end of Wadi N. And as for the rocky-hills-8-Nov-labyrinth; pah! Not even on the menu.

The landscape west of Timimoun wasn't the Sahara's most scenic. Basically low, crumbly, chalky and given to dips filled with sebkha; and the sand was very fine, a dull greyish-beige like that unspeakably dreary bit between Ghardaia and El Golea so that if you pulled off the road to have a snack lunch you'd find yourself having to engage 4x4 to get moving again like the smart young men in their Daewoo. But it firmed up and made more of a pictorial effort as I neared the Reggan-Bechar road, a giant T-junction where people waited to get lifts to the place their original ride wasn't going on to. There should surely have been an enterprising little lean-to café here, but the usual small-trader entrepreneurial flair did not extend to this spot any more. On my last motorcycle trip in 1991, on a 350cc Suzuki that I swore was out to kill me, there had been something here and it had sold me a litre of paradise; a thousand gullet-cooling, life-saving millilitres of orange fizz that so impressed me I took an arty photo of it on my dwindling stock of film.

Turning right towards Bechar, I paused after a few miles and looked to my left. Now that was a bit better. Still a bit crumbly but that Sahara magic hovered. It certainly was there when I was last here. The landscape was perking up; a hint of drama and a soothing, extended overlay of wind-blown, gently-curving sand. And there had been the light. The alchemy of light.

... the alchemy of light.

17. Pieces of silver

The score 'At Arak Road ... ', as In-the-Know sports reporters in the media would probably have it, was 1-0 to the Rain Floods; the Road Engineers, suffering a crushing defeat in the second half – with scattered culverts, broken tarmac and exposed optical cable to prove it. A return match, at Foum el Kheneg, however, saw the tables turned, a 100-metre torrent failing to overcome some excellent teamwork by the Road Engineers. Moreover the *Oued* Saoura was no ordinary opponent. As the gendarme at the Kerzaz checkpoint, 130km up the road from the Reggan-road junction west from Timimoun, told me later, when there was heavy rain in Morocco, the *Oued* Saoura, pool-stagnant and dryish most of the time, let fly with a certain vigour.

Here at Foum el Kheneg, some way before Kerzaz, it was clear that the *Oued* Saoura was indeed flexing its muscles, rampaging through a gap in the rocky ridge like a Red Arrows formation of express trains. A score of culverts firmly concreted into a substantial causeway handled the onslaught well - all the more impressive for me since the last time I

Oued Saoura in sprightly mood at Foum el Kheneg.

207

was here you could have driven through the dry wadi bed without bothering with the causeway. The huge pipes' foaming, angry outflow looked like those pictures you see of giant irrigation dams with the sluices open. The turgid brown water, once through, gathered itself together and curled slowly out into a wide flood-wadi that disappeared out into the desert and dunes beyond, there to sink, presumably, into some forgotten water table or aquifer hundreds of metres down.

As if to hammer home the man-conquers-nature aspect, a sleek, blue, air-conditioned, long-distance bus crept across northbound to Bechar, passengers dozing behind sun-screens and either unaware or unimpressed by the elemental riot passing beneath the wheels and the roadway.

Farther up the road by 120km, north of Kerzaz, I again had cause to gulp and be grateful, for here, once more in dramatic contrast to the situation in 2003 when it was being built, a new bridge was providing the solution to what would have been something of a problem. Now slow, swirling and mean, with those areas of surface roiling and whirls that would have been a clarion 'keep out' to swimmers and canoeists, the *oued* was again in purposeful mood. Had the bridge still been under construction I really don't know what the alternatives would have been. As it was, leaning on the rails to take pictures of it all, I felt, to my mounting alarm, the bridge begin to pulse up and down rhythmically like a dolphin swimming. I looked up to find a 42-tonner coming slowly over and took on board another lesson in engineering and structural flexure that had not occurred to me before.

How we take all this kind of thing for granted in Europe. If a bridge is needed then a bridge is somehow there; built by somebody or other, and everyone complains, in their usual, dilettante, teeming-ants-in-a-box-of-sugar way, that it causes traffic jams, is all a bit of a bore and they get on with yet another superfluous call on their cool, don't-be-seen-without-it mobile phones. Memorably typical of our all-too-often technophobic zeitgeist and media was my recollection of the BBC's coverage of the opening of the Channel Tunnel – a Herculean engineering feat – during which the only thing the reporter could find to say was that the first train through it was 20 minutes late. Oh, that will never do.

Despite the going-north and end-of-trip blues on the hover, waiting to settle on my shoulder, there was much to see and quietly enjoy about the big western loop. It predicated a certain mental attitude – relaxed, receptive, slow-down – which was usually easier for me after the main exploring, remote-area section of a trip had been covered. Timimoun was a hard act to follow but it put you in the right frame of mind: the specially nice people, the look and feel of the place and its being, to use John Major's wonderfully evocative phrase, at ease with itself, perfectly content and quietly proud to be Timimoun.

Going on north-west and north there was Kerzaz and its huge dune, a kind of giant, immaculately knife-edged, unchanging sentinel at the western edge of the Grand Erg Occidental; Beni Abbes, again squeezed between the *Oued* Saoura and the *erg*, its white, crenellated, story-book fort overlooking the wadi (now also with a smart bridge since the early times), the place where we had called in 1961 with three Land Rovers and the Matchless motorcycle and where the French army officers had welcomed the 'rosbifs' (if that's what Brits were called in those days too) with a bottle of Vat 69 whisky from the cellar – at 10 in the morning. Beni Abbes was the location of the first hermitage and chapel

of Père Charles de Foucauld, still lovingly preserved and looked after by members of the brotherhood he founded. There was also a tragically dilapidated and dusty natural history museum diligently put together by the French in the 1950s and '60s, its detail still fascinating and identifiable but the whole looking like Miss Havisham's cobweb-covered wedding feast and watched over by two *guardiens* who, by some miracle, retained their sanity despite the brain-crushing boredom of their job awaiting visitors, a total of whom probably amounting to no more than a dozen a year. Beni Abbes's Rym Hotel was originally designed by Pouillon – and it showed – but it had a modern addition, comfortable, effective, but with all the flair of a packing case. Beni Abbes, though, was an essential stop for its location, what remained of its history and the Foucauld hermitage.

Beni Abbes, the archetypal desert village in real life. Père Foucauld's simple chapel is a moving memorial to a man combining faith and humility with dynamism.

This time, though, I was not able to linger and as I headed for Ain Sefra, it brought to mind Taghit, 140km farther on, which I would also, after a final night's camping, pass along the way – a kind of smaller Beni Abbes but, if anything, even more attractive.

I was also having to think ahead. Exceptional as it was in terms of atmosphere, facilities, location, pride and welcome from the staff, staying at Algiers' unique El Djazair hotel was expensive. I chose to stay there principally for its proximity to the port and its enclosed, secure, car park where the equipment-laden Mercedes could rest easy without the attention of local thieves. Originally opened as the Saint George in 1889, a wintering resort for rich Europeans of the time, a historical fact of which the management took every opportunity to remind customers, the hotel was renamed in recent years.

As interesting as the city was, spending time there was not the main aim of visiting Algeria – albeit central Algiers and Oran were fascinating places to see. Thus if I wanted to catch the ship sailing on a given day I would attempt to get teed-up to arrive the day before, having made the bookings and phone calls in advance – and stay just the one night. Easier said than done, but the excellent Annabelle Jimenez at Southern Ferries in London had agreed, in response to my call on the satellite phone, to contact SNCM in Algiers and pencil in a booking which I would zip down to confirm immediately on arrival.

I also rang Russ Middleton in the Embassy to ask if any progress had been made regarding the recovery of my maps. Disappointed but not entirely surprised, I learned that the answer was no, but his suggestion of a visit to the MFA (Ministry of Foreign Affairs) in person initially sounded a good idea. I hoped they would see I was not exactly out of the James Bond or Philby mould, mitigate the gendarmerie perception of my dastardly intent and perhaps get things moving a bit. It would be a very busy Saturday – indeed my brief stay was to yield more than I expected – but it seemed to be a good use of the time.

Overshadowing all of this, as I drove on, were thoughts for what the future held. Would there be another trip? The Libya scenario kept reminding me that whatever the rights or wrongs of the case, once you attracted any kind of attention from the folks in uniforms, there would likely be 'a file' that would surface any time I applied for a visa from here on; a file marked 'trouble-maker' with, doubtless, a big finger-of-suspicion motif too.

They had no way of knowing, and even if they did I am pretty sure there would be no understanding, but trips of this kind were my whole life. Whilst there was much else of interest out there, this kind of thing was, still is, at the centre of it for me: being out in wild, remote landscape, alone with the elements, the better to appreciate it. The very essence of our planet combined with that something in the human psyche with which it resonated so well. And if all this were stopped, what then? What was the point having a two-tonne 4x4 sitting in the garage? Boxes of spares, tool kits, recovery gear, cooking gear, maps, nav-aids, rescue-alerting items, camping equipment?

On the way south, coming through Ain Oussera, a smart white Toyota pickup pulled alongside, its driver waving frantically that I should stop. Rachid Benyahia was the man; him and his two sons. A local entrepreneur with a small factory and a huge machine he had bought in Taiwan that made concrete-reinforcing metal mesh, a traveller in the Middle East for parts and machinery and a dedicated fan of Mercedes-Benz G-Wagens which he wanted to buy second-hand. Mine was fantastic. Did I want to sell it? What modifications had I done? Where did the bits come from? What about those wheels? Automatic! Eeeeh! Would I stay for lunch? Would I come back and stay with his family on my return?

Outbound I had politely declined to get involved at all but now it all came back. If there really were going to be no further trips wasn't this the time to sell? Two thirds of my added equipment would be applicable to operating a G-Wagen in Algeria. It would not be impossible to call at Ain Oussera as I wended my way back towards Algiers.

Whilst the pragmatic part of me thought this was the realistic thing to do – even 40 years' desert journeying had to come to an end some time – part of me was disgusted; a betrayal of my own ideals. Pieces of silver. There was always hope. These thoughts were with me for the next few days and spoiled them for me. Very unsettling and a sorry end to a trip that had, for all its challenges and potential dangers – or perhaps because of them – been rich in experience. I would see how it went and phone Benyahia in the next day or two to sound out the possibilities and implications. After all, how could there not be complications; there would be the customs side to think about, among others.

•   •   •

On what was to be my final night under the stars, I was back in low-profile mode, shields on the windows, minimum lighting in the cab. If I was honest, despite the beauty of observing the heavens before I went to sleep, the rising of Orion, the departing moon, I was getting weary of creeping about like a fugitive in case some passing official (or bandit, as those same officials would have it?) should see and come over to investigate – either then to apprehend me or expound (or demonstrate) the dangers of camping in the desert.

But my spirits were in for a boost. This was, in effect, the Bechar bypass – an official one this time. A minor road via Igli and Taghit that avoided Bechar and New Bechar, the hideous light-industrial sprawl that seemed, when I had gone that way a few years before, to go on forever, an endless procession of industrial waste, rubbish dumps, ring-roads fringed with grey concrete blocks and trucks dispensing dust and grit behind them.

Now, waking to a muted dawn, I went on down the narrow tarmac strip to Igli, not much more than a village, but situated where the mighty *Oued* Saoura branched off north-west to become the *Oued* Guir and was met from the north by the south-flowing *Oued* Zousfana. A low bridge, perilously close to the high-water-level, I thought, spanned the swollen wadis, but a mile on, Igli, remote, small, unspoiled, was coming to life.

Igli was sweet. At this early hour the children were going to school. A joyous little girl, beautifully turned out, skipping down the road with her huge backpack satchel of school work on her back. Boys, 12-14 years old, smiling, full of life and fun. Big smiles. Make the foreigner smile, I thought, and you get points. They did. And I hoped they got them. Just round the corner, a man stringing heavy electricity cable from one pole to another; all over the road. No problem. Big smile. A newly-made velvet-smooth tarmac road meandered north from Igli the 66km towards Taghit. Secretly, I thought, they must have hired the French firm that made the 20-mile billiard table that runs around Saint Exupéry airport south-east of Lyon, the smoothest road I have ever travelled on. I came across the very un-French gang working on it some way down the road and waved my appreciation.

I fuelled at Taghit, coming down the steep approach road I had T-junctioned into, the backroad from Bechar. The service station was full of *bouchons bleus* (I had to smile), and the underpowered blue two-tonners were crammed with sheep going somewhere to market. They would make a production of going up that steep approach road, I thought. The waistcoated, pantalooned and be-turbaned crews out-gunned the *moutons* for decibels and some huge debate or argument – with actions – seemed to be ricocheting back and forth while the slow glug of the pump filled the dented fuel tanks with diesel.

Taghit was always a delight, bigger than Igli but still more of a village than a town, ranged right up against the Grand Erg that seemed to be a backdrop to everything, with a

Taghit, a small,
quiet gem.
Somehow the
Grand Erg
Occidental knows
where to stop.
The fuel station
is far left, centre.

Taghit's hotel; by Pouillon. With some astonishing rock art just down the road.

single main street of tiny shops that you entered after zigzagging up from the wadi Zousfana a little bit farther on from the filling station. The wadi had come a long way from up the north-east but didn't have the might, majesty or capacity of the major wadi, albeit when I last visited Taghit it was the year before and it would not have been under the same provocation.

Taghit's hotel was a Pouillon and a charmer built with a tower, as was his wont, to reflect local style; not as a white concrete box. Though it suffered now, like the rest, from rather dire plumbing and rattly air-conditioners, the balcony of my room permitted the tying-on of my parachute-cord clothes line so that, without turning the place visually into a tenement, I was able to produce five-star laundry to match what was now my rating for the wounded hotel. Again, alas, I was the only guest.

I had long seen annotations even on the Michelin map about rock carvings to the south of Taghit and was surprised to be told at the hotel, not that one needed a guide and convoy, but that you just went 18km straight down the now-tarmacked road to the next villages along the Zousfana wadi and there they were, '*En face ...* ' at the end of the road. And so indeed they were, beautifully executed on boulders of hard durable rock that over the millennia showed no weathering at all despite being exposed to the elements. One had been polished to a dull sheen and, examining the rock, it was humbling to realise how long the work must have taken. Once again, the carvings were of ostrich, eland, gazelle and even a lion, a sobering commentary on how bereft of wildlife the wadi was today in comparison. Here at the site of the engravings, though, the hunters must have had a birds' eye view of what would have been a fertile plain below, down to the edge of the wadi. Not the shelter of the site I had found north of Tekenberet, but a good hide from which to observe and then stalk prey – after the sculpture.

●   ●   ●

But that had been 2005. Now, with something of a *bête noire* mile-athon ahead as I homed in on Ain Sefra to the north, I was heading past Taghit to join the road that would have earlier threaded Bechar and its developmental turmoil. The old Cadbury TV ad, '*Only the crumbliest, flakiest chocolate ...* ', always came to mind when I passed the extraordinary rock formation in the *Oued* Djedida / Ben Zireg gorge before the main road junction at Ben Zireg. It was as though some gargantuan, primordial prototype Cadbury's Flake production line had gone berserk and spilled the initial run down the hillside after getting the size parameters wrong by a factor of 10^4. The junction of this tiny, innocent little sideroad going off down to Taghit from the Bechar road was the position of a military checkpoint and the last time I was here, going south, there had been a great sucking of teeth, rolling of eyes and wringing of hands about how *très dangereuse* it all was. Even as I had noted a dusty, ordinary little civilian VW driven by a weary worker coming along from the direction

Ben Zireg's rocks – clearly Gulliver's chocolate factory for an early version of Cadbury's Flake.

of Taghit, I was being regaled with the dangers of *loups* along the way. It took my dreadful French some time to dredge the fact I was thus to face the horrors of slavering wolves, no less. In the end, it being Ramadan, the evening meal being on the way, and as I had flatly refused to countenance another traverse of what I presumed was the Bechar ringroad (or weave-your-way-through road), the portly, cheerful lieutenant, whose brief must have been to keep foreigners to the main roads only, gave in and let me go. The Ben Zireg geology and the general evidence of torrents in the past tearing through the rocks were worth the wait, however, and I camped just beyond the end of the ravine, poised for the approach of the fanged carnivores' gleaming green eyes in the night.

Now, I drove headon into a strong north-east wind that blew fine dust into the air as the road paralleled the Djebel Grouz and then wound, now north-west, around Djebel Mekter (and the border with Morocco) to Ain Sefra. Ain Sefra looked as if it had suffered this fine dust since time immemorial or been downwind of a distant volcanic eruption; everything was a kind of grey-brown colour. Recalling, from my previous visit to the town on a motorcycle 20-odd years before, that the hotel was both interesting and difficult to find, I stopped to ask a man on the pavement the way. The problems, and with the right attitude, rich comedy, of not knowing each other's language made our conversation mutually hilarious but once again the will to communicate and some vigorous gesticulating won the day. I had made my first friend at Ain Sefra.

Ain Sefra is a kind of equilateral triangle balanced on one point. The straight bit on top is the road going over the *Haut Plateau* towards Algiers, the two other sides roughly define the edges of the town. The point it's balancing on is where you start to probe around up a little winding road to find, among magnificent eucalyptus trees that must be not a jot under 130 feet high, another Pouillon gem, the Hotel Mekter. As at Kerzaz, Taghit and Beni Abbes (where Père Foucauld's influence might have been a factor), I reckoned someone associated with the building of the hotel – maybe the local imam, too, for you could see the mosque from the hill on which it stood – must have drawn up an agreement with God about keeping the sand dunes at bay. For not a hundred yards behind the hotel was a huge dune together with an entourage of lesser dunes which you could struggle up to obtain breathtaking views over the town and Djebel Aissa beyond. I thought they must have been brave to build the hotel just here with the dune so close but someone obviously knew the

history of it all and the trees would certainly help. With the early morning temperature a bracing 3.7°C, I began to realise that the *haut* of the *plateau* here was getting to be quite lofty; as I drove on north it would touch 4000 feet according to the GPS.

Again sadly underpopulated, the hotel was nonetheless clearly cherished by the manager and staff and was well kept. The swimming pool even had clear blue water in it – despite the temperature. The design was classic mischievous, keep-you-guessing Pouillon – no corridor had straight sides; recessed doorways, small buttresses, split-levels, steps up and steps down abounded. As you entered your tiny room you broke into a smile at the ingenuity. Five steps up from the door off the corridor put you into the bedroom; turn around and another five steps up to a high sliding window let you onto a balcony, by now on the roof of the corridor you had just left, and giving you a view of the pool and surrounding purple bougainvillea. Behind, tall cypresses had been planted and the razor-edged dune backed it all elegantly. I noticed too that God had also supplied a stationary, constantly regenerating, standing-wave white cloud obviously flipped skyward and maintained by one of the proliferation of scenic long-ridge *djebels* on the surrounding plateau. Despite the wind at surface level, the cloud never moved all the time I was there.

As well as the usual collection of individuals who sat around the front door gossiping in that cigarette-smoking, brown-coat-or-leather-jacketed Algerian way, Hotel Mekter had a standard-issue Algerian hotel cat, smarter than a brand-new 1000-dinar note. It knew who the new guests were, was alert to the timing of their meals and would come and sit at their feet affecting a pleading, pathetic expression that would melt them into sacrificing a choice morsel of their roast chicken at intervals. As silky-furred and cuddly a cat as I've ever seen, the procedure was clearly successful.

The high plateau that sat between the Atlas Tellien 50 miles inland from Algiers on the coast and the Atlas Saharien a couple of hundred miles farther south was not a region of scenic splendour. Devoid of anything except scrub, a rare tree or two and the very occasional low hill, its unattractiveness was exacerbated by the wind and low temperatures with which it was usually afflicted. The northern part, however, was agriculturally viable and unimaginably large single tracts – to British eyes at least – were under the plough, tiny distant green tractors driven by farmers in traditional coarse, brown, hooded cloaks doggedly at the wheel leaving immaculately precise lines of furrows in their wake. Here the roads were all tarmacked but narrow, and as usual my gentle pace was an irritant to the drivers of the yellow Peugeot taxis that flew at frightening speed along them. They were good to follow through the villages, though, for they knew where the 'sleeping-policeman' bumps were; plus pedestrians kept out of their way. Inevitably, the rearmost row of passengers would turn round to look at the curious foreign-registered vehicle that had been blocking their progress. No wonder it's slow, the driver's on the wrong side, they seemed to say, straight-faced, in response to my tentative wave.

The 165 miles from Ain Sefra to Saida seemed a lot longer, and with the temperature and the lack of any place to camp unobtrusively in these parts I was into hotel night-stop mode now for what remained of the journey. Saida's Forsane Hotel was definitely not Pouillon, a functional stack of boxes apparently trying, without much success, to poach Pompidou Centre panache by having most of its plumbing, air-conditioning and associated pipe work externally strapped to the building. Functional, though, it was; with exceptionally hot water and a sinister hole in the bathroom ceiling above the wash basin as though a previous guest had responded to the hot-tap's temperature by going straight into low earth-orbit.

The Forsane was also enlivened by its Security Manager, a nervous, manic, small man who lost no time in telling me my safety was in capable hands and, tapping his revolver, which he did every 10 seconds or so, I could rest easy for the night. This not being an area noted for any security issues, I did wonder if he was a victim of what, on earlier trips, I had dubbed the frequently-manifested 'WASP-therefore-TISP' syndrome (We Are Security People therefore There Is a Security Problem). He inserted himself into the Mercedes while I was unloading and began turning things over which was not especially welcome and, next morning, still brandishing his revolver, tried to pressure me into giving someone a lift to somewhere. I always felt guilty about not giving people lifts – language, pace, room, stops for photography etc – but this time less so. I felt he must have been an understudy for Pink Panther's Superintendent Dreyfus or indeed been the character's inspiration and prototype.

My route to Algiers from here was like a right-pointing arrow – east to Tiaret, on to Bou Saada where I hoped to get some special photographs and then north-west up to the capital. I phoned Annabelle at SNCM London again and her goodwill and helpfulness had been torpedoed by the usual (in my experience) bloody-minded response from SNCM in Marseilles. When I had had my ticket stolen in 2003 I phoned SNCM to cancel it the better part of a week before the due sailing date and asked if they could give me credit to get another one – especially since my funds had been stolen too. No, I would have to wait a full year before I could get a refund and what else had been stolen was my problem not theirs. Thus I now found I could not benefit from Annabelle making a provisional booking for my open ticket and the maximum time between provisional and confirmation that they could allow was 24 hours. So I had to sock in to the high-price Algiers environment and if things didn't work out I could be waiting a week to get on a ferry.

In terms of, as I said to Geoff on one trip, 'scenic grandeur' – a term used only if the opposite prevailed – Saida to Tiaret to Bou Saada was similarly uninspiring. Northern Algeria was not like Algeria south of the Atlas Saharien, and grey-brown prevailed both

Lada Niva and
kit, in need of
attention.
25°15'N, 0°29'E;
buyer collects.

literally and in terms of mood. A Lada Niva came from the other direction on the narrow road and a smile lightened my disposition. Hassi bel Gebbour is not much more than a collection of shacks (one of which, vitally, is part of a fuel station), and is situated at the remote, very sandy end of the long, 357km Gassi Touil corridor south from the oil megapolis of Hassi Messaoud. 'HBG', as we called it, population probably 15-20, appeared to have let the 20th century pass it by and was unaware there was a 21st. Driving what was then a spanking new Discovery, Geoff and I looked down somewhat on the humble Ladas that flourished once in Algeria. Later we saw two together. 'Ah,' said Geoff, 'Off, no doubt, to the Hassi bel Guebbour Lada Niva Owners' Club annual whist drive and dinner-dance!' A quaintly hilarious thought, but not fair, really, for the Niva had a basically sound spec; the suspension, though, lacked articulation and was brutally stiff. Poor Niva; some still survived and did well enough in their hard, bouncy way. Well, most of them. I'd seen the remains of one out on the Tanezrouft.

My mind was still in turmoil about the G-Wagen. The more I thought about it the less certain I was about even entertaining a sale in Algeria. Though there should be nothing insuperable about the logistics of getting my kit home without the vehicle, I could imagine it burgeoning into a huge bureaucratic production; whilst the customs pantomime over disposing of a temporarily imported vehicle could only be guessed at.

In preparation for a possible sale I had phoned Rachid Benyahia with a view to meeting him at Ain Oussera en route to Bou Saada, but now the schedule was getting tight too – especially if I had to allow time to go directly to the SNCM shipping office in Algiers immediately on arrival. I agonised. Or went through the motions of agonising, for I knew what I had to do.

It was now nine o'clock so I stopped, stepped out into the biting cold wind and tried to make contact on the satellite phone above the racket of passing trucks and cars. Rachid was more than a little put out that I wanted to cancel our meeting. Unusually so, I thought. I mentioned customs implications and I had the impression that he had something up his sleeve; something instinct told me I would not wish to get involved with. I said time was tight, that I would make contact when I got to the UK and we could examine how best to go forward: maybe me delivering the vehicle to Marseilles for him to pick up. Still he demurred. He had cancelled a trip to Algiers to meet me, he said. I felt bad about it.

'Rachid,' I said, 'I'm really sorry. But I can't make it. I'll be in touch. Promise.'

218

18. Casbah

Hachette and Nagel produced proper guide books written by people, teams of people, who had been there and also knew their stuff. Recently-aired stories about the genesis of some of the current rash of travellers' guides leaves you agape – and cautious about picking through what is often also some very good material. I was approached for tips after one of my journeys by a relative of a young girl who had been commissioned to 'do the chapter on Algeria' in one such series (Algeria in the one chapter!) and was horrified to learn she had never visited the country before. Steeped in history, different cultures, extremes of landscape, terrain and climate, extending over no less than 18 degrees of latitude and bigger than the whole of western Europe ... I often wondered how the write-up turned out. Her nubile demeanour and the size of her backpack would doubtless get her through.

Apart from extended walkabouts in Algiers and Oran (Oh, *dangereuse!* they said), I had only fractional, drive-through knowledge of narrow ribbons of Algeria north of the Atlas. But though it obviously lacked the unique grandeur of, and was quite different from, the Sahara, the region had a scale and character that contrived to rise above the fragmented initial impression of haphazard shabbiness, erratic development, bustle and the overall ambience of grey-brown dust left by some of the minor towns along its routes. The great sweep of the hills, the beauty of its natural vegetation, the grace of the agriculture and nature's beneficence in response to man's industry, however, conveyed a calm and tranquillity that soothed the traveller.

Hachette's *guide bleu* and Nagel's award-winning Encyclopedia-guide on Algeria, precious 1986 and 1973 copies of which I still had, enthused about Bou Saada and a 'Pouillon special' hotel, one of his best with extraordinary gardens: a popular weekend resort for *Algerois* of the time. Despite being now tied to a schedule, I was ever willing to postpone what might be considered the end of the trip and decided that Bou Saada and its Le Caid hotel should be an en route photographic assignment.

In passing – lest I accede to accusations of rose-tinted spectacles or qualify for Gilbert and Sullivan's *Mikado* Lord High Executioner list (the man who 'praises every country but his own') – I found, with these much-respected guidebooks, comfort and justification that Nagel's observation on Algerians was very much in accord with my own. After listing individuals from guides to waiters, to booksellers, to landladies, to 'children at (Tipasa's) Tomb of the Christian Woman', Nagel observes: 'All of them have shown a friendliness and helpfulness which the authors ... have rarely found equalled in any other country.'

And: 'Whether (the visitor) is dealing with a taxi driver, a student of progressive ideas, a civil servant in Algiers, one of the village elders in some remote part of the country or the ordinary man in the street in one of the towns, he will find everywhere the same eagerness to express in concrete form the traditional hospitality of the Arab.'

I drove the long route to Bou Saada, still feeling bad about having to disappoint Rachid Benyahia at Ain Oussera but nevertheless certain I had done the right thing. The policeman at the big roundabout on the northern outskirts of Bou Saada, as if he knew what Nagel expected of him, could hardly have been more welcoming or helpful when I asked where the Hotel Le Caid was. Clear instructions, a big smile and the offer to accompany me there to ensure I found it, were part of the package. As was, the next day when I drove north, a wave and instant recognition.

Arriving with high expectations, alas and agonisingly, the hotel was a desperate disappointment. Not merely from the point of view of my personal comfort – for it later donated a stomach bug to the like of which I had not succumbed on any previous trip. It was the general state of dereliction. Gardens, lauded in the guidebooks, that had reverted to

a dense, impenetrable jungle; a one-time swimming pool that now resembled a cesspit and all surrounded by a rusting chain-link fence breached only by a rickety locked gate. I should have been more tactful but, inside, I remonstrated with the under-manager and showed him what the guidebooks of 20 years before had had to say. It was the Tidikelt syndrome all over again; 'security' problems, few visitors, so no money: and staff cuts. It was heartbreaking. As if this were not enough, he showed me photographs of a disastrous fire they had had in 1996. The

Pouillon in tune: modern profile, yes; traditional colour, correct; split levels, of course; Algerian hand-painted tiles – naturellement

uncharacteristic offhand manner and obvious disillusion of the staff were palpable.

But all was not lost. The building was there. Not in the same league as Timimoun's Gourara by any means, it was still a most attractive design with considerable potential and had not slid irreparably downhill like the Boustane at El Golea where, by a ratio of probably a thousand to one, the guests were outnumbered by the mosquitoes. The Hotel Le Caid would come back in due course.

•   •   •

No such cause for sadness prevailed at the Algiers El Djazair. Brimming with guests, energy and professionalism, success shouted from every corner. I had gone in virtually on bended knees. Phoning ahead a couple a days before, the El Djazair had had no room for the day I required; nor had the Aurassi, the huge, boxy architectural anomaly on the hill that Algerians humorously called *le climatiseur* (the air-conditioner) which indeed it resembled. The location was critical. First I had to get to the SNCM offices at the port, probably on foot, to nail the ferry booking – an area so congested and unparkable even taxis had to go into a kind of holding orbit while you got off and conducted your business. Second, it was vital to have a secure car park for the Merc, and third, it was important to be near the port for when I actually went for the ferry early in the morning. As sometimes happened, appearing in person at the El Djazair's reception mysteriously produced a room. I was pathetically grateful; not least because the Le Caid's farewell bug had left me with a fever and needing something flat and soft to lie on for quite a protracted period. Russ Middleton at the Embassy had nobly offered me accommodation but his location was miles away and being ill as a house-guest is awkward for all the parties concerned.

For various reasons my one-night stay plan had to fold because I couldn't get on the next ship out and had to take one that would involve three nights at the hotel. Despite the unplanned cost, fate was actually arranging a bonus for it would have invaluable spin-offs.

Twenty-four hours can produce remarkable changes when combined with the miracles the human body can bring about when it fires up the immune system and an appropriate brew of antibodies. When my fever and wobbliness had subsided I went downstairs and before long was accosted effusively by someone calling me 'Colonel'. Said Chitour, an Algerian journalist, was something of a human dynamo and apparently remembered me from the Michael Palin filming session four years earlier in the Hoggar. In the course of our animated exchanges I had mentioned my attempts to get some interest in a Sahara Protected Area from the Algerian authorities – bearing in mind what was happening in Libya and the cultural devastation that had taken place in Tunisia with the excessive inflow of mass European tourism. Chitour enthused about the idea and immediately reeled off who I should see and where. With the ship now a day and half off, I had the time.

The first person I phoned was Su Sheppard at the Embassy. No, there was nothing yet on the maps but she'd make a special effort to elicit action on the grounds that I was shortly to jump onto a northbound ship. Internally I fumed; it was now a full month since they had been taken from me and we appeared to be getting nowhere. Darkly, I assumed the Embassy were getting brassed off with the whole saga and were not doing anything very energetic to get results, but in fairness the delays were almost certainly further down the line and constant badgering can often be counterproductive.

It was not a question of cost. It was not as if the maps could be replaced. All the confiscated sheets were now out of print and unobtainable. More than that, they bore navigational notes and data on a succession of journeys dating back 27 years. I had a mental picture of the maps lying, probably damaged and creased, on some dusty shelf in Tamanrasset where they will have been sent for examination by the chief gendarme of the *wilaya*. It all depended if any action had been taken by the Ministry of Foreign Affairs in response to Su's letter; and how far down the line the instructions, if any, had got.

While she was on, was there any remote chance, I asked, that she – or anyone in the Embassy – could fix an interview with the people Said Chitour had mentioned? She promised to get back to me.

Monument des Martyrs overlooks the bay in Algiers, sombre reminder of the carnage of the war for independence 1954-62.

It's an odd thing but you seldom feel better than you do after feeling bad and my antibodies, or whatever it was, had not only fixed the Le Caid bug but put a spring in my step. I now had a couple or three hours spare and did not want to waste them. For reasons only of time (for I had walked there before and it had taken nearly three quarters of an hour), I got the same rickety taxi that had taken me to the ferry people, SNCM, the day before to take me to the Monument des Martyrs that stood dramatically on the hillside overlooking Algiers and the harbour below. Impressive, sweeping architecture sat atop a poignant and thought-provoking museum of the war of independence; a war that started, countrywide on 1st November 1954 and lasted until Algerian independence was granted in 1962. With any knowledge of Algeria's history it is impossible not to see both sides of the conflict.

Few subjects tap all-or-nothing, black-or-white oratory more predictably than

colonialism's pros and cons, yet nowhere could there be a greater contrast, and mix, of the good and bad than in Algeria. The jaw-dropping arrogance of the geo-political carve-ups of the mid to late 19th century led in due course to genuine nation-building, coherence and the creation of a national infrastructure, albeit often against a background of assumed superiority, lack of consultation and an all-too-frequent insensitivity to local cultural issues.

Thus Algeria as a country was created by the French, starting in 1830, its borders expanding south, in effect, to fill the vast area that yawned between it and other putatively more desirable tracts of Africa that other colonial powers had their foot on at the time. It subsumed, without regard, fiercely individual tribal entities such as the Berber in the north, the Chaamba and the Touareg in the south, yet the French prevailed – at a horrifying cost in lives on both sides for the 'pacification' process. They made Algeria a country, they created an infrastructure, they administered it, painstakingly mapped it – including its vast achingly beautiful deserts – they made roads and, though the much promoted trans-Saharan link never did get built, railways too.

And above all, they loved it. They lavished French culture, architecture, agriculture, viniculture upon the country. It was part of France. It was beautiful, ordered and it worked. And as night followed day, as with the British in India over a more extended timescale, the country they had created decided that if it was to be a country it would be so on its own. If the pacification of the fledgling country in the 19th and early 20th centuries had cost bloodshed, it was nothing compared with the scale, ferocity and hideous savagery of the war for independence that concluded in 1962.

The museum at the Monument des Martyrs spares no detail. Photographs of death at its most brutal are on display. Relics and war machinery are there too. It is moving and food for deep thought. At the most basic and oversimplified level you can understand the French, who had poured so much work, love, planning and application into making Algeria a coherent country, not wanting to relinquish what they had created. And this in an age where colonialism – rightly or wrongly – was virtually the norm. And you can, equally, well understand the Algerians' explosive resolve to right the wrongs, to avenge the arrogance and seize control of their own soil from the colonialists who, whatever benefits they had brought, had taken so much – not least a sense of individual pride.

If this is all a sobering and frightening lesson, how amazing is the steady emergence of reconciliation and cooperation 50 years later. Doubts, grudges and some bitterness linger on in pockets and the slate is not totally clean, but the progress into the 21st century is mature, pragmatic and redolent, at last, of mutual respect. No less amazing, and worth repeating, is the inherent, default, niceness of the Algerians. It is worth repeating what, only 10 years after the end of the conflict, Nagel observes: 'All of them have shown a friendliness and helpfulness which the authors of the Guide have rarely found equalled in any other country.'

•　　　•　　　•

Algiers by night. Ferry docks centre left, Monument des Martyrs upper right. Le climatiseur, the Aurassi Hotel (inset), had its uses as a perch to take the picture.

Su rang back. Rachida Benyahia, the Ambassador's secretary (no relation, I assumed, of Rachid Benyahia at Ain Oussera), had arranged an appointment at the Ministry of Culture for the next day which I looked forward to with hopeful anticipation. Moreover Su recommended also a contact who would show me round the casbah. 'The casbah in Algiers' is almost enough of a cliché to make you smile. Yet it is in fact old Algiers *par excellence* and of fascinating historical interest: an apparent jumble of old buildings crushed together on the hillside overlooking the harbour; tiny, steep, narrow walkways overhung by jutting upper stories; dark alleyways with steps to trip over in the dim light; almost subterranean shops. A disorientating maze of narrow streets. Minuscule mosques cheek-by-jowl with shops and bakeries, the occasional house of extraordinary artistic merit, and wrecks that have collapsed in the rains or earthquakes over the centuries.

Unfortunately tales have grown around the casbah, which, like many, doubtless have a basis of fact, however thin – a den of thieves and muggers was the overview of the taxi driver-cum-self-appointed guide who took me briefly around the last time I was here. So paranoid was he that he concealed a cudgel in his jacket and bade me similarly keep my camera out of sight lest it be snatched by a passing ne'er-do-well. Camera-snatching is something of a sport among a devoted few. I had already experienced it on a grand scale. In 1990 when Geoff Renner and I arrived off the ferry in a Discovery loaned by Land Rover only to make our own discovery, namely that between leaving the UK and arriving at the port a new rule prevailed: Brits needed visas.

The tiny Sidi Abdellah mosque in the casbah, built in the Ottoman period. Not a thief or mugger in sight. The lad in the red is wearing an England shirt. Football: panacea internationale.

Compelled to return to Marseilles to get one from the consulate there, we left the vehicle in the police compound at the port. On our return the vehicle had been broken into and three sets of camera gear and a (then) high-tech GPS unit taken, loaned also. I met someone who, in Oran, had simply been standing outside his hotel, when a lightning-quick young man scorched by and whipped the camera out of his hand.

I had half expected these dire warnings to be complemented by hostile looks and snarling groups of delinquents, but the people me and my nervous taxi man met

Solemn, dignified reminder of the war for independence. Memorial to Ali la Pointe where he and his colleagues died.

seemed casual, helpful, friendly and not specially interested in what I was or was not carrying. Off the bustling main-street market the steep winding alleyways were quiet, rather like the old town in Tripoli.

Variously chronicled as a one-time thug and petty criminal, viewers of the harrowing 1965 Gillo Pontecorvo film *The Battle for Algiers* will recall Ali la Pointe, the Algerian guerrilla leader, now folk hero, cornered in the casbah, refusing to surrender and being bombed out by the French paras taking his son Omar and, reputedly, 20 others with him. A solemn memorial with a plaque and Algerian flag marks the spot where it all took place on 8 October 1957.

For me, a year later, It was time to get a proper look at the casbah. And Su's contact, Mr Boualem, was the man. Of Boualem Belachehab's' many attributes and talents, one of the most immediately notable, perhaps, was the fact that he seemed to be a walking tranquilliser. He exuded a calm good nature that rolled over you and over those we were

Memorial to colonial insensitivity. The casbah's Ketchaoua mosque was taken over and turned into the Cathédrale St Philippe in 1832 but restored to Moslem use in 1962. Superb baguettes are happier reminder of French influence.

Memorial to colonial presence 1830-1930; House of the Centenary opposite the Ketchaoua mosque elegantly reflects local style. Architect Claro, built 1930; now an office of the Culture Department of Algiers.

Boualem Belachehab, guide extraordinaire, human tranquilliser, who seemed to know everyone in the casbah. Behind, the Djamaa Djedid (New Mosque) built in ... 1660 (!) for the janissaries, a kind of Ottoman Revolutionary Guard.

later to meet. He was in charge of the National Museum of Antiquities and Islamic Art just down the hill from the El Djazair – a jewel box of astonishingly fine work, minuscule paintings, manuscripts, carvings and regal attire adorned with unimaginably fine embroidery in silver thread, but as, alas, is sometimes the case, a somewhat bare and underused jewel box. That it existed at all, like the Bardo Museum not far away, was cause for small celebration and hope that its contents would be preserved for future generations and visitors to see.

Though he must have done, there was no evidence that Mr Boualem had done all this a hundred times before; mostly with groups. I was very lucky to have him to myself. We caught a bus to a strategically convenient jumping off point and he strolled me through countless winding alleyways and streets, past tiny shops, a craftsman hammering out those great brass trays that hold the giant 'mutton-grab' meals of rice, couscous, chicken and lamb on occasions of communal celebration. We met (another) friend of his, in front of his deeply carved front doorway with his two little girls, who recorded Algerian popular rai music on CDs.

Doubtless it was Mr Boualem's aura but everywhere we went people were quiet, friendly and relaxed. How could these same people – or people just like them – turn into elbowing, pushing, shoving, petty-minded, dedicated queue-jumpers when, not 400 metres from here, they awaited processing at the port to board the ferry? When I went to the port (as I would in 36 hours' time) I concentrated on relaxing and trying not to let it all bug me. But it never really worked. Especially as, this time, I would be taken apart and the Merc probed by customs who suspected I was, with my neat boxes, an archaeologist smuggling fossils out of the country. A change from being a map-toting spy, I supposed.

But for now, the calm of the casbah and the beneficent Mr Boualem prevailed in this oldest part of Algiers. As the Libyans had done in old Tripoli and had started to do in old Ghadames – and the Saudis had criminally failed to do in old Jeddah – I hoped the Algiers

Casbah shop. The care, the industry, the pride. What ever time does he have to get up in the morning to prepare all this?

planners would cherish the casbah, invest in it, renovate it and keep the bulldozers and diggers out forever.

19. Clancy Woods

Ten to one. Not the time or the odds on a racehorse but my preferred minimum ratio, when on a trip (15:1 is better), of NUTS to HUTS – Nights Under The Stars to nights spent in hotels. But I guess after weeks camping in the desert, as uniquely and ineradicably uplifting to the soul as that is, you do get to appreciate (with a desert trip's inevitable logistic limitations) what hotels, however basic, have to offer – the practical things like the shower (even the sorry dribble you often get), a laundry or at least a place to wash and, with suitable ingenuity, hang out to dry, your clothes.

As I have already remarked, I have the sense of wonder of a nerdy 13-year old and regard myself thrice-blessed as a result. You notice things. I am fascinated by how things are; and how, if applicable, they are made – anything from Velcro to the Millau bridge. The grandeur or neat perception of the overall concept and then the crucial interplay of function, ergonomics, aesthetics and the astonishing ingenuity and technical skill – invariably undervalued – that goes into production techniques. (Have you ever considered the precision, stamping tolerances and tool-life involved in producing the little groove that makes an aluminium ring-pull drinks can work – and be as easily opened by a beefy

The El Djazair hotel, Algiers.

construction worker as by a child? Or, more challenging still, a steel can with a pull-off lid?). Cars, pens, furniture, saucepans, buildings, plastic mouldings, architecture; even the ordinary is interesting. The best is astonishing and brings on that slow smile.

And, of course, when considering NUTS and HUTS, an all-enveloping human living-experience like a hotel sharpens the perceptions a little. That the original, creative and sympathetic designs of Fernand Pouillon should resonate with my consuming curiosity was inevitable.

From the outside the *El Djazair* hotel in Algiers looked competent and functional enough, sheltering behind a wall and trees of some kind on the bustling, traffic-saturated Avenue Souidani Boudjemaa in the busiest part of the city, perched on a hill overlooking the harbour and distant Mediterranean. Traditional early-colonial architecture, with echoes of aspirational baroque twiddly bits but nothing to get too excited about. For me, the meaningful security gate and walled-in, guarded car park had been the initial attraction. In all honesty I had never otherwise been entirely at ease in five-star hotels. A bit over the top, the ones I'd seen. And then I went inside.

Even then the detail did not hit you immediately. Yes, a room please. One, maybe two nights. Depends on bookings on the ferry. Passport? Yes, of course. Can you change dinars? Understand there is a *guardien* on the car park all the time? No, I can carry the bag OK. What time is the ... my goodness, that tile work is ... ah, OK, so I have time for a shower then ... astonishing. Six squat rectangular pillars in the huge reception area kept the ceiling from hitting the floor. Each side of each pillar was covered in a separate and unique collection of hand-painted Algerian tile-work; intricate designs that had clearly been tailored to the size and shape of the pillars. And as I looked up it was clear the ceiling plasterwork too was something special. Ethnic, Maghreb, Spanish-Moorish, I wasn't an expert but certainly not out of a box in a U-build hotel kit. Deeply carved dark wood fronted the counters.

Reception (above) and conference room (below) at the El Djazair. Tilework, plasterwork, design. Someone took a cultural ambience on board, dreamed it, and drew it.

All this had been the first time I visited. I had been taking photographs. Now, three years later, the receptionist behind the information counter lit up. 'Ah! The photos! Welcome!'

'Halem!' I said. I remembered his name because it was similar to that of a colleague in the Air Force. But how many hundreds, thousands even, of blurry white faces had passed his desk in three years? Groucho at Timimoun was a delightful surprise after all that time. Here it was little short of amazing.

But no less so than the hotel's reception rooms when, almost deferentially, you began to look around. Hotel Saint George, 1889, is

232

'Hard to believe this is a hotel,' I said. 'It's more like a palace.' 'Yes,' he said, 'It was.' (0 .3", f8, 400 ASA, set, 17-40mm lens at 17mm. No tripod, just Fuji's simple beanbag pressed against a pillar.)

where it began, or rather was the first milestone from its distant origins as Palace of the Dey of Algiers to charismatic hotel of choice in the centre of the capital. Initially residence for guests of British and French in Algiers at the time, it became a hotel in name in 1889 and a popular winter resort for Europeans boasting a prestigious visitors' book of which it is still proud: the King of Greece, Rudyard Kipling, Winston Churchill are names casually dropped in the brochures. From November 1942 to December 1943 General Dwight Eisenhower, C-in-C of Allied Expeditionary Forces in North Africa maintained his headquarters at the Saint George.

Severe bomb damage later in the war led to its closure and it was not reopened again until 1948. Further expansion was called for in 1974, and this time the magic touch of architect Pouillon was brought to bear. Proud of its heritage to a man, the staff lose no opportunity to remind guests that the place was once the Saint George. I suppose after time in the desert I was ready to be impressed. I

Heads of state would feel at ease – and honoured. The special reception room at the El Djazair.

was.

There was much on my mind, however, in the dwindling time left before I got the ferry for Marseilles. I fervently hoped that before I left we would get to some kind of definitive rung on the ladder towards getting my maps back from the Algerian authorities – whoever it was that was now involved. Less obvious but almost as important, I also needed to nail the provenance of 'the letter' sent to the Embassy (from no-one to nobody in particular?), the broad drift of which I had been told but, with its talk of '... *be removed from the country'* had to be pinned down and expunged at an official level if there was ever to be a chance of my visiting the country again. I was, for heaven's sake, a bona fide traveller and not a spy and someone somewhere must have the guts to admit the mistake.

And then there was the visit to the Ministry of Culture to squeeze in as well. Tomorrow at 10. Luckily I had brought a copy of my own 'letter' – a letter and paper of a different sort altogether – and it would be good to talk, face to face, to someone about my proposals.

In the meantime, with their permission, I roamed the public rooms and grounds of the El Djazair with my now trusty and much-loved Canon EOS 5D. Its superb wide-angle zoom captured the scale, the detail, the lighting and the elegance of this extraordinary building and my personally-voted best accessory of the entire millennium – the £10 Fuji squashy bean-bag that could be dumped on, rested against, or cushioned-against-lumps from almost anything – enabled me to get a steady-camera shot without a tripod.

I had the impression the staff were used to visitors, open mouthed, traipsing around with little-bitty digital cameras but the EOS 5D seemed to come across as a 'serious' camera and caught the interest of the people who made the El Djazair work. One, in the dining room, where there was a whole 19th-century fishermen's wharf scene in hand-painted tiles, was doubly interested.

'Ah,' he said, 'You are just like that American film actor. You know, the one in that ... '

'American film actor?!'

'Yes! Photographer. Tall, thin, the hair also, little bit grey at edges. You know him. Clancy Woods.'

'Say again? Who? Clancy Woods?'

'Yes. Also in western movies. But this was film about bridges. Wooden bridges, I think.'

From his description I was getting a hazy picture of that film called something-or-other Bridges. Not Toko-Ri or River Kwai, not that old, but another one. Yes, that was it; tall guy, thin, lined face, greying hair, taking pictures? Ah, yes; pictures of what's-her-name, Beryl Street? No, Meryl Streep: *Bridges of Madison County*. Then – oh, good heavens – it dawned on me. 'Clin', with French pronunciation would come out 'clan'. Elided with 'teaswood' or 'teastwood' plus some minor desecration of consonants and my lousy hearing that would be it: Clint Eastwood. *Clint Eastwood* for Pete's sake! Hey; cool! We both fell about laughing.

But I left the dining room walking a little taller, a shade more impressive, a whisker more dignified, eyes narrowed and steely, holding my camera with a certain dignity. Pale rider with a Canon. Yes; the new me: Clancy Woods. I may even cancel my order for the brown trilby and bull-whip.

20. Algeria, the uncut gem

Algeria is for the most part, a jewel box. Let it not become a Pandora's box opened to let in foreign hordes and let out a putrefaction of overcrowding and cultural pollution. Xenophobic hyperbole? Misanthropic excess? Go to a cinema to see a good film. Then double or treble the audience in the same space; and throw in a bunch of rowdies. Look at the picture below. A small town west of Algiers. Then think of Benidorm.

I recall the kindness of the people and the tranquillity in Timimoun, then recollect my experience of Hammamet and elsewhere in Tunisia: politely declining the offer of a flower from a 12-year old boy and being told to fuck off; being approached by male prostitutes repeatedly in Tunisian hotels; small boys at Sbeitla's Roman site throwing a broken bottle under the wheels of my vehicle; children making rude European gestures and throwing stones at the sight of an approaching car with foreign number plates. This is absorbed popular reaction to, and learned from, the behaviour and tastes of overseas visitors.

When, in 1998, I visited the remote oasis of Kufra in Libya, the country was emerging from 30 years' isolation from the west. The children in the street were well behaved, shy, respectful and gave me, as a visitor, little gifts. It was almost heartbreaking; for its innocence, for how precious it was and for the integrity of basic Arab family values.

Is there no crime against foreigners in Algeria? Yes, there is. With their unemployment there is crime against quite a few people in Algeria. I was comprehensively robbed at El Golea in 2002 by a teenager at a filling station, and the kids in the villages near the Tunisian border throw stones at vehicles. But the general situation is nothing like tourist-saturated Tunisia.

The little town in the picture here is almost too perfect to let any developer set eyes on; what is its future?

Tiny town west of Algiers. Would you dare show this picture to a 'developer'? Market gardens within 100 yards of the shore. Bowling alley, disco and a tasteful casino should fit in there nicely. Maybe couple of hotel tower blocks.

Local lads fishing off the beach at Tipasa. The almost empty Hotel de Baie lies behind.

The current semi-vacuum of tourism has left Tipasa shore unmolested; an idyllic bay with local lads fishing off the beach. For how long? The legacy of what the French achieved over 130 years has, in the main, been preserved. It must be cherished and brought back to life. Carefully. The Algerian Government has been mature in its approach to what it inherited. Streets have been renamed but nothing has been knocked down out of post-colonial pique. Let this attitude be applauded and nurtured.

Whilst I might not have recently been seen wearing a black turban, a beard, a wild stare or cradling an AK, nor am I advocating a draconian, neo-Taleban excision of western modes of relaxation. Nevertheless, uncomfortable things have to be said. A glance at Europe's more popular resorts hints at what they are. And even that is not the whole story. What Europeans do in Europe, arguably, is their affair but to export or emulate this for commercial reasons in countries of a different, more conservative, culture is another matter if that culture is not to be 'diluted' – to use the most tactful word.

Internationalism is a fine thing but it doesn't mean everyone has to be the same. 'The West' has no right to establish or expect a monoculture; nor is it remotely desirable. 'Rich' and 'big' isn't always best and countries aspiring to increase tourist volume for economic, or reasons of diversification, would surely be wise to consider carefully how they do it and whether to adopt alternative roads to the well-trodden one of aping the US concepts of 'luxury', 'entertainment' and what to many will simply seem excess.

Algeria is particularly fortunate in being financially very well off thanks to its oil and gas revenues so can afford to be picky. It also has a multitude of unrivalled, and so far mostly unspoiled, locations. It has existed without tourism's assumed benefits for the last nearly two or three decades while it was wracked with internal unrest and extremism so there is surely no rush to tumble into superficially-considered development in this field. Caution – and a hard, close look at Tunisia, the Greek islands and southern Spain – must arguably be the watchword before any gates are flung too wide. The main heading is diversification; the subtext is protection.

Visitors' calling cards.

So what of the Sahara? Development? Protection? Not exactly overrun with visitors at this writing – albeit enough to trigger amber warnings. But there, in those wide spaces, is a

legacy unique not just to Algeria but to the whole planet. A wilderness known to few but so pristine and unspoiled that a simple awareness of it must be the first step. An awareness less easy for Algerians against a historical background of the great desert's perceived dangers and hostility. Is it all uniquely beautiful? No. But the pictures in this book touch fractionally on some areas that are.

Who is going to harm it; what is there to damage? Sadly, the answers to both these questions are on the record: yahoo motor rallies tearing through sub-Saharan villages, leaving wrecked vehicles, litter and mayhem behind in the desert; tourists crowbarring rocks bearing rock art away from their original sites – and litter, litter, litter. And the cultural damage which is, quite simply, irreversible: big groups, loud, inappropriately dressed, often insensitive to local customs, codes and behaviour.

What can be done? What *should* be done? Nothing more revolutionary than moderation should be the aim. And that – one of the uncomfortable things that have to be said – means keeping out the wrong people. Understandably, Algeria has plans for redevelopment of their once-active tourist industry, has allocated funds and set targets. Only this way will its string of hotels be revitalised. It can also be a source of sorely-needed employment. But it has no need to lure the masses. Its culture and its landscapes are far more important than that. Check out Oman.

•　　　•　　　•

Mademoiselle Hebache Nadhera looked too young and fragile for her job description. Sitting behind her desk in her black *hijab* head-scarf, modestly dressed in the Muslim fashion, with a peach-perfect complexion, her profile reminded me of those smooth-contoured Russian dolls. I had been met by Mr Khalfaoui who took me upstairs to Mlle Nadhera's office. She held the position of *Directeur du Patrimoine Culturel, Ministère de la Culture* – Director of Cultural Heritage, no less, at the Ministry of Culture.

It was more than just politeness. They understood my concern for the Sahara.

Fragile. Delicate.
Handle with care.
Silence please.
No noisy groups.
No litter. Tidied,
rearranged by
the management
weekly. Perfection
assured. Views of
Garet el Djenoun
(right, 2330m):
no charge. Please
leave only
footprints or
tyre marks.
Moist eyes
permitted.

Mr Khalfaoui listened intently, translating for Mlle Nadhera. I told them the time was now, before the improving security situation permitted an influx. I told them of Tunisia and Mr K permitted himself a just perceptible nodding smile of recognition. I told them of theft and vandalism of rock art in the Akakus region of Libya, and in Algeria's own Tassili National Park. I highlighted, as tactfully as I could, the present apparently irrational regulations applying on the road to Tamanrasset and drew the distinction between protection and simply fencing everything off so that nobody could see anything. I said that the aim must be to ensure only well-equipped, properly motivated people had access and that they should, when so vetted, be able to visit remote areas on their own if they wished – as if, you might say, they were visiting a mosque or cathedral. No-one goes to the Scottish highlands, the Alps or a US National Park to be escorted by a clock-watching guide. It can work.

'This is not America,' Mr Khalfaoui said. To my secret delight! Good on you, I thought. I explained I was making the point that safety need not be compromised by being on your own and that one of the main attractions of such vast wilderness was the utter peace and solitude. The visitor equipment criteria should include satellite phone, EPIRB, laid down minima on water and fuel, a vehicle inspection followed by issue of a Permit to Travel. And all preceded by payment, at visa-application stage, of a Security Bond costing in the region of €1500-2000, 90 per cent refundable on exit without incident. Mr Khalfaoui's eyebrows rose with a hint of approval. Within me there were reservations that here we were, back to

the crude default situation of what the excellent Mr Jones, my economics master at Bristol Grammar School, used to term rationing-by-the-purse. Statistically and demographically, though, it is what seemed to work. Older, more responsible people would have the funds and discipline to abide by the guidelines and prerequisites. A way would have to be found for the young, adventurous and no less motivated and appreciative, to take part; responsibly.

€2000 would ensure visitors took care to prepare properly and not invoke an 'incident' that would scotch their 90 per cent refund. An 'incident' would include breaking down and leaving a vehicle in the desert; plus the customs implications of not re-exporting. Abiding by the demanding equipment scales would similarly make certain they paid attention and took care. Auto rallies and *raids* would be banned. The size of groups would be limited, as in certain US recreational reserves. There would be multilingual handouts regarding total prohibition of litter, a simple briefing on local customs and sensitivities – all at the visa-application stage.

None of this would be onerous to those who had the right attitude and the breadth of vision to see what mistakes had been made elsewhere in the world. None of this would be hard to organise or implement. The sheer size of Algeria is always a challenge but implementation would be simply a matter of communication to police posts, army units and gendarmeries that manned checkpoints in the area affected. And communicating, above all, to visa-issuing consulates. But *'area affected'*? What area?

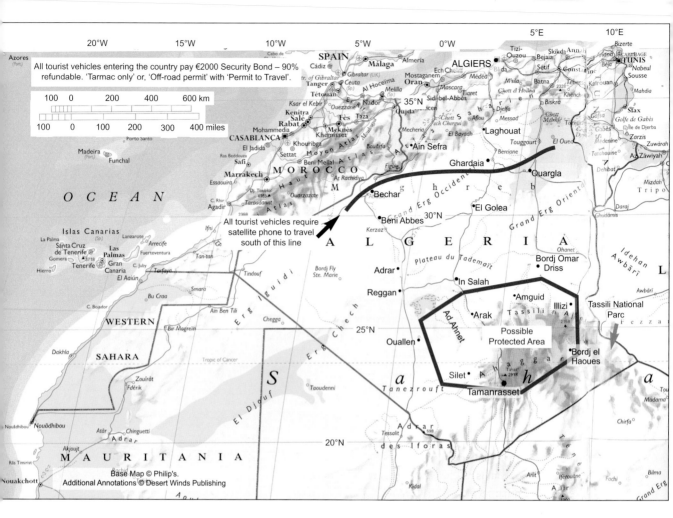

All tourist vehicles entering the country pay €2000 Security Bond – 90% refundable. 'Tarmac only' or, 'Off-road permit' with 'Permit to Travel'.

All tourist vehicles require satellite phone to travel south of this line

Possible Protected Area

Base Map © Philip's.
Additional Annotations © Desert Winds Publishing

Protected Area proposal: initial submission.

This: the red polygon. At least provisionally. Defining the extent of the protected area is at once easy and hard. Where, literally, do you draw the line? The area here is reasonable and pragmatic. It would be a start. There would be others; pockets, but to take a stand on this area would indicate intent. Tourist vehicles travelling south of the wavy red line parallel to the Atlas Mountains would need to carry satellite phones.

As much as our language differences would permit – my poor French and Mr Khafaoui's far better English – I desperately wanted to get across to Mlle Nadhera my awareness that I might be seen as another busy-body foreigner telling them what they should do. My concern was heartfelt and genuine.

They listened and I think we had made contact. They even nodded when I brought up the subject of 'guides'. Not really guides, most of them; just drivers with patchy knowledge of the country and no ability to read a map or a GPS. Mr Boualem, who had spent time working in the Tassili National Park, had agreed.

Though they were, like many hereabouts, very good at it, I don't think Mr K and Mlle Nadhera were just being polite. Could I put it all in writing? Through the Ambassador in London? They'd need to get the Ministry of Tourism involved. No, co-sponsorship by BP or Sonatrach, the Algerian national oil company, would just hold things up … . I could hardly

242

believe what I'd just heard. The straw of optional procrastination had not been grasped. My spirits soared.

Back in the UK later I would find it took time. And a little money. There was no point submitting a paper in elegant English. Especially if it had to be passed around offices in the Ministry of Tourism in Algiers. There was the formal copy for the Ambassador in London with 'info' copies – in truth, the ones that would get results if any would – to be sent to Mlle Nadhera and Mr K in Algiers. How do you go about getting a reliable Arabic translation? Any number would doubtless aver their expertise but the subtleties of the English had to be understood before it could be translated. I went to the top. The Foreign and Commonwealth Office used translators and I plugged in. It cost the thick end of £500 but I did not want to submit a half-baked translation of the kind, inverted, we are all too used to seeing in the UK – foreigners trying to write English; ho, ho, ho. Very droll.

Trying to get a proposal for protection of the almost unimaginable plethora of rock art at Libya's Jebel Uweinat off the ground had taken me, via UNESCO, five *years*. I was used to being patient. Nothing, though, is so utterly, up-the-wall, frustrating as just getting no reply. I've even labelled it here in the UK 'The New British Disease' or 'The NERB Syndrome' – No-one Ever Rings Back. Doubtless Mr K and Mlle N were having the same troubles at the Ministry of Tourism where the whole thing would have considerably less immediacy, not having met the idea's proponent and maybe feeling that this kind of scheme was up to them to spark, not some unknown Brit.

Nevertheless, the dreary UK winter, the beautiful spring, the rainy summer and another winter dragged by, dotted with tactful prods and reminders and efforts by the noble Rachida on my behalf – and still no real response. At times I almost wished they would say, 'Sorry, but this proposal is not for us.' At least I would know.

A year, 16 months; 18 months, 19. Nothing.

Su Sheppard's efforts with the maps were easier to keep track of. Actually they weren't for, although I could contact her between her other duties, I had no idea of where it had all got to – and nor had she. The letters and requests and phone calls had all gone out but it was hard for her – and even harder for me – to know if any of the seeds had germinated. Had the shockwaves of an Embassy letter to the Ministry of Foreign Affairs had any effect or was the MFA inured to every mildly inconvenienced foreigner kicking up a stink?

The phone rang. 'They're here. Out of the blue. They just arrived. Two cases.' It was Su. I felt I must have been dreaming. She had no means of answering my immediate follow-up questions: Are they all there? Are they damaged? Covered in coffee stains? 'Channels' were dilated briefly to let them through and helpful people at the FCO rang to say they had a couple of packages for me if I would care to collect them.

Only one map was missing and, cause for just a hint of unease, the satellite images with my previous routes marked on were also absent. I hoped there was nothing sinister about this. But 86 other maps, still filed in the right order were there, undamaged. Precious, irreplaceable French IGN maps printed 50 years earlier and bearing the pencilled notes of nearly a score of previous journeys. Later that evening, a small libation of Blossom Hill was called for. I drank to them all. Thank you Su; thank you FCO, thank you Captain Rahmouni and his boss who had clearly realised the mistake and taken care of my maps.

'The letter', and the *persona non grata* status with which it seemed to label me, was another matter. The Libya EPIRB test and the visa-inhibiting 'File' that ensued came to mind – a small incident, a small mistake, all satisfactorily explained but enough to stop another visa. I wanted to be sure that no black mark remained on some list in a dusty computer in Algerian passport control. The maps' return was indication and admission enough that I was not, after all, engaged in nefarious doings with 'military maps'. But my attempts to find out exactly what was said and by whom were hitting a brick wall in the Embassy. As the potentially injured party, I can't say that this was especially welcome; I surely had a right to know what was being levelled at me. Foot shuffling was followed by straight obstruction and I began to suspect there were security overtones. There were; not relating to me but in the end, after going to the highest level and getting a broad explanation, I could see what the problem had been. No-one could guarantee there being nothing on any file anywhere but at least I knew the letter had been low-to-mid level and more an attempt at face-saving after the somewhat overzealous affair at Ain al Hadjadj.

• • •

And in the end, now that I was home, what of the hero of the whole story? The force that carried it forward and without which none of this could have happened? Were there no accolades? Was there any residual damage after so challenging an adventure? Any, to use the fashionable phrase, post-traumatic stress? Would there be a next time?

It was all a bit private, really. No-one but me knew what had gone on, what had been achieved. Where would the accolades come from? From me. For only I knew what a pillar of strength and reliability the G-Wagen had been. It was the embodiment of standards of engineering integrity that were a glowing reflection on those who had designed and manufactured it. It had had its faults. The dodgy electrical harness that caused the EDC light to illuminate on its first trip had been a housekeeping, storage fault not a design fault. There had, after all, been a safety net, and whilst limping home from 23°N had not been much fun, it didn't stop me from taking the old route north from Arak and seeing Tiguelgamine where the 40-foot crocodiles lurked in the scary black water. This time a broken spring surfaced on the Merc's annual check, but the geometry of the design was such that I wasn't even aware of it.

And I certainly hoped there would be a next time.

• • •

Andrew Henderson is the new British Ambassador in Algiers, a down-to-earth, no-nonsense, very human being, brimming with enthusiasm to get out to see his new patch but eye-rollingly, finger-itchingly resigned to the inevitable security constraints with which he is beset. The FCO have even had the wisdom to appoint him for a far longer stint than his predecessors. Hearing of my travels, he and his wife Julia came to see me before his appointment. He was supportive of my Protected Area proposals, but I knew that he could not get involved officially – even apart from having neither the remit nor the luxury of a Cultural Attaché. Nevertheless he made contact recently with ideas as to how it might be moved forward, drawing on his new-found circle of acquaintants.

There aren't many clouds in the Sahara but I think the sun is just coming out from behind one of them. Forever? Eh, Mohammed?

Another Sahara
day begins; with
a modest,
routine
spectacle.

The small print

First published in the United Kingdom in 2008 by
Desert Winds Publishing, 44 Salusbury Lane, Hertfordshire SG5 3EG, England

Written, illustrated, and designed by Tom Sheppard, MBE
Text, photographs, artwork, design and layout copyright © Tom Sheppard 2008
Maps reproduced by kind permission of Philip's and Michelin

The moral right of Tom Sheppard to be identified as the author of this work has been asserted in accordance with the Copyright, Designs and Patents Act of 1988.

A CIP catalogue record for this book is available from the British Library.
ISBN 978-0-9532324-5-1

Printed and bound by Printer Trento S.r.l, Italy
Typeface: Tiepolo Book 9 on 13 pt
Illustrations: High definition stochastic (screenless) printing

Acknowledgement and heartfelt thanks

It is customary to gush, as they do at Oscar ceremonies and the like, about who did what, and what, without whom, could never have been achieved. I have already given repeated and well-deserved praise for the progenitors of the Mercedes-Benz G-Wagen, a classic of integrity, simplicity and effectiveness for an expedition such as the one that forms the main thread of this book.

But there would have been no book at all without the typically unsung wizards and digital technorati at Apple Computer, QuarkXPress, Adobe (Photoshop CS3) software and at Canon's Camera Division. Heroes all – careful, meticulous heroes; may they prosper, sup wine and peel grapes to a contented old age and garner richly deserved satisfaction for their contributions to what we see and read every day, worldwide.

Desert Winds